Hiking

Northern Arizona

Bruce Grubbs

Second Edition

FALCON®

GUILFORD, CONNECTICUT

An imprint of The Globe Pequot Press

Cover photo, interior photos, and maps: Bruce Grubbs

Library of Congress Cataloging-in-Publication Data
Grubbs, Bruce (Bruce O.)
    Hiking northern Arizona / by Bruce Grubbs.—2nd ed.
      p. cm. — (A Falcon guide)
    Rev. ed. of: The trail guide to northern Arizona. c1994
    Includes bibliographical references.
    ISBN 0-7627-1209-0
      1. Hiking—Arizona—Guidebooks. 2. Arizona—Guidebooks. I. Grubbs, Bruce
(Bruce O.) Trail guide to northern Arizona. II. Series.

GV199.42.A7 G78 2001
917.91'30454—dc21   2001040246

Manufactured in the United States of America
Second Edition/Second Printing

To buy books in quantity for corporate use
or incentives, call **(800) 962–0973, ext. 4551,**
or e-mail **premiums@GlobePequot.com.**

Hiking

Northern Arizona

Help Us Keep This Guide Up to Date

Every effort has been made by the authors and editors to make this guide as accurate and useful as possible. However, many things can change after a guide is published—trails are rerouted, regulations change, techniques evolve, facilities come under new management, etc.

We would love to hear from you concerning your experiences with this guide and how you feel it could be improved and kept up to date. While we may not be able to respond to all comments and suggestions, we'll take them to heart and we'll also make certain to share them with the authors. Please send your comments and suggestions to the following address:

The Globe Pequot Press
Reader Response/Editorial Department
P.O. Box 480
Guilford, CT 06437

Or you may e-mail us at:

editorial@GlobePequot.com

Thanks for your input, and happy travels!

Contents

Acknowledgments

I'd like to thank all the USDA Forest Service and other agency personnel who reviewed this book and made valuable comments and suggestions. Thanks once again to Jean Rukkila, an experienced Arizona hiker who read the manuscript and caught my embarrassing mistakes. Warm thanks to Duart Martin for encouraging this project, not to mention hiking with me. And thanks to all my other hiking companions over the years. It wouldn't have been nearly as much fun without you. Thanks to David Lee, Molly Jay, Leeann Drabenstott, and Hrissi Haldezos, my editors, for working with me to make this second edition the best possible book. And I greatly appreciate the production people at Falcon Publishing who turned my rough manuscript into another fine FalconGuide.

The red rocks of Bell Rock and Courthouse Butte catch the last rays of the evening sun in an aerial view.

Map Legend

Interstate	(15)	Town or City	○	▦
US Highway	(66)	Campground	⛺	
State or County Road	(47) (190)	Building	■	
Forest Service Road	4165	Ranger Station	⚑	
Interstate Highway	⟹	Peak	⛰ 9,782 ft.	
Paved Road	⟹	Elevation	9,782 ft. ✕	
Gravel Road	═══	Hill	⛰	
Unimproved Road	▪══════	Butte	🏔	
Described Trail	∼∼∼	Crater	⬭	
Route Along Road	═════════	Cliffs	⌇⌇⌇	
Other Trail	∼∼∼	Gate	•—•	
Cross-Country Route	⋯⋯⋯⋯	Power Line	•——•——•	
Pass/Saddle	) (	Mine Site	⚒	
Trailhead	○	Overlook or Point of Interest	◙	
Parking Area	Ⓟ			
River/Creek/Falls	⟋⟍	National Forest or Wilderness Boundary	—·—·—·—	
Intermittent Creek	∼·∼·∼			
Bridge	⋈∼∼	National or State Park	▨	
Lake	⬬			
Spring	⚲	Map Orientation	N ◢	
Marsh	⚶	Scale	0 0.5 1 Miles	

USGS Topographic Maps

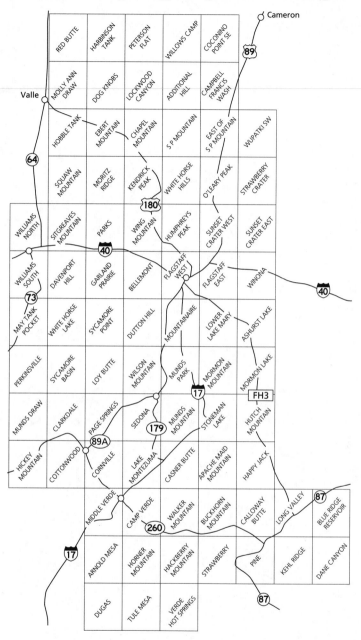

Overview Map

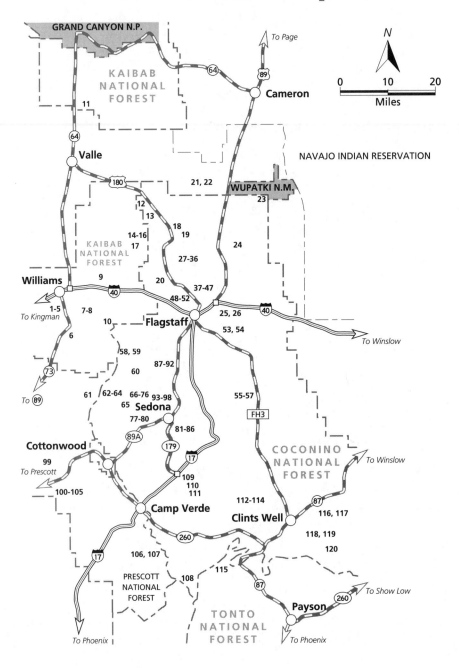

Introduction

Northern Arizona offers almost unlimited opportunities for hiking and exploration. There are dense pine forests and sparse deserts, alpine peaks and desert sandstone canyons, trout streams and isolated springs, volcanic plateaus and rugged granite mountains. Because of Arizona's friendly climate and the great elevation range within the area, it is possible to hike year round. During the summer, desert dwellers from Phoenix and Tucson come north to explore the high plateaus, cool canyons, and towering peaks. During the winter, residents of the high country can descend to the desert areas of Northern Arizona and enjoy great hiking in pleasant weather, an hour's drive away.

In this completely revised second edition, I describe 120 of the best hikes in north-central Arizona. There are hikes near the towns of Williams, Flagstaff, Sedona, Camp Verde, Cottonwood, and Jerome. The hikes range from short, easy day hikes on level trails to demanding backpack trips. Most of the hikes follow established trails, while a few involve cross-country hiking. Some hikes require walking for short distances on roads in order to complete a loop. Trails in designated wilderness areas and in national parks and monuments are closed to bicycles as well as all motorized vehicles and provide the most serene hiking experience. Other trails are open to bicycles, and many are open to horses and pack stock. (By the way, mountain bikes are an excellent means of exploring backcountry roads which are unappealing on foot.)

My intent is to present you with the best and most interesting hikes, rather than catalog all possible trails as separate hikes. To do this, whenever possible I combine trails into loops or other forms in order to create the most interesting hike. I also mention side hikes and other options. Once you have hiked the routes I present here, you will be well equipped to plan your own hikes. Please regard this guide as an invitation to begin your personal discovery of this wonderful area. I hope you always travel with a light pack.

WHY HIKE?

Hiking is an activity that is enjoyable for all ages and abilities, especially if the group walks at the speed of the slowest member of the group. Faster hikers can use the extra time to explore or indulge in activities such as plant and animal identification, fishing, rockhounding, or loafing. Families and groups can find much to share in the outdoors as long as hiking is not allowed to become a competitive event. We can all use more exercise, and hiking is a great way to get it. Walking in wild country also promotes self-reliance, a feeling that is sometimes hard to come by in our modern civilization. And, finally, the best argument of all: Roads just don't go to the most interesting places. To get to the places in this beautiful state that are unspoiled and undeveloped, you have to walk.

CANYONS, MOUNTAINS, AND PLATEAUS

The geography of Northern Arizona is fascinating and varied. The Mogollon Rim begins northwest of Sedona and runs east nearly 200 miles into New Mexico, dividing the area covered by this book into two distinctly different regions. The Colorado Plateau lies north of the Mogollon Rim and includes parts of Arizona, Utah, Colorado, and New Mexico. Layer upon layer of sedimentary rocks have been laid down over millions of years. Some of the rocks were formed under water, while others were deposited in Sahara-like deserts. Mountain-building forces have raised the plateau one to two-and-a-half miles above sea level, warping and fracturing the rocks. Running water from rain and snow melt has eroded these weaknesses into thousands of canyons. These range in length from a few miles to the 290 miles of the Grand Canyon. Volcanic forces have also intruded into the weak zones in the rock, creating hundreds of volcanic hills and mountains. Instead of a flat, featureless landscape, the Colorado Plateau is a region of narrow canyons, tall mountains, and vast vistas.

The fault escarpment of the Mogollon Rim faces generally south along its length. Below the rim lies the most rugged portion of Arizona, the central mountains. In contrast to the high plateaus found north of the Mogollon Rim, this region consists of rugged mountain ranges and deep valleys. Some of these ranges rise more than 4,000 feet. The Verde River, one of Arizona's last free-flowing rivers, drains this area. Numerous side canyons cutting into the mountains and the Mogollon Rim create fine opportunities for hiking and exploration.

A major avalanche path on the north side of Fremont Park.

Climate

The elevations in the area covered by this guide range from 3,000 feet along the Verde River to 12,633 feet at the summit of Humphreys Peak. Because of this, temperatures and climate vary greatly. The wet seasons are December through March, when winter storms can be expected, and July through mid-September, when summer thunderstorms are common. Fall and late spring are usually the best hiking seasons.

Starting in late November, snowstorms can be frequent, and there are often several feet of snow on the higher portions of the Colorado Plateau and much more on the mountains by January. Occasionally the first snowfall is delayed into January. Many high-elevation areas then remain open for hiking well into winter, but the late season traveler should be prepared for possible winter snowstorms. The lower desert areas may experience an occasional snowfall, but the snow doesn't usually stay on the ground for more than a day or two. Between storms, the weather is bright and sunny. Winter rain turns normally dry desert into lush areas with running streams, green grass, and colorful flowers. As a result, the desert can be a very rewarding place to hike in the winter.

Spring weather is changeable as the storm track starts its seasonal swing to the north. By April the weather is usually dry but still cool, making spring a very good time to hike. Springs, water pockets, and streams are often full, which makes it easier to plan backpack trips. In wet years, the desert becomes a riot of wildflowers.

In May the weather usually takes a serious turn toward the heat of summer. Desert temperatures over 100 degrees F are common by June. The high plateau and mountain country, where high temperatures seldom exceed 90 degrees F, is the place to hike. This is also a good time to explore desert canyons that require wading and swimming.

Around midsummer, moisture moves in from the Gulf of Mexico, marking the start of Arizona's summer monsoon season. From July through mid-September, afternoon thunderstorms commonly occur over the high country. Mornings dawn cool and clear, inviting early starts—very necessary for hikes into the highest mountains. You should be off exposed ridges and summits by noon to avoid serious lightning hazard. Flash floods are common during the monsoon, and you should avoid hiking in narrow canyons. On the plus side, the summer rains bring a resurgence of flowers to the forest country and are a welcome change from the hot, dry days of June.

The monsoon usually ends by mid-September, and autumn is clear, cool, and dry. The fine weather and changing fall colors make hiking at all elevations an absolute delight. Dry weather usually continues into November. Hikers in the mountains in late fall should keep a close eye on the weather. The first winter storm is sometimes a large one, dropping several feet of snow on elevations above 5,000 feet.

Making It a Safe Trip

Wilderness can be a safe place, if you are willing to respect your limitations. Once you develop confidence in your technique and equipment, you should become comfortable in the backcountry. The hiker should be self-reliant; this capability can be safely developed by starting out with easy hikes and progressing to more difficult adventures as your experience broadens. Many wilderness accidents are caused by individuals or parties pushing too hard. Instead, set reasonable goals, allowing for delays caused by weather, deteriorated trails, slow members of your party, unexpectedly rough country, and dry springs. Be flexible enough to eliminate part of a hike if your original plans appear too ambitious. Don't fall into the trap of considering a trip plan "cast in stone"—rather, take pride in your adaptability. With experience, operating in the backcountry becomes a welcome relief from the complex tangle of civilized living. Wilderness decisions are usually important but also basic in nature. While "out there," things that seemed important in civilization lose some of their urgency. In other words, we gain a sense of perspective.

A modest amount of good equipment, along with the skill and technique to use it, make hiking safer and more enjoyable. Experienced hikers with good equipment also have less impact on the backcountry. Good gear is not cheap, but it does last a long time. See Appendix E, Hiker's Checklist.

The rim of the Dry Creek basin seen from Brins Mesa.

Day hiking is very popular because it can be enjoyed without investing in much time or specialized equipment. Often beginners find that they already have all the gear needed. For many hikers, the step from day hiking to backpacking is a large one, and it is often not taken. Somehow, the thought of sleeping out is daunting, as is the additional time, equipment, and skill required. However, the hiker who never stays out overnight is missing as much as the swimmer who only dangles his toes in the water. Start out easy, by camping near a trailhead on a familiar trail, and then gradually extend your range by camping farther from the road and staying out longer.

MINIMUM EQUIPMENT

On all hikes that are more than a casual stroll, you should carry some minimum equipment: water, food, rain/wind gear, sunglasses, sunscreen, knife, lighter or other reliable fire starter, map, compass, and a flashlight. These items can easily be carried in a small fanny pack and may save your life if you are delayed or the weather changes.

FOOTWEAR

For short, easy hikes on good trails, nearly any comfortable footwear, such as tennis shoes or running shoes, will work. It's important that the shoe or boot fits snugly but offers plenty of toe room. Double check children's hiking shoes, since they can't determine the proper fit for themselves and won't complain until it is too late.

If you become an avid hiker, you may want to buy a pair of lightweight hiking boots. These are suitable for longer, rougher trails. There are many models available in women's, men's, and children's sizes, constructed of nylon with leather reinforcing and molded rubber soles. Some of the more sophisticated and expensive designs use waterproof/breathable fabrics.

For difficult hiking with heavy loads, some hikers prefer all-leather boots with soles that can be replaced when they wear out. Others (including myself) prefer lightweight boots even for difficult cross-country hiking.

Good-quality, well-fitting socks are critical to hiking comfort. They provide not only insulation but also padding. A good combination is a light inner sock of cotton, wool, or polypropylene, with an outer medium or heavy weight sock of wool with nylon reinforcing. The outer sock will tend to slide against the inner sock, rather than directly on your skin, reducing the chance of blisters. Inner socks of cotton are comfortable in warm weather, while polypropylene socks will wick moisture away from your skin in cool weather. Wool is still the best fiber for the outer, cushioning sock, though small percentages of synthetic fibers make the sock more durable.

Blisters should be treated *before* they happen! A large or deep blister can be immobilizing. At the first sign of a hot spot or other discomfort on your feet, stop and have a look. A hot spot can be protected with a piece of felt moleskin. Often a change of socks will help as well. Once a blister has fully developed, it should be protected by a piece of moleskin with the center cut out around the raised area of skin, like a donut.

CLOTHING

Nearly any durable clothing will do for hiking in good, stable weather. On hot, sunny days, keep your skin covered with long sleeves and long pants, or use a good sunscreen. In the mountains, strong sun and high altitudes can produce painful sunburn in a short time, even on tanned skin; a brimmed sun-hat is a good defense. Long pants will also protect your skin from scratches when hiking a brushy trail.

Give a little more thought to your clothing in cool, windy, or changeable weather; several layers of light, flexible clothing work better than single heavy, cumbersome layers such as winter parkas. In cool weather, a warm wool or synthetic watch-cap or balaclava makes an amazing difference in comfort— up to half your body's heat is lost through your head. Protect your hands with wool or synthetic gloves or mittens.

The layer system becomes even more important while backpacking, because you'll want to keep your load as light as possible. The "four-layer" system can handle nearly any weather condition. The first, inner layer consists of lightweight, synthetic, moisture-wicking long underwear. A pair of sturdy pants (with shorts as a warm weather addition) and a sturdy shirt that will hold up to brush and rocks forms the second layer. The third layer consists of an insulating jacket or parka. Down is the lightest, most durable insulation, but once wet, it dries very slowly. When you expect wet weather, consider a jacket insulated with a synthetic fill. Synthetic pile or fleece is the warmest, driest insulator for very wet conditions. Even when soaked it can be wrung out and worn immediately. Finally, the fourth layer consists of a good set of rain pants and jacket with hood. If this outer layer is constructed from a waterproof and breathable fabric, then it will do double duty as a wind shell.

Don't put up with being overheated or chilled; while hiking, stop to add or subtract layers as necessary to stay comfortable.

FOOD

You should bring some food on all but the shortest hikes. High-calorie food keeps your energy level up. You can make sandwiches and other picnic items, or take fruit, cheese, crackers, nuts and drink mixes. I like to keep an athletic energy bar or two in my pack, just in case.

Although a great deal of dehydrated food is made especially for backpacking and lightweight camping, it's very expensive. You can find many items in supermarkets that make good backpacking food at lower cost. Using just supermarket food, I have done countless backpack trips with 1.5 pounds of food per person per day. Some suggestions: for breakfast: low-bulk cold cereals with powdered milk, hot cereals, dried fruit, breakfast bars, hot chocolate, tea, and coffee bags. For lunch: munchies such as nuts, cheese, crackers, dried fruit, candy bars, athletic energy-bars, dried soup, hard candy, beef or turkey jerky, sardines, and fruit-flavored drink mixes. For dinner: dried-noodle or rice-based dishes, either prepackaged, or made up at home, possibly supplemented with margarine and/or a small can of tuna, turkey, or chicken.

6

Before leaving home, remove excess packaging such as cardboard boxes. Plastic bags with zipper closures make excellent food-repackaging bags. Messy items should be double-bagged. Pack margarine and peanut butter in reliable, wide-mouth plastic jars (available from outdoor suppliers). Unless you really trust the seal, put the container in a plastic bag as well! Extra bags are useful during the trip for double-bagging messy trash such as sardine cans. Dedicate one or more nylon stuffsacks to food storage; don't use them for anything else during the trip. The idea is to confine food odors as much as possible.

In camp, hang your food sacks from a 10- or 15-foot-high tree limb, if possible. The most foolproof technique is to divide your food into two equal sacks. Use a stone to toss the end of a piece of nylon cord over a limb, well out from the trunk, and tie half your food to the end. Pull the food up to the limb and tie your remaining food sack onto the cord as high as you can reach. Stuff the excess cord into the food sack. Then use a stick to push the second sack several feet higher than your head. The first sack will act as a counterweight and descend a few feet, but it should remain at least as high as the second sack. In the morning, use a stick to pull down one of the sacks. This method is foolproof against most animals.

WATER

On day hikes, bring water from home. It's easier than purifying the backcountry water sources. Many of the day hikes in this area don't have any reliable water sources during the dry season. Remember that each hiker may drink a gallon or more during a long, difficult, hot hike.

Backcountry water sources are not safe to drink. Appearance is no indication of safety—even sparkling clear water may contain dangerous parasites. Contamination comes from wild and domestic animals as well as increasing human use. Infections from contaminated water are uncomfortable and can be disabling. Giardiasis, for example, is a severe gastrointestinal infection caused by small cysts which can result in an emergency evacuation of the infected hiker. Giardiasis is spread by all mammals, including humans. Purify all backcountry water sources; you have no way of telling if a given source is safe. Iodine tablets, available from outdoor shops, are the most effective wilderness water-purification system. (See *Medicine for Mountaineering* in Further Reading.) One iodine tablet per quart will kill nearly all dangerous organisms, including *Giardia,* within 30 minutes. Carefully read and follow the directions on the bottle to ensure effective use. In order to retain their potency, the tablets must be kept dry until used, and it's a good idea to discard opened bottles after a trip. Some find the iodine taste objectionable; an iodine-taste–remover tablet is now available that restores the original color and taste of the water without altering the iodine's effectiveness. Since the active biocidal agent is removed by these tablets, make sure you wait until the iodine tablets have had time to purify the water before adding these remover tablets. Fruit and sport drinks containing ascorbic acid (vitamin C) have the same effect. Some people use such drink mixes to mask the taste of the iodine; if you do so, wait 30 minutes, until the iodine tablets have done their work, before adding the drink mix.

Water filters are a popular alternative to iodine treatment, largely due to the better-tasting water they produce. They are heavier to carry than iodine tablets, and also take longer to use. Filters alone cannot remove viruses because the pores in the filter elements are too large to trap them. There are some filter systems that use an active iodine element to kill viruses. These are usually called water purifiers, instead of filters.

Water can also be purified by bringing it to a rolling boil. The time required to heat the water to a boil is sufficient to kill disease organisms even at high altitude. (See *Medicine for Mountaineering* in Further Reading.) Two disadvantages of boiling are that it uses extra fuel and gives the water a flat taste. You can improve the taste by pouring the water back and forth between two containers several times. This restores the dissolved air that boiling removes.

The best water containers are plastic bottles with leak-proof caps, carried inside your pack. Another popular arrangement is a fanny pack with external bottle carriers. Metal canteens carried on your belt or on a shoulder strap are uncomfortable, and the water is quickly heated by the sun.

KNIFE

A knife is necessary for many routine tasks, such as cutting cord, and is vital for emergency fire building. Some hikers prefer the Swiss Army or multipurpose tool type with scissors and other implements, while others like a simple, large-bladed knife such as a folding hunter.

SUNGLASSES

A good pair of sunglasses is essential when traveling in open areas during the summer. Good glasses are optically correct and remove invisible ultraviolet and infrared light, reducing eyestrain and headaches. Ultraviolet protection is especially important at high altitude and on summer snowfields. The tag on the glasses will specify whether ultraviolet and infrared are filtered. Cheap sunglasses with no ultraviolet protection are worse than no sunglasses. They reduce visible light, causing the eye's iris to open and admit more damaging ultraviolet rays. Excessive ultraviolet exposure causes snowblindness, a temporary but very uncomfortable condition. Hikers who are dependent on prescription glasses or contact lenses should carry a spare pair of glasses. You can protect your expensive lenses with a hard-shell plastic case.

SUNSCREEN

Sunscreen is another essential item. Lotions are rated by their Sun Protection Factor, or SPF, which approximates the amount of protection provided by the sunscreen as compared to unprotected skin. For example, a sunscreen rated at SPF 15 gives about 15 times your natural protection. An SPF of 30 is not excessive for hiking in the mountains in the summer. Few things can ruin a hike more completely than a bad sunburn.

PACK

A well-fitting, well-made day pack goes a long way toward making your hike a pleasant experience. Look for firm foam padding on the back panel and on the shoulder straps. Larger day packs usually have a waist belt, which may or may not be padded, and a reinforced bottom. Fanny packs are another popular alternative. They are especially nice in warm weather because your back has free air circulation. Their main drawback is limited capacity, which makes them unsuited for long hikes in remote areas or in changeable weather. Fanny packs work well for young children, who can carry a token amount and will feel included in the group.

Packs for backpacking fall into two categories: internal frame and external frame. Internal-frame packs have the frame built into the pack; the pack rides closer to your body and balances well for cross-country hiking. External-frame packs are usually made of aluminum tubing with a separately attached pack bag. They are easier to pack and to load for extended trips. They also give better back ventilation in hot weather. A good backpack of either type carefully distributes the load between your shoulders, back, and hips, with most of the weight on your hips. Correct fit is critical. Models are now made specifically for men, women, and children, so getting a good fit is easier than ever.

A loaded pack means that you'll walk at a slower pace, especially uphill. Remember to allow for this when planning overnight trips versus day hikes. A walking stick can be helpful, especially at stream crossings or other places where the footing is uncertain. Walking sticks can also be used to push brush and low branches out of the way, as a prop to turn a pack into a back rest, or to support a tarp for shelter from the weather.

SLEEPING BAG

Your sleeping bag is one of the most important items in your pack. With a good one you'll most likely have a comfortable sleep; a poor bag will guarantee a miserable experience. The length of the manufacturer's warranty is a good indicator of quality. The occasional user may be happy with a backpacker's-style mummy bag insulated with one of the current synthetic fills. Synthetic fills have the advantages of lower initial cost and of retaining some of their insulating ability when soaking wet. High-quality down fill, though expensive, is still unsurpassed in insulating capability for its weight. Since it is more durable, down is actually less expensive than synthetics over the lifetime of the bag. People who backpack often prefer down bags. Down is also more water resistant than commonly thought, as anyone who has tried to wash a down bag by hand can tell you. Sleeping bags are rated by temperature and sometimes by recommended seasons. A three-season bag is adequate for most backpacking. If you sleep cold, consider a warmer bag.

9

SLEEPING PAD

Since lightweight sleeping bags don't provide much insulation or padding underneath, you'll need a sleeping pad. The best type currently available is the self-inflating, foam-filled air mattress. These are less prone to punctures than a traditional air mattress, much warmer, and very comfortable. Closed-cell foam pads are a cheaper alternative. They insulate very well but are not especially comfortable.

SHELTER

Most hikers depend on a tent for shelter. Sound construction and high quality is important. A three-season, two-man dome or free-standing tent is the most versatile. Larger tents are more awkward to carry and require more spacious campsites. Nearly all tents use a separate waterproof fly over the tent canopy, which provides rain protection and also allows moisture to escape from within the tent. Small children can share a tent with their parents, but as they get older, kids often enjoy their own.

Some experienced hikers avoid the weight and expense of a tent by carrying a nylon tarp with a separate groundsheet. A tarp provides good weather protection if set up properly and is versatile enough to use as a sun shade or wind break during lunch stops. Using a tarp effectively does take some practice. Also, a tarp provides no protection from mosquitoes and other insects.

FIRST AID KIT

A small first-aid kit will do for day hikes, but you'll definitely need a more complete kit for backpacking. Make sure that you get one intended specifically for wilderness sports. You may want to include a few repair items, such as spare bulbs and batteries for your flashlight, stove and pack parts, and a sewing kit.

ACCESSORIES

A camera is probably the most common "extra" item carried on day hikes. You can use small, nylon ditty bags or plastic bags to protect it and other fragile items from rain and dust. Even the most waterproof packs can leak through seams and zippers, and dust and sand seems to get into everything.

EQUIPMENT SOURCES

Consider supporting the local outdoor shops when they are staffed by people who use the gear and are willing to share their knowledge with you. Mail order is an alternative if you can't find a good local shop. See Appendix B for a list of local shops and mail order companies.

TRIP PLANNING

Maps are essential for trip planning and should be obtained in advance of the trip. Guidebooks allow you to learn about an area more quickly than you could with maps alone. Once you are comfortable with an area and have done many of the hikes in the guidebooks, you will be able to plan your own hikes using maps and information from other hikers to help you.

When planning a backpacking trip, think about alternatives to traditional campsites. Dry camping, or camping with just the water you carry, is a valuable skill with many advantages. Dry camping virtually eliminates the possibility of contaminating wilderness streams and lakes. You can avoid heavily used campsites and their camp-robbing animal attendants such as skunks, mice, gray jays, and insects. Dry camping also opens up many beautiful, uncrowded campsites. The technique is simple: use a collapsible water container to pick up water at the last reliable source of the day and use minimum water for camp chores. If possible, plan your route so that you pass at least one reliable water source each day of the trip.

Note that certain areas are closed to overnight camping. These closures are mentioned in the "Permits and restrictions" section of each hike description; check with the listed agency for the latest information.

BACKCOUNTRY NAVIGATION

Maps

Several different types of maps are available for wilderness navigation. Topographic maps are the most useful because they show the elevation and shape of the land through the use of contour lines. All of northern Arizona is covered by the quadrangle series published by the US Geological Survey. Each hike description in this book lists the USGS topographic maps that cover the hike. The USGS maps are produced from aerial photos to high standards of accuracy. At a scale of 1:24,000 (2.6 inches to the mile) and printed in sheets that cover about 7 by 9 miles, these are usually the most detailed maps available. The only catch is that the USGS can't update the maps all that often, so manmade details such as trails and roads may be out of date. USGS maps are sold at some outdoor shops and bookstores and are also available by mail order from the USGS map distribution center in Denver. See Appendix D for the current address. Request a free Arizona index and catalog of the topographic maps.

The USDA Forest Service publishes maps of the Coconino, Prescott, and Kaibab National Forests. These maps show the forest road system at a scale of 1:126,720 (0.5 inch to the mile). It also shows the official road numbers shown on road signs. These maps are useful for finding the trailheads but don't have enough detail for hiking.

Some national forests publish topographic maps of designated wilderness areas, though none are available for northern Arizona as yet. In time the Kaibab and Coconino National Forests may start to produce such maps.

Several private companies produce hiking maps. Beartooth Maps publishes an excellent trail map for the Sedona area. National Geographic (formerly Wildflower Productions) publishes computer-based maps that cover the areas in this book at the same level of detail as USGS maps. See Appendix B for contact information.

Lockett Tank reflects nearby quaking aspens.

Map reading is a skill that requires practice, but it pays off in increased safety in the backcountry. The best way to learn is to get a map of an area that you already know. Go to a place with an overview of the terrain and spend some time relating what you see to the map symbols. Before entering the backcountry, study the maps to become familiar with the general lay of the land. Trail signs may be vandalized or inaccurate. It is wise to stay aware of your location at all times, and use the trail signs as confirmation. While hiking, refer to the map often and locate yourself in reference to visible landmarks. If you do this consistently, without relying on trail signs, you will never become lost.

Compasses

Always carry a reliable, liquid-filled compass so that you can determine directions in dense forest or bad weather. Because backcountry navigation in the generally open terrain of northern Arizona consists primarily of map reading, your compass will probably languish in your pack for years before you use it. When you finally do need it, you will need it badly—not a good time to find out that the needle has fallen off.

Global Positioning System

The satellite navigation system maintained by the Department of Defense makes it possible to find your location nearly anywhere on earth. GPS consists of a set of 21active satellites orbiting 12,000 miles above the earth. Low-cost, portable receivers are available that are designed specifically for ground navigation. The readout shows your position within about 33 feet (10 meters). Weather conditions do not affect the accuracy of GPS, but the receiver must have a clear view of the sky. This means that dense forest, narrow canyons, or poor satellite geometry can prevent an accurate fix. A GPS unit is no substitute for a good map and a reliable compass. Keep in mind that the GPS unit is useless if the batteries die; take spares! When buying a unit for hiking, make sure it uses the Universal Transverse Mercator (UTM) coordinate system as well as latitude and longitude. UTM is found on USGS topographic maps and is easier to use than the latitude and longitude system. Any map accurate enough for wilderness navigation will have at least one coordinate system.

WALKING

Walking in wild country is not just a matter of "picking 'em up and putting 'em down." Most novice hikers try to go too fast and then find themselves out of breath and having to stop frequently. The group should move at a speed that allows easy conversation among all members. Long hikes, especially uphill sections, should be paced so that rest breaks are needed only about once an hour. That's not to say that you shouldn't stop at scenic viewpoints or other points of interest. If you find yourself taking a great many breaks, you're probably going too fast. Keep rest stops short so that you don't become chilled. It's harder to get going after a long break.

As you walk, always pay attention to the stretch of ground immediately in front of you. Hazards such as spiny plants, overhanging sharp branches, and sunbathing rattlesnakes are easy to miss if you only have eyes for the scenery. On the other hand, daydreaming is an important part of hiking. There are always sections of trail that aren't that interesting. The experienced hiker can let her mind wander far away but still pay attention to the trail underfoot and the route ahead. Or, she can focus on aspects of the environment such as listening to a bird song or identifying trees from a distance by their general shape. Either technique lets the miles pass almost unnoticed.

Hikes taken with young children should have extremely modest goals. A day hike of a few hundred yards may be far enough. Children find all sorts of interesting things in a small area that their parents would not otherwise notice. Introduce your children to short day hikes at an early age, gradually lengthening the distance as they grow older and their stamina and interest increase. The first overnight hikes can be kept short, as they should be for any novice hiker, child or adult. Once a child is old enough to carry a pack, keep its load light. If you progressively introduce your children to backpacking, by the time they are energetic teenagers they'll be addicted to hiking. Then, maybe you can persuade them to carry some of your own load!

TRAIL COURTESY

Never cut switchbacks on trails. Short-cutting actually takes more physical effort than staying on the trail. It also increases erosion and the need for trail maintenance. Give horses and other pack animals the right of way by stepping off the trail downhill. Talk in a normal tone of voice; don't make sudden movements or loud noises, which can spook an animal.

Mountain bikes are not allowed on trails in wilderness areas or in most national parks. You may encounter bikes outside these areas. Since they're less maneuverable than you, it's polite to step aside so the riders can pass without having to veer off the trail. On the other hand, mountain bikers should respect your desire for a quiet backcountry experience and refrain from making excessive noise.

Smokers should stop at a bare spot or rock ledge and make certain that all smoking materials are out before continuing. Please remember that cigarette butts are not biodegradable—they should be packed out with the rest of your garbage. Never smoke or light any kind of fire on windy days or when the fire danger is high because wildfires can start easily and spread explosively.

Dogs are not allowed on trails in national parks. In the national forests, dogs are allowed but must be kept under control. A leash is a good idea. If your dog barks or runs up to other people, it should be left at home. Barking dogs disturb other hikers, and their presence places unnecessary stress on wildlife.

Cutting live trees or plants of any kind, blazing or carving initials on trees or rocks, picking wildflowers, and building rock campfire rings are destructive activities. We all need to consider the next hiker, and leave everything as we would like to find it ourselves. Everyone should read *Leave No Trace,* the official manual of the American Hiking Society, for the latest minimum-impact techniques (see Appendix A).

Never disturb ruins or other old sites and artifacts. All such sites are protected by the National Historic Preservation Act and the Archeological Resources Preservation Act. These laws are intended to preserve our historic and prehistoric heritage. Archaeologists study artifacts in their settings because the context reveals more information than the artifact alone. Once a site is disturbed, another piece of the puzzle is gone forever.

CAMPING

Start looking for a campsite at least a couple of hours before dark. Campsites become harder to find as the group size increases—a good reason to avoid groups larger than five or six people. The best camps are on reasonably level sites with dry, sandy soil, bare rock, or forest duff. Avoid fragile, easily damaged sites such as grassy meadows, lakeshores, and stream banks. Select a site that's screened from trails, meadows, and other campsites. As a rule of thumb, camp out of sight and sound of others and respect their desire for wilderness solitude. Land managers sometimes close specific areas to camping or entry to allow it to recover from heavy use. Please respect these closures.

During hot weather, look for shade, especially from the morning sun. In heavy forest, check overhead for "widowmakers," large dead branches that may break off and crash down. If bad weather threatens, look for a

Many times it is possible to camp without a tent and enjoy a bedroom with fifty-mile views.

campsite sheltered from wind and blowing rain, preferably with natural drainage and an absorbent surface such as forest duff or sand. Heavy forest provides protection from rain at the beginning of a storm, but the trees drip for hours after the rain stops. Never dig drainage ditches or excavate dirt to level a campsite; these obsolete practices cause erosion and severe damage. A slight slope will keep groundwater from pooling under your tent. Modern sleeping pads make it possible to camp on gravel or even rock slabs in comfort.

CAMPFIRES

Don't build campfires, except in an emergency. The Norwegians have a saying: "There's no such thing as bad weather, just bad clothing." Too much of northern Arizona is already scarred by campfire rings and heaps of trash and aluminum cans that campers have tried to burn. Campfires are prohibited in some areas and are likely to be outlawed elsewhere. Campfires are also prohibited in the national forests during periods of high fire danger.

TRASH

If you carried it in, you can also carry it out. Lightweight food that has been carefully repacked to eliminate excess packaging produces little trash even after a week or more in the backcountry. Avoid burying food or trash. After you leave, animals will smell it, dig it up, and scatter it all over the place. Don't feed wild creatures; they will become dependent on human food, which is not good for them and can lead to their starvation during the winter. Also, animals that become used to human food become more aggressive in seeking out those sources, which leads to unpleasant encounters between people and wildlife.

SANITATION

Wilderness sanitation is a critical skill that we all need to possess. Naturally occurring diseases such as Giardiasis are aggravated by poor human sanitation. Facilities are often available at trailheads and campgrounds; use them. In the backcountry, select a site at least 100 yards from streams, lakes, springs, and dry washes. Avoid barren, sandy soil, if possible. Next, dig a small "cat-hole" about 6 inches down into the organic layer of the soil. (Some people carry a small plastic trowel for this purpose.) When finished, refill the hole, making the site as natural as possible. Land managers now recommend that all toilet paper be carried out. Use double zipper bags, with a small amount of baking soda to absorb odor.

FIRST AID

At least one member of the party should have current first-aid skills. *Medicine for Mountaineering* and *Wild Country Companion* (see Appendix A) are excellent sources of wilderness medical information.

WEATHER

During the summer, heat can be a hazard, especially at the lower elevations. In hot weather, each hiker will need a gallon of water, or more, every day. To avoid dehydration, drink more water than required to quench your thirst. Sport drinks that replace electrolytes are also useful. Protection both from the heat and the sun is important: a lightweight sun-hat is an essential. During hot weather, plan hikes at higher elevations, or hike early in the day to avoid the afternoon heat.

Thunderstorms may occur during the summer. Towering cumulus clouds appear first and warn of the heavy rain, hail, high winds, and lightning that is likely to follow. In thunderstorm season, plan your hike to avoid high ridges and peaks during the afternoon. If a thunderstorm does occur, get off exposed ridges and stay away from lone trees. If lightning begins to strike in your immediate area, crouch on a sleeping pad or other insulating object, keeping your contact with the ground to a minimum. The idea is to reduce your exposure to the ground currents caused by a lightning bolt, which spread out from the point of the actual strike.

Avoid continuous exposure to chilling weather, which may subtly lower body temperature and cause sudden collapse from hypothermia, a life-threatening condition. Cool winds, especially with rain, are the most dangerous because the heat loss is insidious. You can prevent hypothermia by wearing enough layers of clothing to avoid chilling, and by eating and drinking regularly so that your body continues to produce heat. Snow may fall at any time of year on the higher mountains. Be prepared for it by bringing more layers of warm clothing than you think you will need. During the winter season, use synthetic garments made of polypropylene or polyester fibers, because these fibers retain their insulating ability when wet better than any natural fiber, including wool.

INSECTS AND THEIR KIN

Insects are not a major hazard in northern Arizona. Mosquitoes are occasionally around after snow melt at the higher elevations. Scorpions are found nearly everywhere, but the species found in this area are not especially hazardous. (There are more venomous scorpions in the desert of southwestern Arizona.) Other insects such as bees, wasps, and the like also give non-threatening but painful stings. A new hazard has appeared in the last few years: the Africanized bee. Accidentally released into the wilds of South America, they have since spread north into Arizona. Identical in appearance to the common honey bee, these bees are very aggressive in defending their hive. Never approach any beehive or swarm, wild or domestic. Be wary about peering into rock crevices or holes in dead trees. If attacked, drop your pack and run. Protect your eyes and don't swat at the bees. If shelter such as a building or vehicle is available, use it. Otherwise, run into heavy brush, which confuses the bees.

People who have a known allergic reaction to specific insect stings are at special risk. Since this reaction can develop rapidly and be life-threatening, such people should check with their doctor to see if desensitization treatment is recommended. They should also carry insect-sting kits prescribed by their doctors.

SNAKES

Rattlesnakes are not common at the highest elevations but may be encountered in the lower country. They can be avoided easily because they usually warn off intruders by rattling well before striking range. Never handle or tease any snake. Since rattlesnakes can strike no farther than approximately half their body length, avoid placing your hands and feet in areas that you cannot see, and walk several feet away from rock overhangs and shady ledges. Bites usually occur on the feet or ankles, so ankle-high hiking boots and loose-fitting long pants will prevent most injuries. Snakes prefer surfaces at about 80 degrees F. This means they like the shade of bushes or rock overhangs in hot weather, and in cool weather they prefer open, sunny ground. Don't confuse common, nonpoisonous bull snakes with rattlesnakes.

WILDLIFE

Wild animals normally leave you alone unless molested or provoked. Don't feed any wild animal, as they rapidly get used to handouts and then will vigorously defend their new food source. Around camp, problems with rodents can be avoided by hanging your food from rocks or trees. Even the

The ponderosa pine forest on the Coconino Plateau is home to many different creatures.

18

Poison ivy in Secret Canyon. It is easily recognized by its three glossy leaves and its favored habitat of cool, moist stream beds and dry washes.

toughest pack can be wrecked by a determined mouse or squirrel that has all night to work. Heavily used campsites present the worst problems.

PLANTS

Spiny plants are a hazard, especially at lower elevations. Always watch where you place your hands and feet. Spines can be removed with a pair of tweezers, a good item to have in your first aid kit. Stinging nettle is harder to deal with because the irritating hairs are so fine. Apply a strip of adhesive tape over the affected area and remove it to pull out the nettle hairs. Never eat any plant, unless you positively know what you are doing. Poison ivy may be found in the lower canyons; it is easily recognized by its shiny leaves, which grow in groups of three. If you accidentally make contact with poison ivy, wash the affected area with soap and water as soon as possible. Plain water is better than nothing. Calamine lotion may help relieve the itching. Remember that dogs and clothing that have come into contact with the plants can spread the volatile acid that causes the skin reaction.

RESCUE

Anyone entering remote country should be self-sufficient and prepared to take care of emergencies such as equipment failure and minor medical problems. Very rarely, circumstances may create a life-threatening situation that

19

requires an emergency evacuation or a search effort. Carry and know how to use a signal mirror. Mirror flashes are visible for 50 miles or more in good weather. Always leave word of your hiking plans with a reliable individual. For backpack trips, you should provide a written itinerary. The responsible person should be advised to contact the appropriate authority when you become overdue. In your instructions, allow extra time for routine delays. The appropriate county sheriff is responsible for search and rescue. In national parks and monuments, the National Park Service shares responsibility for search and rescue with the sheriff's department. The USDA Forest Service cooperates with the sheriff's departments and may also be contacted in the event of an emergency.

Don't count on a cellular phone for communications in the backcountry. The cellular phone system is dependent on a closely spaced network of short-range radio transmitters designed for use in cities and populated areas. Cell phone coverage is not continuous in rural areas and may be non-existent in wilderness. Even if you can alert authorities to your problem, you will have a better chance of surviving until rescuers arrive if you are self-sufficient.

Author's Recommendations

Easy day hikes	
2	Clover Spring Trail
4	Buckskinner Trail
8	Davenport Hill Trail
17	Beale Road Historic Trail
22	Colton Crater
23	Doney Trail
32	Kachina Trail
39	Rocky Ridge Trail
44	Sandy Seep Trail
45	Fatman's Loop
48	Lower Oldham Trail
49	Buffalo Park
53	Sandy's Canyon Trail
55	Mormon Lake
56	Ledges Trail
67	Doe Mountain
68	Fay Canyon Arch
69	Boynton Canyon
70	Long Canyon
74	Vultee Arch
76	Devils Bridge
80	Jim Thompson Trail
81	Huckaby Trail
84	Courthouse Butte
91	West Fork Trail
98	Wilson Canyon
99	Woodchute Trail
114	Willow Crossing Trail

Very easy day hikes for parents with small children	
7	Dogtown Lake Trail
9	Keyhole Sink Trail
12	Red Mountain
44	Sandy Seep Trail
49	Buffalo Park
53	Sandy's Canyon Trail
56	Ledges Trail
64	Robbers Roost
77	Eagles Nest Trail
78	Apache Fire Trail
91	West Fork Trail
96	Allens Bend Trail
98	Wilson Canyon

First night in the wilderness	10 Sycamore Rim Trail
	58 Kelsey–Dorsey Loop
	60 Secret Mountain Trail
	109 Bell Trail
	112 Tramway Trail
	113 Maxwell Trail
	116 Horse Crossing Trail
	117 Kinder Crossing Trail
Long day hikes	3 Bill Williams Trail
	10 Sycamore Rim Trail
	15 Bull Basin and Pumpkin Trails
	26 Walnut Canyon Rim
	28 Bear Jaw–Abineau Canyon Loop
	31 Humphreys–Kachina Loop
	36 Flagstaff Spring
	54 Anderson Mesa
	60 Secret Mountain Trail
	63 Mooney–Casner Loop
	65 Loy Canyon Trail
	71 Secret Canyon
	75 Brins Mesa
	85 House Mountain
	86 Jacks Canyon
	94 North Wilson Mountain Trail
	97 Wilson Mountain
	102 Yaeger Canyon Loop
	105 Black Canyon Trail
	106 Chasm Creek Trail
	107 Cold Water Spring
	118 U-Bar Trail
	119 Houston Brothers Trails
	120 Barbershop Trail
Winter hikes	45 Fatman's Loop
	49 Buffalo Park
	67 Doe Mountain
	68 Fay Canyon Arch
	69 Boynton Canyon
	70 Long Canyon
	77 Eagles Nest Trail
	78 Apache Fire Trail
	79 Mormon Canyon
	80 Jim Thompson Trail
	81 Huckaby Trail
	83 Little Horse Trail
	84 Courthouse Butte

Summer hikes with water	71 Secret Canyon
	77 Eagles Nest Trail
	78 Apache Fire Trail
	81 Huckaby Trail
	87 Pumphouse Wash
	91 West Fork Trail
	96 Allens Bend Trail
	109 Bell Trail
	112 Tramway Trail
	113 Maxwell Trail
	115 Fossil Springs Trail
	116 Horse Crossing Trail
	117 Kinder Crossing Trail
Hikes for peak baggers	1 Bixler Saddle Trail
	3 Bill Williams Trail
	5 Benham Trail
	6 Summit Mountain Trail
	8 Davenport Hill Trail
	11 Red Butte
	13 Slate Mountain Trail
	14 Kendrick Peak Trail
	18 Saddle Mountain
	20 Wing Mountain
	21 SP Crater
	30 Humphreys Peak Trail
	34 Schultz Peak
	46 Elden Mountain Loop
	66 Bear Mountain
	82 Munds Mountain
	85 House Mountain
	86 Jacks Canyon
	94 North Wilson Mountain Trail
	97 Wilson Mountain
	99 Woodchute Trail
Cross-country challenges	17 Beale Road Historic Trail
	18 Saddle Mountain
	20 Wing Mountain
	24 Bonito Crater
	27 Abineau Trail–North Ridge Humphreys Peak
	33 Weatherford Canyon
	34 Schultz Peak
	59 Winter Cabin–Kelsey Loop
	61 Parsons Trail
	73 Dry Creek
	75 Brins Mesa

Using This Guide

HIKE DESCRIPTIONS

The hikes are presented in an easy-to-read format with at-a-glance information at the start. Each hike description contains the following information:

Hike number and name: The hike number is also shown on the Overview Map, to help you visualize the general location of the hike. I've used the official, or at least the commonly accepted, name for a trail or hike wherever possible. Hikes that use several trails are usually named for the main trail.

Description: This is a general description of the hike, which includes special attractions and the name of the designated wilderness or other specially protected area, if any.

Location: This is the distance, in miles, and direction from the nearest large town.

Type of trail: Out-and-back hikes are two-way hikes in which the return is done by backtracking the trail. Loop hikes start and end at the same trailhead, but avoid retracing the trail. There may be some repeated sections in order to connect a loop hike. Shuttle hikes are one-way hikes starting and ending at different trailheads. You will have to leave a vehicle at both trailheads, or arrange for reliable pickup at the exit trailhead. The term "cross-country" means that there is no trail for all or a part of the route. Refer to the hike's Key Points and Description for details.

Type of trip: Day hike or backpack trip. Some day hikes can be expanded into easy backpack trips, and ambitious hikers may cover a backpack trip in one day.

Difficulty: All the hikes are rated as easy, moderate, or difficult. This is a subjective rating, but in general, easy hikes can be done by nearly anyone and take a few hours at most. Moderate hikes take all or most of a day and require moderate physical abilities. Difficult hikes are long with significant elevation changes, require a full day or several days to accomplish, and may involve cross-country hiking and route finding. These hikes should be attempted only by experienced hikers in good physical condition.

Total distance: Distances given in miles. For out-and-back hikes, this distance includes the return. (This is a change from the first edition of this book, where out-and-back hike distance was given for the outbound hike only.) For loops and shuttle hikes, this is the one-way distance.

Elevation change: The total altitude change in feet, not including ups and downs along the way.

Elevation graph: Each hike with significant elevation change has a graph showing a profile view of the hike.

Time required: A subjective estimate of the number of hours or days required for an average hiker to walk the trail, not including lunch stops or other diversions. I've tried to err on the conservative side. Experienced, fit hikers will take less time; novices may take considerably more.

Water: Known and usually reliable sources. Don't ever depend on a single water source, no matter how reliable it's been in the past. Remember that *all* backcountry water should be purified.

Best season: This is the recommended season to do the hike. The season may be longer or shorter in some years. "All year" hikes may be hot in summer; you may want to hike early in the morning.

Maps: The appropriate USGS 7.5-minute topographic quadrangles are always listed, and the USDA Forest Service maps if they are useful for the hike or the approach road. The trail may not be shown on the maps, but they are still useful for general orientation. There is a guide to the USGS maps for the entire area on page xi.

Permits and restrictions: Permit requirements and camping and other restrictions are noted here. A Red Rock Pass is required for trailhead parking in the red rock and Oak Creek Canyon areas of the Coconino National Forest. Daily, weekly, and annual permits are available. Also, certain picnic areas used for trailhead parking require a separate fee. This is not a backcountry permit—if you enter the backcountry by other means (bicycle, drop-off, etc.), you do not need a permit. For details, check with the Sedona Ranger Station (see contact information in Appendix D). As of this writing, permits and fees are *not* required for the remainder of the area covered by this book.

For more information: The name of the land management unit having jurisdiction over the hike. For the address and phone number, refer to Appendix D. Before your hike, it's a good idea to check with the agency for the latest trail conditions and other information.

Finding the trailhead: These driving directions are given from the nearest town for all of the hikes. Distances are in miles.

Key points: This is a listing of key points such as trail junctions and important landmarks along the hike. You should be able to follow the route by reference to this section. Distances are given in miles from the start of the hike.

The hike: In this narrative, I describe the hike in detail and provide some interesting natural and human history. The description uses references to landmarks rather than distances wherever possible, since distances are listed under "Key points."

Williams

The town of Williams is on the western portion of the Coconino Plateau at the base of Bill Williams Mountain. Although the Coconino Plateau was part of New Spain for three hundred years, the Spanish had little to do with it. American mountain men such as Bill Williams were the first to put the Coconino Plateau on the map. When much of Arizona was ceded to the United States in 1848, American exploration naturally intensified. Wagon roads were pushed through the area, and in 1883 the coming of the railroad put northern Arizona on the map. A spur track was soon built from Williams to the south rim of the Grand Canyon, replacing the torturous stage ride with a comfortable train trip. Tourism blossomed, and Williams became known as the "Gateway to the Grand Canyon." The small mountain town is surrounded by the ponderosa pine forests of the Kaibab National Forest, which offers many enjoyable hikes. Extinct volcanoes and cinder cones relieve the otherwise flat surface of the plateau; many of the hikes take advantage of these features.

1 Bixler Saddle Trail

Description:	A hike on a seldom-used, easier trail to the summit of Bill Williams Mountain.
Location:	9.4 miles southwest of Williams.
Type of trail:	Out and back.
Type of trip:	Day hike.
Difficulty:	Moderate.
Total distance:	5.0 miles.
Elevation change:	1,500 feet.
Time required:	3.5 hours.
Water:	None.
Best season:	Late spring through fall.
Maps:	Williams South USGS quad; Kaibab National Forest (Williams, Chalender, and Tusayan Ranger Districts).
Permits and restrictions:	None.
For more information:	Williams Ranger District, Kaibab National Forest.

Finding the trailhead: From Williams, drive west on Interstate 40 about 5 miles and exit at Devil Dog Road. Turn left (south) on this maintained dirt road (Forest Road 108). Travel about 0.4 mile and turn left (east) again, staying on FR 108. After about 0.5 mile, the road turns sharply right (south). Watch for an unsigned, unmaintained road (FR 45) turning left (east). Turn here; this is the Bixler Saddle Road, which is rocky in places. A high-clearance or four-wheel-drive vehicle is recommended. Follow this road about 3.5 miles to its end at Bixler Saddle and the signed trailhead.

Bixler Saddle Trail • Clover Spring Trail
Bill Williams Trail • Buckskinner Trail • Benham Trail

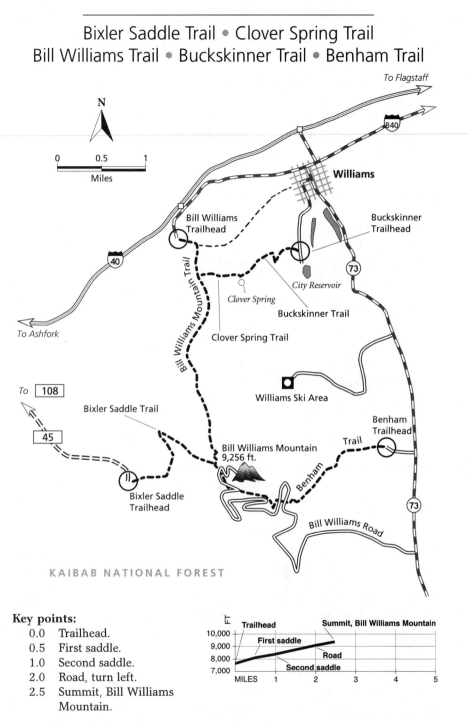

Key points:

- 0.0   Trailhead.
- 0.5   First saddle.
- 1.0   Second saddle.
- 2.0   Road, turn left.
- 2.5   Summit, Bill Williams Mountain.

The hike: The Bixler Saddle Trail starts up the gentle ridge to the northeast then follows a minor drainage through cool fir forest. There are close views of some impressive rock formations. After reaching a saddle, it traverses the west slopes of Bill Williams Mountain through open pine-oak forest with great views. A few short switchbacks lead to another saddle. The trail then swings southeast across the mountainside. In a little under a mile it reaches yet another saddle; the radio towers on the summit are clearly visible above. The trail descends slightly to end at a signed junction with the Bill Williams Mountain Trail. Turn right (east) and follow this trail about 0.2 mile to its end at a road. It's now about 0.5 mile along the road to the summit.

The actual summit is crowded with radio buildings and towers. There are excellent views of the western Coconino Plateau and the Mogollon Rim. Sycamore Canyon is visible to the south, as is Mingus Mountain. The Forest Service fire lookout is staffed during high fire danger. Be sure to ask permission from the staff member before climbing the tower.

2 Clover Spring Trail

See Map on Page 29

Description:	A pleasant, easy hike through pine and oak forest on the southeast slopes of Bill Williams Mountain.
Location:	1 mile west of Williams.
Type of trail:	Out and back.
Type of trip:	Day hike.
Difficulty:	Easy.
Total distance:	2.2 miles.
Elevation change:	160 feet.
Time required:	1.5 hours.
Water:	Clover Spring.
Best season:	Spring through fall.
Maps:	Williams South USGS quad; Kaibab National Forest (Williams, Chalender, and Tusayan Ranger Districts).
Permits and restrictions:	None.
For more information:	Williams Ranger District, Kaibab National Forest.

Finding the trailhead: From Williams, drive west on Bill Williams Avenue (Business Interstate 40) and just before the I-40 interchange west of town, turn left at the turnoff for the Forest Service Ranger Station. Turn left again at the next signed turnoff for the ranger station and follow the signs to the Bill Williams trailhead, which is next to the ranger station.

Key points:
  0.0   Bill Williams Trailhead.
  0.6   Turn left on Clover Spring Trail.
  1.1   Clover Spring.

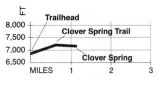

The hike: The trail is not shown on the topographic map, but it's a good trail that's easy to follow. Follow the signed Bill Williams Trail as it leaves the parking area and crosses a meadow. Shortly the trail begins to climb moderately in a series

Clover Spring.

of switchbacks. The forest is especially fine in this area, with an interesting mixture of the ever-present ponderosa pine, Gambel oaks, alligator junipers, and even a few white fir.

White fir trees are much less common than Douglas-fir, and seem to favor cool drainage bottoms. Usually they can be distinguished from the Douglas-fir by their blue-green color. When white fir are growing next to Douglas-fir, the color difference is obvious; otherwise, you may have to look more closely. White fir cones grow upward from the branches, as is the case for all true firs, while the Douglas-fir cones hang down. Some people also confuse white fir with blue spruce, but if you attempt to roll a few needles in your fingers you'll discover that they are flat. Spruce needles are square in cross section and easily roll in your fingers.

After the switchbacks end and the Bill Williams Trail levels out a bit, watch for an unmarked trail forking left (0.6 mile from the trailhead). Turn left here, and follow the excellent trail as it traverses the hillside to the east. Clover Hill is visible ahead to your left through the trees. Another common plant grows along the trail here: the cliffrose. Usually a nondescript shrub that rarely reaches 10 feet in height, in early summer it's a showy mass of small white flowers.

After a slightly downhill walk through the woods, you'll reach Clover Spring 0.5 mile from the trail fork. Although the spring isn't much more than a slow trickle, it used to be an important water source in the early days of settlement. It supplied water for the ranger station for a time and is an important water source for wildlife, as are all springs on this dry plateau. As with all natural water sources, it should be purified before consumption.

3 Bill Williams Trail

	See Map on Page 29
Description:	This trail takes you through cool, alpine forest to the summit of Bill Williams Mountain.
Location:	1 mile west of Williams.
Type of trail:	Out and back.
Type of trip:	Day hike.
Difficulty:	Moderate.
Total distance:	6.8 miles.
Elevation change:	2,380 feet.
Time required:	5 hours.
Water:	None.
Best season:	Summer through fall.
Maps:	Williams South USGS quad; Kaibab National Forest (Williams, Chalender, and Tusayan Ranger Districts).
Permits and restrictions:	None.
For more information:	Williams Ranger District, Kaibab National Forest.

Finding the trailhead: From Williams, drive west on Bill Williams Avenue (Business Interstate 40), and, just before the I-40 interchange west of town, turn left at the turnoff for the Forest Service Ranger Station. Turn left again at the next signed turnoff for the ranger station, and follow the signs to the Bill Williams trailhead, next to the ranger station.

Key points:

0.0   Bill Williams Trailhead.
0.6   Junction with the Clover Spring Trail.
2.9   Bill Williams Road, turn left.
3.4   Bill Williams Mountain.

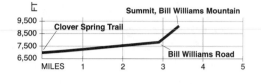

The hike: The first section of this hike is the same as the Clover Spring Trail. From the Clover Spring Trail junction, the Bill Williams Trail continues south, climbing gradually. As it nears the steep north slopes of the mountain, it heads into a north-facing canyon and starts to climb more steeply. The forest changes from open ponderosa pine stands to denser Douglas-fir with a scattering of aspen. A series of switchbacks leads up to the trail's end at the Bill Williams Road. To reach the summit, turn left and walk 0.5 mile to the end of the road.

4 Buckskinner Trail

See Map on Page 29

Description:	This is an easy trail that starts from Buckskinner Park in the town of Williams. It can be used for a short, easy hike as described here, or used to reach the Bill Williams Trail for a more ambitious hike.
Location:	In Williams.
Type of trail:	Out and back.
Type of trip:	Day hike.
Difficulty:	Easy.
Total distance:	2.0 miles.
Elevation change:	320 feet.
Time required:	1.5 hours.
Water:	None.
Best season:	Late spring through fall.
Maps:	Williams South USGS quad; Kaibab National Forest (Williams, Chalender, and Tusayan Ranger Districts).
Permits and restrictions:	None.
For more information:	Williams Ranger District, Kaibab National Forest.

Finding the trailhead: From Bill Williams Avenue, Williams's main street, turn south on Fourth Street. Go two blocks and turn right. After two more blocks, turn left onto Sixth Street. Follow this street a short distance out of

33

town. Keep left at the Forest Service complex, and follow the road (now maintained dirt) to Buckskinner Park, which is on the right just before the end of the road at City Reservoir. The trailhead is behind the ramadas, on the west side of the park.

Key points:

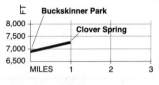

- 0.0   Trailhead at Buckskinner Park.
- 1.0   Clover Spring.

The hike: The well-defined trail heads south-southwest into a ravine and works its way to the top of a volcanic terrace. A few Douglas-fir mix with the ponderosa pine–Gambel oak forest here, but when the trail reaches the flatter terrain above, the Douglas-fir disappear. The trail continues west-southwest, crosses another ravine, and reaches Clover Spring. This is a logical turnaround point for a short, easy hike. If desired, you can continue on Clover Spring Trail 0.5 mile to Bill Williams Trail and turn left to hike to the top of Bill Williams Mountain. This is a climb of more than 2,000 feet, and it adds 6 miles to the round-trip distance. See Hike 3 for information.

5 Benham Trail

See Map on Page 29

Description: An enjoyable walk on a well-graded trail through beautiful ponderosa pine forest to the summit of Bill Williams Mountain.

Location: 4.1 miles south of Williams.

Type of trail: Out and back.

Type of trip: Day hike.

Difficulty: Moderate.

Total distance: 8.0 miles.

Elevation change: 2,000 feet.

Time required: 5 hours.

Water: None.

Best season: Late spring through fall.

Maps: Williams South USGS quad; Kaibab National Forest (Williams, Chalender, and Tusayan Ranger Districts).

Permits and restrictions: None.

For more information: Williams Ranger District, Kaibab National Forest.

Finding the trailhead: From Bill Williams Avenue, Williams's main street, drive 3.9 miles south on Fourth Street (County Road 73) and turn right (west) at the sign for the Benham Trail. Continue 0.2 mile, turn right just before you reach a gate with private property signs, and park at the signed trailhead.

Key points:

  0.0   Trailhead.

  1.9   First road crossing.

  3.5   End of trail on
          summit road.

  4.0   Summit.

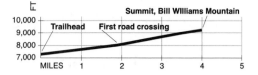

The hike: According to the Forest Service sign at the trailhead, the Benham Trail was originally constructed in 1920; it was abandoned in 1951 when the present road was opened to the top of the mountain. The trail was reopened in 1976 as a recreation trail and named after H. L. Benham, the forest ranger on the Williams Ranger District from 1910 to 1911. The United States Forest Service was created in 1903 to manage the National Forest Reserves that had been designated in the 1890s. Early forest rangers were responsible for enforcing the new (and often unpopular) conservation laws over an entire ranger district, an area of hundreds of square miles. Usually working alone, the rangers built trails, suppressed fires, and monitored timber-cutting activity.

The Benham Trail is not shown on the topographic map but is easy to follow as it wanders up the gentle slope to the west through an open ponderosa pine and Gambel oak forest. Gambel oaks are deciduous and average only 10 to 20 feet in height, with slender gray trunks. About 1.5 miles from the trailhead, the trail crosses a gully then crosses through an ugly but short section of logged forest. Shortly afterward, the trail enters a dense section of Gambel oaks, where there are a few Douglas-firs. Among the Gambel oaks there are a few much larger Emory and Arizona White oaks.

The trail begins to climb the southeast side of the mountain in a series of switchbacks, and the quality of the trail is evident in the massive amount of construction. This was probably the main supply trail for the fire lookout tower on the summit, as the slightly shorter Bill Williams Trail is blocked by snow later in the year than the Benham Trail. The trail crosses a switchback in the vehicle road and then reaches the south ridge of the mountain. Continuing to climb in switchbacks, the trail skirts another road switchback, where the Forest Service rerouted the trail. Above this point there is an interesting stand of Gambel oak that is being crowded out by a young, dense stand of Douglas-fir. The trail crosses the road again and passes a small patch of quaking aspen. After a fourth road crossing, a few final switchbacks lead through a stand of small aspen. An unmarked trail to the left leads about 50 feet to the road and the head of the Bill Williams Trail. The Benham Trail goes right and ends on the road in about 100 yards. From here it is 0.5 mile to the summit along the road.

6 Summit Mountain Trail

Description:	A hike to the top of Summit Mountain that has great views of the southern Coconino Plateau.
Location:	10.9 miles southeast of Williams.
Type of trail:	Out and back.
Type of trip:	Day hike.
Difficulty:	Easy.
Total distance:	2.0 miles.
Elevation change:	640 feet.
Time required:	1.5 hours.
Water:	None.
Best season:	Summer through fall.
Maps:	Williams South, May Tank Pocket USGS quads; Kaibab National Forest (Williams, Chalender, and Tusayan Ranger Districts).
Permits and restrictions:	None.
For more information:	Chalendar Ranger District, Kaibab National Forest.

Finding the trailhead: From Williams, drive 8.4 miles south on Fourth Street (County Road 73) and turn left on Forest Road 110. Continue 2.0 miles and turn right on FR 706. Go 0.5 mile to the trailhead, which is on the right.

Key points:
- 0.0 Trailhead.
- 1.0 Summit Mountain viewpoint.

San Francisco Mountain floats above a sea of pines, viewed from the Summit Mountain Trail.

Summit Mountain Trail

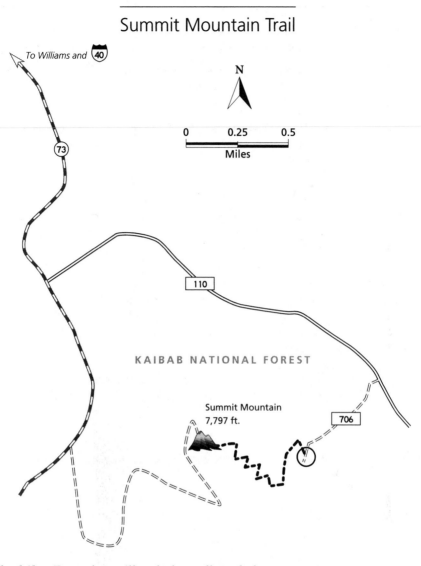

To Williams and 40

73

N

KAIBAB NATIONAL FOREST

110

Summit Mountain
7,797 ft.

706

The hike: From the trailhead, the well-graded trail climbs west above the parking area and then swings south above an old cinder pit. It then switchbacks up the southeast ridge through pleasant ponderosa pine and Gambel oak for-

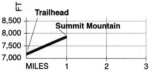

est. This forest is open and you'll get occasional glimpses of the forested plateau. Higher up, there's a great view of Kendrick Mountain and San Francisco Mountain to the northeast. When the trail emerges onto the summit plateau, it heads west. Shortly, it ends at a viewpoint looking southwest toward Mingus Mountain and the Sierra Prieta near Prescott.

This trail was built more than 80 years ago to reach a fire lookout, but was abandoned until 1997, when it was rebuilt as a recreation trail.

7 Dogtown Lake Trail

Description:	An easy walk around the shores of Dogtown Lake.
Location:	7.9 miles southwest of Williams.
Type of trail:	Loop.
Type of trip:	Day hike.
Difficulty:	Easy.
Total distance:	1.8 miles.
Elevation change:	None.
Time required:	1 hour.
Water:	Dogtown Lake.
Best season:	Late spring through fall.
Maps:	Williams South USGS quad; Kaibab National Forest (Williams, Chalender, and Tusayan Ranger Districts).
Permits and restrictions:	None.
For more information:	Chalendar Ranger District, Kaibab National Forest.

Finding the trailhead: From Williams, drive 3.9 miles south on Fourth Street (County Road 73) and turn left (east) on Forest Road 140. Follow this maintained dirt road 3.0 miles and turn left onto maintained FR 132. Continue 1 mile to Dogtown Campground. Bear left in the campground and park in the trailhead parking near the boat ramp.

Dogtown Lake Trail • Davenport Hill Trail

Key points:
- 0.0 Trailhead at Dogtown Lake.
- 0.7 Wash.
- 1.0 Dogtown Wash.
- 1.8 Trailhead.

The hike: This is an easy, pleasant walk through the pine forest along the shore of Dogtown Lake. Start north from the trailhead to walk the loop counterclockwise. At the northwest corner of the lake you'll cross an unnamed, normally dry wash that feeds the lake. Dogtown Wash, at the southwest side of the lake, is the main inlet to the lake. Like most stream courses on the Coconino Plateau, these washes carry water only during snow melt in early spring and intermittently after heavy summer thunderstorms.

8 Davenport Hill Trail

See Map on Page 38

Description: A day hike to the top of Davenport Hill, featuring a pleasant, shady, pine and oak forest and views of the Williams area.

Location: 7.9 miles southwest of Williams.

Type of trail: Out and back.

Type of trip: Day hike.

Difficulty: Easy.

Total distance: 5.0 miles.

Elevation change: 685 feet.

Time required: 3 hours.

Water: None.

Best season: Summer through fall.

Maps: Davenport Hill USGS quad; Kaibab National Forest (Williams, Chalender, and Tusayan Ranger Districts).

Permits and restrictions: None.

For more information: Chalender Ranger District, Kaibab National Forest.

Finding the trailhead: From Williams, drive 3.9 miles south on Fourth Street (County Road 73) and turn left (east) on Forest Road 140. Follow this maintained dirt road 3 miles and turn left onto maintained FR 132. Continue 1 mile to Dogtown Campground. Bear left in the campground and park in the trailhead parking near the boat ramp.

Key points:
- 0.0 Trailhead at Dogtown Lake.
- 1.5 Start up Davenport Hill.
- 2.5 Summit.

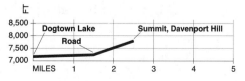

The hike: The first section of the trail is signed as the Ponderosa Nature Trail. The Davenport Hill Trail junction is signed and is at the back of the nature trail loop about 0.3 mile from the trailhead. Turn right at the fork in the nature trail for the shortest route to the Davenport Hill Trail junction. Neither trail is shown on the topographic map, but both are shown on the Forest Service map. At first, the trail follows Dogtown Wash below the dam that forms the lake, but after the nature trail ends it climbs onto a broad, gentle ridge. This area is covered with an open ponderosa pine and Gambel oak forest. About 1.5 miles from the campground, the trail crosses an old road and starts the ascent of Davenport Hill. Built for recreation, the trail climbs the slopes at an easy grade in a series of switchbacks. There are occasional views of the forests and meadows below during the ascent. A section near the top is on the north side of the hill—notice how the change in exposure allows white and Douglas-fir to mix with the pine. The trail finally reaches the ridge crest and turns north a few hundred yards to the summit. Just where the trail turns north, a lightning-shattered pine attests to the violence of the summer lightning storms. At the summit, the view is limited to tantalizing hints because of the surrounding trees.

9 Keyhole Sink Trail

Description:	A very easy trail to a unique petroglyph site near Sitgreaves Mountain.
Location:	10 miles east of Williams.
Type of trail:	Out and back.
Type of trip:	Day hike.
Difficulty:	Easy.
Total distance:	2.0 miles.
Elevation change:	100 feet.
Time required:	1 hour.
Water:	None.
Best season:	Spring through fall.
Maps:	Sitgreaves Mountain USGS quad; Kaibab National Forest (Williams, Chalender, and Tusayan Ranger Districts).
Permits and restrictions:	None.
For more information:	Chalender Ranger District, Kaibab National Forest.

Finding the trailhead: From Williams, drive east on Interstate 40 about 8 miles to the Pittman Valley Road exit. Cross the interstate to the north and turn right (east) on Arizona Highway 66. Continue 2 miles and park on the right (south) in the Oak Hill Snowplay Area parking lot.

Key points:
0.0   Trailhead.
1.0   Keyhole Sink.

Trailhead
8,000
Keyhole Sink
7,500
7,000
6,500
MILES   1   2

The hike: The signed trail (which is not shown on the topographic map) starts on the north side of the road

Keyhole Sink Trail

at a gate. It descends very gradually through open ponderosa pine forest and small meadows. The trail then turns northeast and passes a small stand of aspen before ending in a box canyon. A rail fence, interpretive sign, and visitor's register mark the spot. The low, colorful volcanic cliffs, the aspens

Rock climbers at Keyhole Sink.

and pine, and the pool of water combine to make this a pleasant spot, especially in the late afternoon sun.

Look carefully, and you will find a number of petroglyphs along the base of the wall. One of these clearly depicts a herd of deer entering the canyon. Usually the exact meaning of ancient rock art is more elusive. Please don't touch or otherwise disturb the petroglyphs; they are protected by federal law as a fragile link to the unwritten past. Such artwork is one of the few signs of prehistoric human habitation in this section of the Coconino Plateau. While hunting parties probably passed through from time to time, there is little evidence of any permanent settlement. Probably the short growing season and the lack of water were discouraging.

10 Sycamore Rim Trail

Description:	A long and enjoyable walk on a scenic trail along the rim of Sycamore and Big Springs Canyons. Part of the trail is within Sycamore Canyon Wilderness.
Location:	13 miles southeast of Williams.
Type of trail:	Loop.
Type of trip:	Day hike.
Difficulty:	Moderate.
Total distance:	9.6 miles.
Elevation change:	790 feet.
Time required:	5 hours.
Water:	None.
Best season:	Spring through fall.
Maps:	Davenport Hill, Garland Prairie USGS quads; Kaibab National Forest (Williams, Chalender, and Tusayan Ranger Districts).
Permits and restrictions:	None.
For more information:	Chalender Ranger District, Kaibab National Forest.

Finding the trailhead: From Flagstaff: Drive about 16 miles west on Interstate 40 and turn left (south) at the Parks exit onto the maintained Garland Prairie Road (Forest Road 141). Drive 12 miles and turn left (south) on FR 131, a signed, maintained road. Continue about 1.5 miles to Dow Trailhead.

From Williams: Drive east on I-40 about 4 miles and turn right (south) at the Garland Prairie Road exit (this is not the same exit for Garland Prairie mentioned above). Drive 8.5 miles on FR 141 to reach FR 131and turn right (south) and continue 0.5 mile to the trailhead.

Key points:

0.0	Dow Trailhead.	4.4	Pomeroy Tanks.
0.1	Sycamore Rim Trail; turn right.	5.2	Sycamore Falls.
1.4	Cross FR 56.	6.6	Sycamore Vista.
2.1	KA Hill.	9.6	Dow Trailhead.

Sycamore Rim Trail

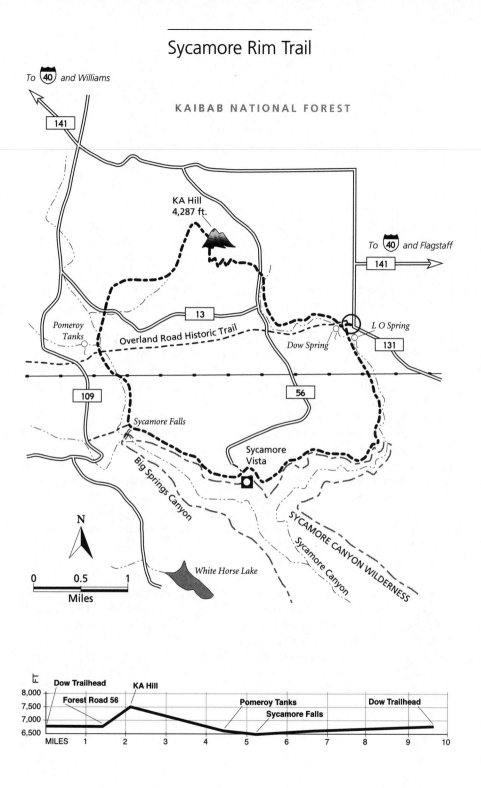

The hike: The Sycamore Rim Trail is not shown on the topographic map. Almost immediately after you leave the parking lot, you'll cross the route of the historic Overland Road. The old road was built in 1858 as part of a route across northern Arizona from east to west. Long abandoned, the route has recently been retraced by the USDA Forest Service and marked with wood posts, brass caps, and rock cairns. From this trailhead, you can optionally follow the old route either east into Garland Prairie, or west toward Pomeroy Tanks.

Continuing on our hike, you meet the Sycamore Rim Trail at a T intersection, where you'll turn left to start the loop. The trail follows the rim of Sycamore Canyon, which is a shallow drainage at this point. A Forest Service sign points out the location of an old lumber mill. Not much is visible now except a few rotting timbers. These temporary logging mills and camps were moved to follow the active logging. The logs were transported on temporary railroad spurs. After the transcontinental railroad reached the area in 1883, railroads were the most economical method of moving cut timber to the mills, as well as men and supplies into the forest. When logging was complete in an area (meaning that all the accessible large trees were cut), the rails would be removed and reused on another spur railroad. The road beds were built to the minimum standard necessary for their short-lived purpose. Today these old railroad grades can be traced for miles through the forest; some have been rebuilt into modern dirt roads.

The shallow canyon gradually broadens into a meadow, which the trail crosses to meet FR 56. On the west side of the road, the trail starts to climb KA Hill in a series of switchbacks. After crossing the forested summit, the trail drops southwest down the gentle, pine-forested slopes and into a shallow drainage. It crosses a road (FR 13) and then passes Pomeroy Tanks, a series of natural basins in the drainage that sometimes hold water. A spur trail goes southwest to Pomeroy Tanks Trailhead on FR 109.

Now the trail follows the drainage, soon crossing back to the east side. The canyon gradually deepens, and the trail meets another spur trail. This one goes to Sycamore Falls Trailhead, also on FR 104. The drainage we've been following is joined by Big Spring Canyon, which in turn drops over Sycamore Falls. The basalt cliffs here are a popular rock climbing area.

As the canyon deepens, the trail heads southeast along its rim, climbing gradually. At Sycamore Vista, you'll have a fine view of Sycamore Canyon Wilderness to the south. Another short spur trail goes to Sycamore Vista Trailhead on FR 56. At this point, the canyon is over 500 feet deep. Now the trail heads east across the broad point separating Big Spring Canyon from Sycamore Canyon. After it meets the rim of Sycamore Canyon, it follows the rim back to the junction near Dow Trailhead. Turn right to return to the trailhead.

Coconino Plateau

The Coconino Plateau is the southernmost portion of the Colorado Plateau and covers the region surrounding San Francisco Mountain, north of the Mogollon Rim and south of the Grand Canyon. Several hundred cinder cones and old volcanoes dot the area, ranging in elevation from 8,000 to 12,633 feet. Most of the hikes in this section explore these old volcanic features. Kendrick Peak and San Francisco Mountain are wilderness areas.

11 Red Butte

Description:	An easy hike to a unique geologic feature.
Location:	About 14 miles south of Tusayan.
Type of trail:	Out and back.
Type of trip:	Day hike.
Difficulty:	Easy.
Total distance:	2.0 miles.
Elevation change:	960 feet.
Time required:	1.5 hours.
Water:	None.
Best season:	Spring through fall.
Maps:	Red Butte USGS quad; Kaibab National Forest (Williams, Chalender, and Tusayan Ranger Districts).
Permits and restrictions:	None.
For more information:	Tusayan Ranger District, Kaibab National Forest.

Finding the trailhead: From Tusayan, drive 12 miles south on Arizona Highway 64 and turn left (east) on Forest Road 320, a maintained dirt road. Continue 1.5 miles and go left on FR 340. After 0.8 mile, turn right onto FR 340A and park at the signed trailhead.

Key points:
- 0.0 Trailhead.
- 1.0 Summit, Red Butte.

The hike: The trail heads up the west slopes of the butte in a series of switchbacks, reaching a shoulder before climbing the summit knob. The small summit plateau is open and the view is good in all directions. A fire-lookout building stands at the northeast edge. If the lookout is staffed, be sure to ask permission before climbing up. Red Butte is formed primarily from reddish Moenkopi sandstone, which is younger than any of the rocks that form the Grand Canyon. Thousands of feet of these younger rocks once covered the plateau around Red Butte but have been eroded away except for this small remnant. A cap of dark-colored, hard, volcanic rocks

Red Butte

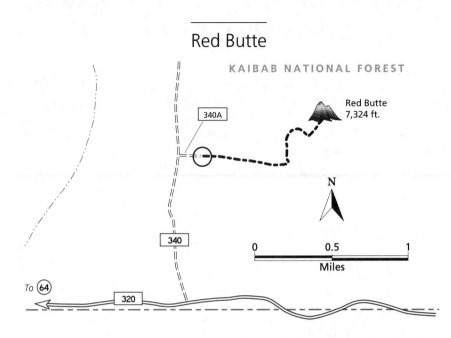

KAIBAB NATIONAL FOREST

340A

Red Butte
7,324 ft.

N

340

0   0.5   1
Miles

To 64

320

protected Red Butte from erosion. Where did all the cubic miles of rock go? Most likely, down the Colorado River to the Pacific Ocean.

Another interesting feature is the old Grand Canyon airport, visible to the north. Although the outlines of the dirt runways are hard to pick out, there are a few old buildings still standing, including a hangar. The site served as the Grand Canyon airport until the 1960s, when the present airport was built just south of Tusayan.

12 Red Mountain

Description:	A short hike to a colorful, highly eroded volcanic mountain on the Coconino Plateau.
Location:	31.6 miles northwest of Flagstaff.
Type of trail:	Out and back.
Type of trip:	Day hike.
Difficulty:	Easy.
Total distance:	1.0 mile.
Elevation change:	150 feet.
Time required:	0.5 hour.
Water:	None.
Best season:	Spring through fall.
Maps:	Chapel Mountain USGS quad; Coconino National Forest.
Permits and restrictions:	None.
For more information:	Peaks Ranger District, Coconino National Forest.

Red Mountain

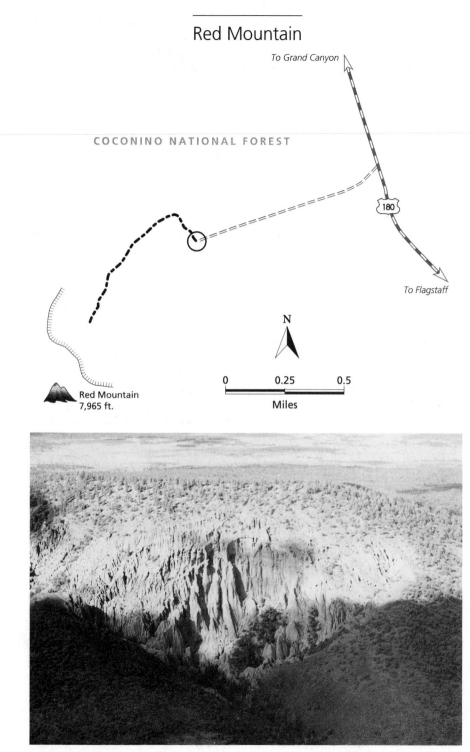

To Grand Canyon

COCONINO NATIONAL FOREST

180

To Flagstaff

Red Mountain
7,965 ft.

N

```
0          0.25          0.5
```
Miles

Aerial view of Red Mountain.

Finding the trailhead: From Flagstaff, drive 31 miles north on U.S. Highway 180 and turn left (west) on an unmaintained dirt road. The colorful face of Red Mountain is visible ahead. Continue 0.6 mile to the trailhead in a large clearing in the pinyon-juniper forest, and park.

Key points:
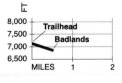

0.0   Trailhead.

0.5   Volcanic badlands.

The hike: From the clearing, contour west around the hillside into the gully that drains the eroded area. Once in the bed of the drainage, walk west into the heart of the reddish badlands. It is easy to imagine a volcanic explosion creating this area, but probably the crumbly spires and hoodoos are the result of water erosion of the old cinder cone. In fact, study of the topographic map shows that Red Mountain is crescent shaped, with the crescent opening to the southwest. Probably the old crater was to the southwest as well, on the opposite side of the eroded area.

13 Slate Mountain Trail

Description:	This hike follows an old road to the summit of Slate Mountain. This is a good place for views of the numerous old volcanoes on the northern Coconino Plateau.
Location:	28 miles northwest of Flagstaff.
Type of trail:	Out and back.
Type of trip:	Day hike.
Difficulty:	Moderate.
Total distance:	4.8 miles.
Elevation change:	850 feet.
Time required:	3 hours.
Water:	None.
Best season:	Spring through fall.
Maps:	Kendrick Peak USGS quad; Coconino National Forest.
Permits and restrictions:	None.
For more information:	Peaks Ranger District, Coconino National Forest.

Finding the trailhead: From Flagstaff, drive about 26 miles north on U.S. Highway 180 and turn left on Forest Road 191. Go 2.0 miles to the trailhead.

Key points:

0.0   Trailhead.

2.4   Summit.

The hike: The hike follows an old road, now closed, around the northwest side of a small hill

48

Slate Mountain Trail

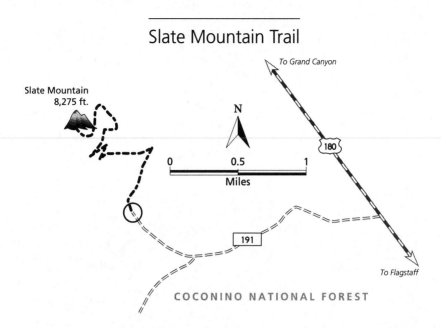

and then starts to climb the south slopes of Slate Mountain. After several switchbacks, the trail swings around the north side of the mountain before winding around the summit cone itself. Little remains of the fire lookout that once stood here, but the views are still excellent. Kendrick Mountain, to the southwest, and San Francisco Mountain, to the southeast, dominate the view. To the north, the Coconino Plateau stretches to the Grand Canyon's South Rim.

14 Kendrick Peak Trail

Description:	This hike follows a well-graded trail to the summit of the second highest mountain in northern Arizona, in the Kendrick Mountain Wilderness.
Location:	22.6 miles northwest of Flagstaff.
Type of trail:	Out and back.
Type of trip:	Day hike.
Difficulty:	Moderate.
Total distance:	8.0 miles.
Elevation change:	2,720 feet.
Time required:	5.5 hours.
Water:	None.
Best season:	Summer through fall.
Maps:	Kendrick Peak USGS quad; Kaibab National Forest (Williams, Chalender, and Tusayan Ranger District).
Permits and restrictions:	None.
For more information:	Chalender Ranger District, Kaibab National Forest.

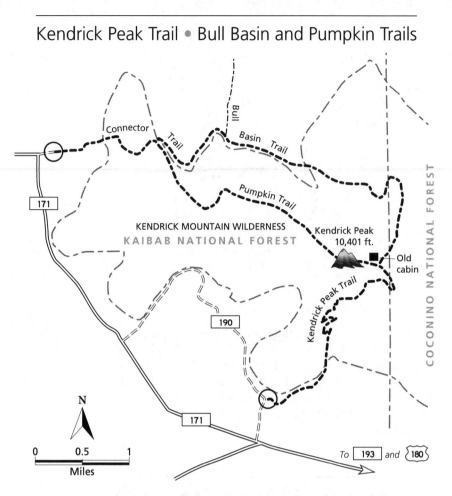

Finding the trailhead: From Flagstaff, drive north about 17 miles on U.S. Highway 180 and turn left (west) on a maintained dirt road (Forest Road 193). Continue 3.2 miles and turn right (northwest) on another maintained dirt road (FR 171). Drive 2.0 miles, turn right onto FR 190, and continue 0.4 mile to the signed trailhead on the right side of the road.

Key points:

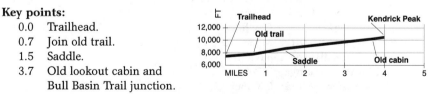

- 0.0 Trailhead.
- 0.7 Join old trail.
- 1.5 Saddle.
- 3.7 Old lookout cabin and Bull Basin Trail junction.
- 4.0 Kendrick Lookout and Pumpkin Trail junction.

The hike: The Kendrick Peak Trail is the easiest of the three trails to the summit of Kendrick Peak. Built for maintenance of the Forest Service fire lookout, it climbs the south side of the mountain in gradual switchbacks.

Fire lookout on the summit of Kendrick Peak.

A devastating wildfire burned much of Kendrick Mountain in 2000. Watch for hazards such as falling trees, as well as logs across the trail. Check with the Chalender Ranger District (see Appendix D) for the latest conditions.

The trail climbs the slope to the northeast, through ponderosa pine stands, to join the original trail just above the old trailhead. This next section of trail was used as a road during a forest fire many years ago, and it is noticeably wider than the remainder of the trail. At first, the trail follows the left side of a drainage; it then begins to switchback. Notice that Douglas-fir appear as the trail climbs this section.

Soon, the trail reaches a saddle and becomes narrower again. The trail climbs a short distance up the ridge to the northeast and starts to ascend the south-facing slope in a series of switchbacks. Limber pine and Arizona cork-bark fir appear, as well as quaking aspen. Occasional open meadows offer extensive views of the forested Coconino Plateau to the south. Eventually, the trail makes a major switchback to the northwest, and there are glimpses of the summit and the squat lookout building. The trail enters a meadow on the east ridge of the peak and meets the Bull Basin Trail near an old cabin.

The cabin was built in the early part of the twentieth century by the fire lookout, who then lived in the cabin and rode his horse to the summit each day to watch for fires. The lookout obtained water from a spring to the south, which is unreliable today. In the early days of the Forest Service, fire lookouts often sat on the bare mountaintop to watch for fires. Amenities like lookout buildings and towers were constructed gradually as the need for permanent fire watches developed.

Continue on the Kendrick Peak Trail about 0.3 mile to the summit. The lookout welcomes visitors unless he or she is busy; ask permission before climbing the stairs. From either the catwalk or the ground, the views are stunning. San Francisco Mountain to the east dominates the scenery, and you can also see many of the hundreds of old volcanoes and cinder cones that dot the plateau. The beautiful pine forest stretches in all directions, scarred here and there by old forest fire burns. To the north, the cliffs of the Grand Canyon's north rim are visible fifty miles away.

15 Bull Basin and Pumpkin Trails

See Map on Page 50

Description: A rugged, seldom-hiked trek through alpine forest through much of the Kendrick Peak Wilderness.

Location: 28 miles northwest of Flagstaff.

Type of trail: Loop.

Type of trip: Day hike or overnight backpack.

Difficulty: Difficult.

Total distance: 10.6 miles.

Elevation change: 3,160 feet.

Time required: 7 hours.

Water: None.

Best season: Summer through fall.

Maps: Kendrick Peak, Moritz Ridge USGS quads; Kaibab National Forest (Williams, Chalender, and Tusayan Ranger Districts).

Permits and restrictions: None.

For more information: Chalender Ranger District, Kaibab National Forest.

Finding the trailhead: From Flagstaff, drive north 17 miles on U.S. Highway 180 and turn left (west) on a maintained dirt road (Forest Road 193). Continue 3.2 miles and turn right (northwest) on another maintained dirt road (FR 171). Drive 7.8 miles to the Pumpkin Trailhead, which is on the right.

Key points:
- 0.0   Pumpkin Trailhead.
- 1.6   Junction with Connector Trail; go left.
- 2.4   Turn right on Bull Basin Trail.
- 4.6   Saddle.
- 5.6   Old lookout cabin; turn right on Kendrick Peak Trail.
- 5.9   Kendrick Lookout; continue on Pumpkin Trail.
- 9.0   Connector Trail junction; turn left.
- 10.6   Pumpkin Trailhead.

The hike: This is a strenuous hike on steep trails. There is no water, so hikers planning an overnight trip will have to carry all the water needed or do the hike in late spring when there are still snowdrifts near the summit.

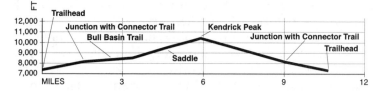

The rewards are worth the effort. None of the trails are shown on the topographic maps, except for the short segment of the Kendrick Peak Trail used by this loop.

A devastating wildfire burned much of Kendrick Mountain in 2000. Watch for hazards such as falling trees, as well as logs across the trail. Check with the Chalender Ranger District for the latest conditions.

The Pumpkin Trail follows an old road east through the ponderosa pine forest and almost immediately starts climbing toward the west ridge of Kendrick Peak. After 1.6 miles, the trail climbs into a saddle and meets the Connector Trail. Turn left (east) here and continue as the Connector Trail contours the north slopes of the mountain along the wilderness boundary. After about a mile the trail passes through another saddle and crosses into Bull Basin. The Connector Trail ends at the junction with the Bull Basin Trail.

Turn right (southeast) on the Bull Basin Trail. The trail contours across the head of Bull Basin and climbs as it heads toward the north ridge of Kendrick Peak. The dense forest gives way to a series of alpine meadows just before the trail reaches the ridge crest at a saddle. Here the trail turns south and climbs steeply to the 10,000-foot east shoulder of the mountain. Now, the

The coyote has successfully adapted to man's presence in northern Arizona.

53

trail climbs more gradually, and ends near the old lookout cabin at the junction with the Kendrick Peak Trail. There are campsites along the tree line at the north edge of the meadow. In early summer or late spring, lingering snowdrifts make it possible to camp without carrying water. The alpine meadow and splendid sunset and sunrise views south are worth the effort of carrying overnight gear up here. Campfires are not recommended, by the way. Trees grow very slowly in the Arctic environment and should not be burned. Carry a backpacking stove to melt snow and cook meals.

Turn right (west) on the Kendrick Peak Trail, and follow it as it climbs to the summit. Look on the west side of the lookout building for the beginning of the Pumpkin Trail, which begins descending immediately. The views are excellent from the upper part of the trail as it switchbacks though several meadows. As the trail enters denser forest, it tends to follow the broad west ridge of the mountain. Watch for the junction with the Connector Trail as the forest becomes nearly pure ponderosa pine once again. This closes the loop—now continue on the Pumpkin Trail to the trailhead.

16 Crater Lake

Description:	A hike to a small lake within the crater of an extinct volcanic cinder cone near Kendrick Peak.
Location:	20.2 miles northwest of Flagstaff.
Type of trail:	Out and back.
Type of trip:	Day hike.
Difficulty:	Easy.
Total distance:	1.0 mile.
Elevation change:	200 feet.
Time required:	1 hour.
Water:	None.
Best season:	Summer through fall.
Maps:	Kendrick Peak USGS quad; Coconino National Forest.
Permits and restrictions:	None.
For more information:	Peaks Ranger District, Coconino National Forest.

Finding the trailhead: From Flagstaff, drive north 17 miles on U.S. Highway 180 and turn left (west) on a maintained dirt road (Forest Road 760). Continue 1.0 mile and turn right at a fork. After 0.2 mile, continue straight ahead at the crossroads as you enter the northeast end of Crowley Park. The road crosses the meadow to the northwest and enters the forest. After 1.0 mile, turn left at a fork. The road enters another meadow near Crater Spring Tank and becomes rough. You may want to park here; otherwise continue to a low saddle, 1.0 mile from the last fork, and park.

Crater Lake

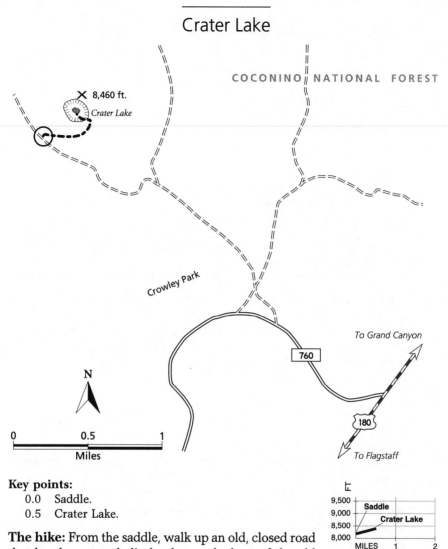

Coconino National Forest

8,460 ft.

Crater Lake

Crowley Park

To Grand Canyon

760

180

To Flagstaff

N

0   0.5   1
Miles

Key points:
0.0   Saddle.
0.5   Crater Lake.

The hike: From the saddle, walk up an old, closed road
that heads east and climbs the south slope of the old
cinder cone. After about 0.2 mile, the trail crosses through a saddle and descends into the crater. Crater Lake is a small pond ringed with aspens and
seems to hold water longer than the other two crater lakes in the area. It is
a pleasant but optional walk around the pond or the crater rim.

17 Beale Road Historic Trail

Description:	An easy walk along the route of a historic wagon road on Government Prairie.
Location:	26.4 miles northwest of Flagstaff.
Type of trail:	Out and back.
Type of trip:	Day hike.
Difficulty:	Easy.
Total distance:	4.8 miles.
Elevation change:	None.
Time required:	2 hours.
Water:	None.
Best season:	Summer through fall.
Maps:	Kendrick Peak USGS quad; Kaibab National Forest (Williams, Chalender, and Tusayan Ranger District).
Permits and restrictions:	None.
For more information:	Chalender Ranger District, Kaibab National Forest.

Finding the trailhead: From Flagstaff, drive north about 17 miles on U.S. Highway 180 and turn left (west) on a maintained dirt road (Forest Road 193). Continue 3.2 miles and turn right (northwest) on another maintained dirt road (FR 171). Drive 2.0 miles and turn left onto FR 100. Continue 4.2 miles to the junction with FR 107, and park.

Key points:
0.0   Trailhead.
2.4   Eastern edge of Government Prairie.

The hike: From the intersection of FR 100 and FR 107, the route of the Beale Road goes generally southeast into Government Prairie. There is no trail tread along this section, but you can follow the route, which is marked with wood posts, brass caps, and rock cairns. As you cross the wide open reaches of Government Prairie, it's easy to imagine what it must have been like to cross this scenic but arid country by horse or wagon. The east side of Government Prairie is a good stopping point because the old route merges with an unmaintained road at this point. You can, if you wish, trace the route all the way to Flagstaff.

The Beale Road was once part of a major interstate route between Fort Smith, Arkansas, and the Colorado River at Arizona's western border. It passed just south of San Francisco Mountain to take advantage of the springs found there.

Beale Road Historic Trail

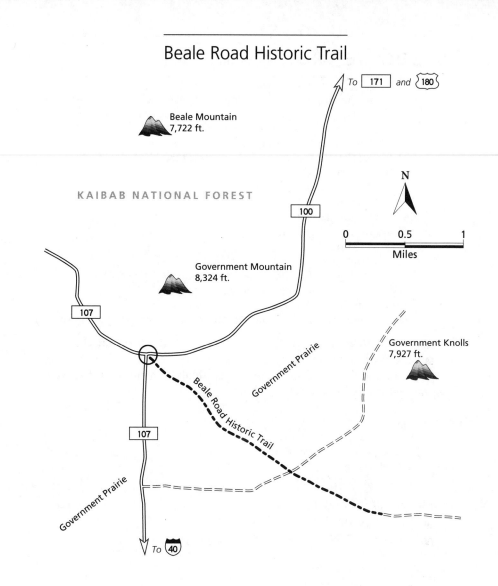

18 Saddle Mountain

Description:	A hike to the top of a volcanic cinder cone featuring unique views of San Francisco Mountain and the northern Coconino Plateau.
Location:	14 miles northwest of Flagstaff.
Type of trail:	Out and back, cross-country.
Type of trip:	Day hike.
Difficulty:	Moderate.
Total distance:	6.0 miles.
Elevation change:	980 feet.
Time required:	4 hours.
Water:	None.
Best season:	Summer through fall.
Maps:	Kendrick Peak, White Horse Hills USGS quads; Coconino National Forest.
Permits and restrictions:	None.
For more information:	Peaks Ranger District, Coconino National Forest.

Finding the trailhead: From Flagstaff drive 14 miles north on U.S. Highway 180 and park near Kendrick Park Picnic Area. (At 12 miles, the highway crosses Kendrick Park. The hill ahead and right, to the northeast, is Saddle Mountain, your destination for this hike.)

Key points:
- 0.0 Start of hike at picnic area.
- 1.1 West ridge of Saddle Mountain.
- 1.6 Turn left on road.
- 3.0 Summit of Saddle Mountain.

The hike: Saddle Mountain is visible to the east from the picnic area. Your initial goal is the southwest ridge of the mountain, which is to the right of the summit. Either follow an old road east to a cinder pit, or walk cross-country through the

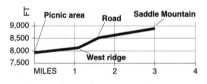

open ponderosa pine forest along the ridge north of Kendrick Park to reach the base of the ridge. Then hike east directly up the ridge (the summit will be to your left). You'll intercept the Saddle Mountain Road where it makes a switchback on the south side of the mountain. Turn left and follow the road to the summit. The last section of the walk takes you around the north side of the mountain, into a cool, dense forest of Douglas-fir—a startling climate change from the dry, grassy slopes of the south side.

The summit itself is crowned with a Forest Service radio tower and building. This facility occupies the former site of a fire lookout tower. At one point, there were three fire towers observing the northern end of the Coconino National Forest and the north slopes of San Francisco Mountain. Today, only one remains in service, O'Leary Peak northeast of San Francisco Mountain.

Saddle Mountain

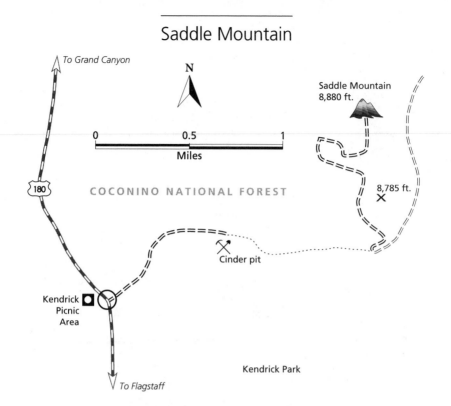

To Grand Canyon

N

Saddle Mountain
8,880 ft.

0   0.5   1
Miles

180

COCONINO NATIONAL FOREST

8,785 ft.
X

Cinder pit

Kendrick
Picnic
Area

Kendrick Park

To Flagstaff

The view is still tremendous from this high perch. The scars from numerous forest fires are visible from here, including the devastating Hochderffer Fire that burned much of the area north of San Francisco Mountain in 1996.

19 Walker Lake

Description:	A short hike to a lake in a volcanic crater, near San Francisco Mountain.
Location:	About 22 miles northwest of Flagstaff.
Type of trail:	Out and back.
Type of trip:	Day hike.
Difficulty:	Easy.
Total distance:	1.0 mile.
Elevation change:	140 feet.
Time required:	1 hour.
Water:	None.
Best season:	Summer through fall.
Maps:	White Horse Hills USGS quad; Coconino National Forest.
Permits and restrictions:	None.
For more information:	Peaks Ranger District, Coconino National Forest.

Walker Lake

✕ 8,511 ft.

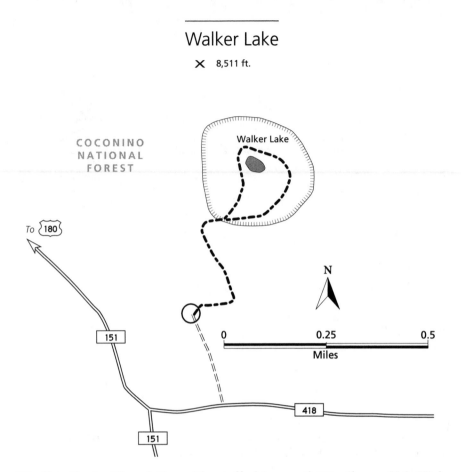

Finding the trailhead: From Flagstaff, drive north 20 miles on U.S. Highway 180. Turn right (east) on the north end of Hart Prairie Road (Forest Road 151). Continue on this maintained dirt road 1.5 miles and turn left (east) on another maintained road (FR 418). Drive 0.2 mile and turn left again (north) on an unmaintained road. Park at the end of the road, in another 0.2 mile.

Key points:
- 0.0 Trailhead.
- 0.3 Saddle on crater rim.
- 0.5 Walker Lake.

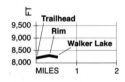

The hike: The trail follows the old road, closed now, up the southwest slope of the cinder cone. It passes through a broad saddle after 0.2 mile and drops gently into the volcanic crater. Walker Lake is fullest in late spring after a snowy winter. In late summer it is little more than a marsh. Considering how porous this volcanic area is, it's surprising that the runoff from the small watershed formed by the crater is enough to form even a small pond. It is worthwhile to walk around the lake. The north slope of the crater is barren due to a human-caused forest fire in the mid-1970s. The fire started near the lake, and high winds swept it up over the

Walker Lake is a shallow pond that lies in the crater left by an old volcano.

rim, where it traveled another 5 miles before being contained by fire fighters. A much larger fire in 1996 burned much of the area again. The views of Humphreys Peak, the highest of San Francisco Mountain, are great from the northwest side of the lake and even better if you climb up the slope through the old burn.

20 Wing Mountain

Description:	A cross-country hike to a scenic, alpine meadow on Wing Mountain.
Location:	9 miles northwest of Flagstaff.
Type of trail:	Cross-country loop.
Type of trip:	Day hike.
Difficulty:	Moderate.
Total distance:	2.2 miles.
Elevation change:	980 feet.
Time required:	2 hours.
Water:	None.
Best season:	Spring through fall.
Maps:	Wing Mountain USGS quad; Coconino National Forest.
Permits and restrictions:	None.
For more information:	Peaks Ranger District, Coconino National Forest.

Wing Mountain

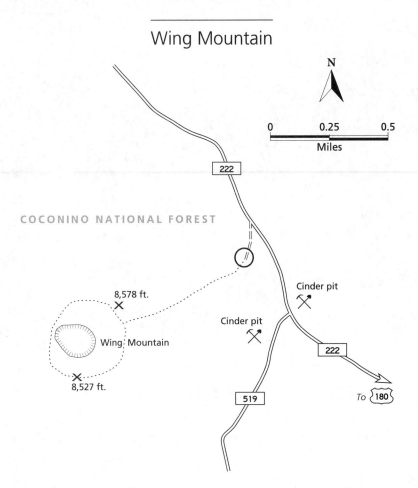

Finding the trailhead: From Flagstaff, drive north on U.S. Highway 180 about 7 miles and turn left (west) on Forest Road 222 (this turnoff is just past the Fort Valley Experimental Forest turnoff). Drive 2 miles, passing the junction of FR 519, and turn left into a small, aspen-bordered meadow that is just past a large cinder pit. Park at the far west side of the meadow.

Key points:

0.0	Start of the hike at meadow.
0.6	Crater rim.
0.7	Summit, Wing Mountain.
1.0	Low point of rim.
1.6	End of loop section.
2.2	Meadow on FR 222.

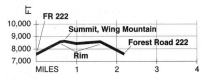

The hike: Walk cross-country southwest directly toward the summit through aspen and ponderosa pine. You'll start to climb the steep slopes almost immediately. In a few places the young pines become almost too thick to walk through, but these patches are easy to avoid. The overcrowded trees are a result of heavy logging that took place in this area around 1900. The stumps

The summit crater of Wing Mountain.

of the large pines are still visible, showing what the forest must have been like before it was logged. After you cross a fence, the forest becomes more open and shows less sign of logging. As you climb, Douglas-fir appear and become more common. These trees are distinguished by their short, flat needles that grow singly. Near the crater rim you may notice an occasional limber pine. Named for its flexible branches that help the tree shed snow, it has medium-length needles that grow five to a bunch. Go straight up to reach the rim and turn right (northwest) to reach the summit, which is only a slight rise without much of a view.

The pleasant walk around the crater rim is the highlight of this hike. The rim dips gradually to its low point on the west side. Along the way, there are views of Kendrick Peak to the northwest and an occasional glimpse of the meadow in the crater. From the southernmost point of the rim, there is an excellent view of Kendrick Peak rising above the grassy crater. Continue around the crater rim until you've completed the loop and then descend northeast to reach the meadow where you parked. The easiest way to do this is to head directly for distant Agassiz Peak, the closest of the summits of San Francisco Mountain.

21 SP Crater

Description:	A cross-country hike to an unusually symmetrical volcanic crater and an associated lava flow on the Coconino Plateau.
Location:	38 miles northeast of Flagstaff.
Type of trail:	Out and back, cross-country.
Type of trip:	Day hike.
Difficulty:	Moderate.
Total distance:	2.4 miles.
Elevation change:	720 feet.
Time required:	1.5 hours.
Water:	None.
Best season:	Spring through fall.
Maps:	SP Mountain, East of SP Mountain USGS quads.
Permits and restrictions:	None.
For more information:	Arizona State Land Department.

Finding the trailhead: From Flagstaff, drive north on U.S. Highway 89 about 30 miles. Go 1.0 mile past the signed turnoff to Wupatki National Monument and turn left (west) on an unsigned dirt road. This unmaintained road is passable to most vehicles except during or after wet weather. To the west, directly ahead, you will see a cinder cone, SP Mountain, which is perfectly symmetrical (it's just to the right and beyond a closer hill). Continue about 6 miles to the east base of SP Mountain and turn left. After another mile, an old four-wheel-drive road leads right (west) up a steep drainage on the south side of SP Mountain. Park here.

Key points:

- 0.0 Start of the hike at four-wheel-drive road.
- 1.0 Saddle.
- 1.2 Rim of SP Crater.

The hike: Follow the dirt road up the drainage to a saddle on the west side of SP Mountain. Now turn east and climb directly up the slope to the rim of SP Crater. It's a steep climb on a loose, cinder surface, but well worth the effort. In summer, this can be a hot hike, so carry water.

From the rim, SP Crater is 400 feet deep, which is just half the height of the cinder cone itself. The volcano is so raw it seems that it could erupt again any time. To the north, the five mile length of the SP Lava Flow adds to the volcanic atmosphere of the place, and gives you an idea what the Flagstaff area must have been like during periods of volcanic activity. SP Mountain is one of the northernmost cinder cones in the San Francisco volcanic field, but lava flows like this one cover much of the area to the north. The black

SP Crater • Colton Crater

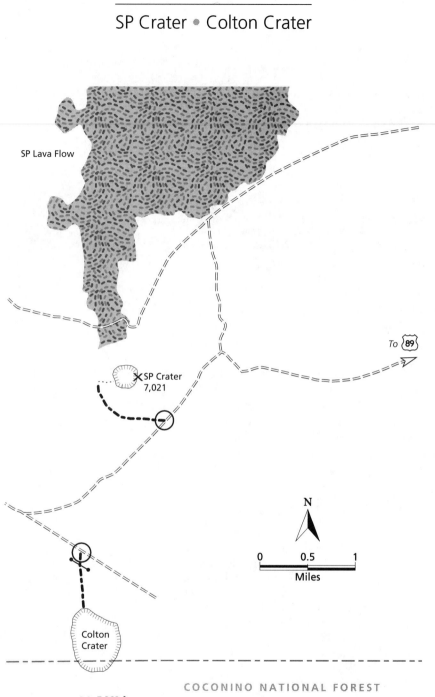

SP Lava Flow

To 89

×SP Crater
7,021

N

0   0.5   1
Miles

Colton
Crater

COCONINO NATIONAL FOREST

× 7,368 ft.

SP Lava Flow stretches 5 miles north from the base of SP Mountain.

rock lies like alien cake frosting on the generally red sedimentary rock. Some of the lava flowed as far north as the Little Colorado River, a distance of 20 miles. The initials, SP, are a cleaned up version of the original name of the cinder cone, which resembles a fixture common in pioneer bedrooms before the advent of indoor plumbing.

22 Colton Crater

See Map on Page 65

Description:	A very easy walk to a large volcanic crater containing a small interior cinder cone on the Coconino Plateau.
Location:	40 miles northeast of Flagstaff.
Type of trail:	Out and back.
Type of trip:	Day hike.
Difficulty:	Easy.
Total distance:	1.4 miles.
Elevation change:	380 feet.
Time required:	1 hour.
Water:	None.
Best season:	Spring through fall.
Maps:	SP Mountain, East of SP Mountain USGS quads.
Permits and restrictions:	None.
For more information:	Arizona State Land Department.

Finding the trailhead: Follow the directions for SP Crater above. From the trailhead, continue on the road another 1.2 miles southwest and turn sharply left (east) onto a little-used road that follows a fenceline. Drive about 0.8 mile to a fainter road that goes right (south) through a wire gate, and park here.

Key points:
- 0.0   Start of the hike at wire gate.
- 0.7   Crater rim.

The hike: Follow the old road south through the gate. Hike 0.7 mile through the scattering of pinyon-juniper and directly up the slope to the rim of Colton Crater. This large and colorful crater is more than half a mile across. A small cinder cone is actually present in the floor of the crater. It must have formed after the more violent eruption that created Colton Crater.

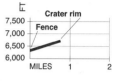

Notice the scattered Utah juniper and Colorado pinyon pine trees. The pinyon pine may be identified by its short needles, which grow in pairs. In good years, the pinyon pines produce a large crop of pine nuts, long a staple food of the native Americans and still popular today. Looking back toward SP Crater, you'll notice that there is almost no pinyon pine or juniper there, but in the short distance to Colton Crater they have become common. This is due to the increasing elevation, which attracts more rain and snow and makes conditions more hospitable for the small trees.

Colton Crater features a wide, deep crater with a small secondary cinder cone at the bottom.

67

23 Doney Trail

Description:	A very easy, short walk to the top of a volcanic cinder cone with an extensive view of the Painted Desert, near Wupatki National Monument.
Location:	About 39 miles northeast of Flagstaff.
Type of trail:	Out and back.
Type of trip:	Day hike.
Difficulty:	Easy.
Total distance:	1.0 mile.
Elevation change:	200 feet.
Time required:	1 hour.
Water:	None.
Best season:	All year.
Maps:	Wupatki SW USGS quad.
Permits and restrictions:	None.
For more information:	Peaks Ranger District, Coconino National Forest.

Finding the trailhead: From Flagstaff, drive north about 30 miles on U.S. Highway 89 and turn right (east) at the signed Wupatki National Monument turnoff. Follow this paved road east 9.2 miles and turn right at the signed picnic area and park at the signed trailhead.

Key points:
0.0   Trailhead.
0.5   Summit and viewpoint.

Distant San Francisco Mountain from the Doney Trail viewpoint.

Doney Trail

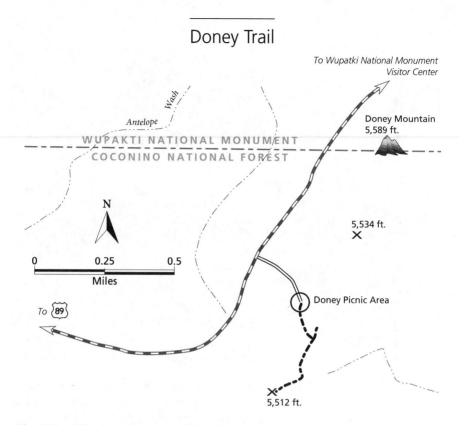

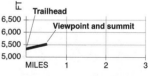

The hike: The broad, easy trail heads south toward the low saddle between two of the cinder cones. From the saddle, you can take a 100-yard side hike to the north for a view from the lower cinder cone. Back on the main trail, continue south about 0.4 mile to the summit. The 360-degree vista includes a sweeping view of the Painted Desert. The soft, rounded slopes, bluffs, and mesa in the distance to the northeast are mostly eroded from soft, pastel-colored shale rocks. At noontime, the harsh, vertical light gives the Painted Desert a washed out, "blah" look. In late evening, when the sun is low in the sky, the colors come alive.

The area to the east is part of Wupatki National Monument, established to preserve numerous prehistoric ruins. After the initial eruption of Sunset Crater volcano in A.D. 1065, the natives living in the Wupatki area were forced to abandon their homes and fields because of the rain of volcanic ash and cinders. A few years later, however, they discovered that the thin layer of ash acted as a mulch to retain soil moisture. This meant they could grow crops in many new areas. The result was a population explosion in the Wupatki area. Members of the Sinagua culture from the south, Anasazi from the northeast, and Cohonina from the west migrated to the area. The three

69

Wukoki Ruin, backdropped by San Francisco Mountain, in nearby Wupatki National Monument.

cultures advanced rapidly due to the sharing of technology and the increased social interaction. But by 1225 the Wupatki area was mostly abandoned. A long drought that began in 1150 was probably a contributing factor.

24 Bonito Crater

Description:	A cross-country hike through a lunar-like landscape in Sunset Crater National Monument.
Location:	16.5 miles northeast of Flagstaff.
Type of trail:	Loop.
Type of trip:	Day hike.
Difficulty:	Easy.
Total distance:	2.5 miles.
Elevation change:	200 feet.
Time required:	1.5 hours.
Water:	None.
Best season:	Spring through fall.
Maps:	O'Leary Peak, Sunset Crater West USGS quads.
Permits and restrictions:	Hiking on Sunset Crater, south of the road, is prohibited.
For more information:	Sunset Crater National Monument.

Finding the trailhead: From Flagstaff, drive north about 12 miles on U.S. Highway 89 and turn right (east) on the signed, paved road to Sunset Crater

Bonito Crater

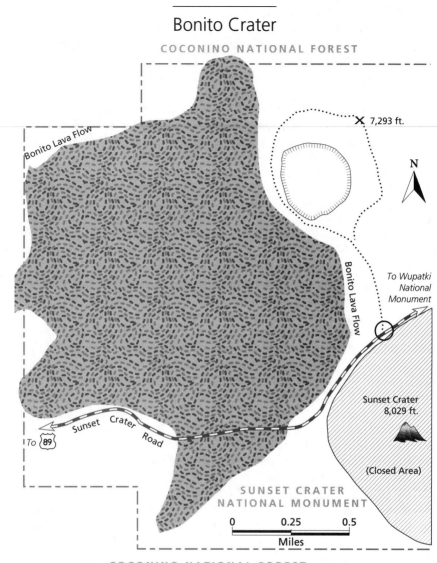

COCONINO NATIONAL FOREST

Bonito Lava Flow

✕ 7,293 ft.

N

Bonito Lava Flow

To Wupatki
National
Monument

Sunset Crater
8,029 ft.

(Closed Area)

Sunset Crater Road

To 89

SUNSET CRATER
NATIONAL MONUMENT

0   0.25   0.5
Miles

COCONINO NATIONAL FOREST

National Monument. (An entrance fee may be required.) Continue 4.5 miles. You will have just passed the Sunset Crater parking area and will now be driving along the north side of Sunset Crater. Park on the left just as the road starts into a cut. The parking is limited to two small pullouts that are not signed.

Key points:

- 0.0   Sunset Crater Road.
- 1.3   Crater rim.
- 2.5   Sunset Crater Road.

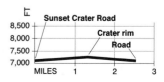

The hike: Please note that Sunset Crater, on the south side of the road, is closed to hiking and climbing. The Park Service implemented this closure around 1976 to protect Sunset Crater from erosion. The rest of the national monument is open to hiking.

Walk west along the highway a few yards until the road-cut ends on the north side and turn right (north). Contour north along the slopes of a small cinder hill to your right and head for a low saddle between this hill and the next, much larger one. On the left, you'll be looking down at the jagged Bonito Lava Flow, which looks like it just poured out of the ground. In fact, the lava is more than 700 years old. Even so, life has found its way onto the shattered rock, as evidenced by the large pine trees.

After the saddle, continue north, staying at about the same level above the steeper slopes to the left. Soon you will see the crater on the right as the slope turns into a definite rim. The rest of the hike follows the rim up and to the right, skirting the edge of the crater all the way back to the point where the rim was first encountered. Although this striking crater has no official name, it seems appropriate to call it Bonito Crater, after the lava flow. The soil seems sterile, but in spring there will often be a few flowers and other plants. Along the highest part of the crater rim, a small community of ponderosa pine and sagebrush has established itself. The exposed ridge seems like an unlikely place for this little patch of life, but if you walk the ridge on a windy day, the explanation becomes clearer. The prevailing wind during snowstorms in this area is from the southwest, which causes snow to pile into drifts on the lee side of the ridges, providing just enough extra moisture for the pines.

As the crater rim turns south, you'll have good views of Sunset Crater across the road. The red cinders along its rim caused Major John Wesley Powell to give the peak its name. In the clear air of the southwest in 1870, the Major was able to see Sunset Crater from the Grand Canyon country, sixty miles to the north. There are a few red cinders scattered along the route of this hike, possibly from Sunset Crater. Also, notice how the cinders are heaped into firm drifts, one to two feet high, along the sections of crater rim not protected by trees and sagebrush. Apparently the wind is strong enough at times to move the cinders because the drifts seem to form only on exposed ridges. A final steep descent of the crater rim, heading southwest, completes the loop. Return by walking south to the road.

25 Walnut Canyon

Description:	An easy walk to cliff-dwelling–style Indian ruins in Walnut Canyon National Monument.
Location:	13 miles east of Flagstaff.
Type of trail:	Loop.
Type of trip:	Day hike.
Difficulty:	Easy.
Total distance:	0.7 mile.
Elevation change:	250 feet.
Time required:	1 hour.
Water:	Visitor center.
Best season:	All year.
Maps:	Flagstaff East USGS quad.
Permits and restrictions:	None.
For more information:	Walnut Canyon National Monument.

Finding the trailhead: From Flagstaff, drive about 10 miles east on Interstate 40 and turn right (south) at the signed Walnut Canyon National Monument exit. Continue 3.0 miles on the paved road to its end at the visitor center.

Key points:
- 0.0   Visitor center.
- 0.3   South end of loop.
- 0.7   Visitor center.

The Sinagua people inhabited the cliffs of Walnut Canyon 800 years ago.

Walnut Canyon

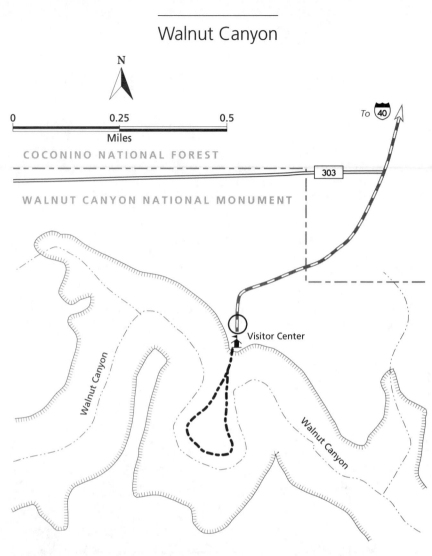

The hike: You may wish to look at the informative exhibits and books in the visitor center before exiting at the back of the building to reach the trail. It descends about 200 feet below the rim and circles a small butte. Interpretive signs along the way explain the ruins as well as the plants and animals found in the area. You'll notice many additional ruins at about the same level as the trail on the opposite walls of Walnut Canyon.

The dwellings in the Walnut Canyon area were built by the people of the Sinagua culture, who apparently arrived in the region about A.D. 700. (*Sinagua* is a Spanish term meaning "without water.") Although the Sinagua people depended on wild plants and animals for food, they also had developed agriculture, which required them to stay in one place. The cliff dwellings were built during the period of maximum occupation of Walnut Canyon, between 1125 and 1250. The Sinagua occupied sites from Wupatki, 40 miles northeast of Flagstaff, to the Verde Valley, 50 miles south. The cliff dwellings and other ruins are clustered, with the ruins on the trail and on the rim near the visitor center being a good example. These clusters were probably occupied by related family groups. An extensive network of trails took advantage of natural routes along ledges and through breaks in the cliffs. Most of the farming took place on the canyon rim, where the Sinagua grew corn, beans, and squash. Artifacts have been found showing that the Sinagua traded with people from all over Arizona as well as southern California and northern Mexico. In fact, the Sinagua may have acted as middlemen because of their central location. About 1250, the Sinagua abandoned Walnut Canyon for unknown reasons, though the long drought that started in 1150 may have been a contributing cause. It is possible that their descendants live on in the Hopi villages to the north, which were founded in about 1200.

26 Walnut Canyon Rim

Description:	This long and scenic hike follows a section of the Arizona Trail along the north rim of Walnut Canyon.
Location:	8.3 miles southeast of Flagstaff.
Type of trail:	Out and back.
Type of trip:	Day hike.
Difficulty:	Moderate.
Total distance:	13.6 miles.
Elevation change:	300 feet.
Time required:	7 hours.
Water:	None.
Best season:	Summer through fall.
Maps:	Flagstaff East USGS quad; Coconino National Forest.
Permits and restrictions:	None.
For more information:	Peaks Ranger District, Coconino National Forest.

Finding the trailhead: From Flagstaff at the junction of Interstate 40 and U.S. Highway 89, drive 4 miles east on I-40 to the Walnut Canyon National Monument exit, and go right (south). Continue 2.5 miles, and just before entering the monument, turn right on Old Walnut Canyon Road (Forest Road 303). Continue 1.8 miles to the Arizona Trail parking area.

Key points:
0.0   Trailhead.
1.9   Cross a side canyon.
2.4   Viewpoint.
5.5   The trail reaches the Walnut Canyon rim again.
6.8   Fisher Point.

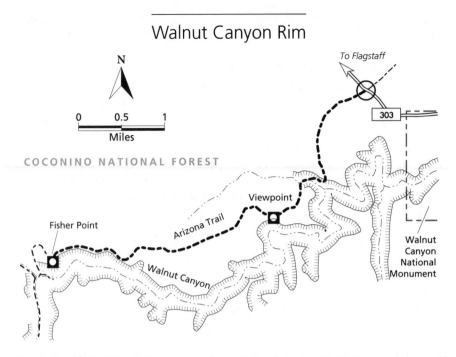

Walnut Canyon Rim

N

0   0.5   1
Miles

COCONINO NATIONAL FOREST

To Flagstaff

303

Fisher Point

Arizona Trail

Viewpoint

Walnut Canyon

Walnut Canyon National Monument

The hike: This hike follows a section of the Arizona Trail. Parts of the trail follow old roads, while other sections are new trail construction; pay close attention to the trail markers. The trail starts off heading southwest through open ponderosa pine and Gambel oak forest, climbing gradually. It turns south and joins an old road for a short distance. New trail construction takes you across a side canyon. On the far side, you'll join another old road. Watch for a spur trail on the right. It goes to a viewpoint overlooking Walnut Canyon. After the viewpoint, the trail follows old roads for over a mile and wanders away from the rim. After the trail leaves the road again, it soon hits the north rim of Walnut Canyon and follows it closely all the way to Fisher Point. This viewpoint, reached by a few yards of spur trail, overlooks the point where the canyon makes an abrupt 90-degree change in direction. It makes an ideal goal for a hike on this portion of the Arizona Trail.

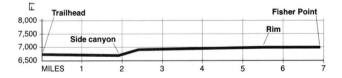

An option is to hike south on the Arizona Trail and exit via the Sandy's Canyon Trail. See the Sandy's Canyon Trail description for details on that section.

San Francisco Mountain

Culminating in 12,633-foot Humphreys Peak, the peaks of San Francisco Mountain are the highest mountains in Arizona. (Though locally known as the "San Francisco Peaks," the official name is "San Francisco Mountain," which I'll use throughout this book.) A horseshoe-shaped ring of peaks surrounds the 10,000-foot Interior Valley, which opens to the northeast. Like all the smaller mountains and hills on the Coconino Plateau, the mountain is an ancient volcano. Many geologists believe that the mountain once reached 16,000 feet or more. There's evidence that the mountain then exploded in a violent volcanic eruption much like that of Mount St. Helens in 1980. Afterward, the present steep canyon was carved by glacial ice. As recently as 10,000 years ago, glaciers were present in the Interior Valley and in the northeast canyons. Glacial features can be seen on several of the hikes. Most of San Francisco Mountain is protected in the Kachina Peaks Wilderness.

In 1889, C. Hart Merriam, a biologist with the U.S. Biological Survey, camped at Little Spring on the northwest slopes of San Francisco Mountain near the new settlement of Flagstaff. He came to study the great variety of plant life that grew on the mountain and its surrounding plateau. He soon noticed that plants tended to grow in associations determined by the climate. The climate grows cooler and wetter as the elevation increases, because the high terrain extracts more rain and snow from storm clouds. Merriam determined that a 1,000-foot elevation gain is approximately equivalent to 600 miles of northward travel. Groups of plants grow at elevations where the climate is to their liking. Animals dependent on certain plants for food are also associated with these plant communities. Merriam invented the term "life zone" to describe plant and animal communities and described the characteristic life zones of Northern Arizona. Although later studies have complicated the simple life-zone concept, it's still a useful way to understand the plant and animal communities of the southwest. Traveling from the Colorado River at the bottom of the Grand Canyon to the top of San Francisco Mountain, you would gain more than 10,000 feet of elevation in 52 miles, equivalent to a journey from northern Mexico to northern Canada.

Hiking on the mountain is somewhat restricted. The Interior Valley forms part of a watershed for the City of Flagstaff and is closed to overnight camping; however, day hiking is allowed. All of the mountain above 11,400 feet (the approximate elevation of timberline) is closed to cross-country hiking; hikers must stay on trails. This closure is to protect an endangered plant, San Francisco Mountain groundsel *(Senecio franciscanus)*, which grows only on this mountain. For more information on these closures, contact the Coconino National Forest, Peaks Ranger District (see Appendix D).

27 Abineau Trail–North Ridge Humphreys Peak

Description:	A hike to a remote glacial canyon and along a scenic alpine ridge in the Kachina Peaks Wilderness. This is an excellent hike to do during hot weather.
Location:	23 miles north of Flagstaff.
Type of trail:	Trail and cross-country loop.
Type of trip:	Day hike.
Difficulty:	Difficult.
Total distance:	5.4 miles.
Elevation change:	3,000 feet.
Time required:	5 hours.
Water:	None.
Best season:	Summer through fall.
Maps:	White Horse Hills, Humphreys Peak USGS quads; Coconino National Forest.
Permits and restrictions:	Cross-country hiking is prohibited above 11,400 feet (the approximate level of timberline).
For more information:	Peaks Ranger District, Coconino National Forest.

Finding the trailhead: From Flagstaff, drive north on U.S. Highway 180 for about 18 miles and turn right on the north end of Hart Prairie Road (Forest Road 151), a maintained dirt road. Continue 1.6 miles and turn left on the Hostetter Tank Road (FR 418), also maintained dirt. Drive 3.1 miles to the signed Abineau Trail turnoff, turn right, and go 0.3 mile to the trailhead.

Key points:
- 0.0 Abineau Trailhead.
- 0.4 Bear Jaw Trail junction; stay right.
- 2.5 Abineau Canyon Road, start of cross-country route.
- 2.9 North ridge of Humphreys Peak.
- 5.4 Abineau Trailhead.

The hike: The trail contours southeast across the pine-forested slope and then enters lower Abineau Canyon and turns upstream. After a short distance, the Bear Jaw Trail joins on the

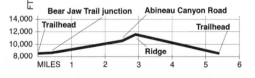

left, but our hike continues to follow the good footpath (not shown on the topographic map) up the dry creekbed uphill through an open ponderosa pine forest. The canyon becomes deeper as you climb, and the open ponderosa pine forest gradually gives way to a denser forest of Douglas-fir, quaking aspen, and limber pine. About 2.3 miles from the trailhead, the forest opens up, with a view of upper Abineau Canyon and the northeast slopes of Humphreys Peak. In June, snow usually lingers on the mountainsides. The Abineau Trail ends at the Abineau Canyon Road after another 100 yards.

Abineau Trail–North Ridge Humphreys Peak
Bear Jaw–Abineau Canyon Loop

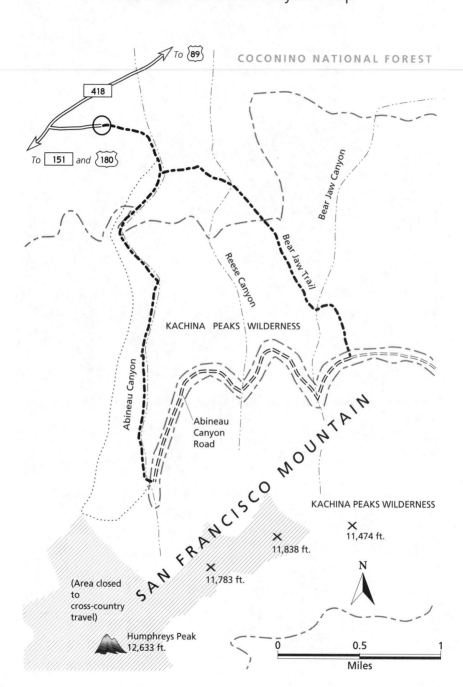

To 89

COCONINO NATIONAL FOREST

418

To 151 and 180

Bear Jaw Canyon

Bear Jaw Trail

Reese Canyon

KACHINA PEAKS WILDERNESS

Abineau Canyon

Abineau
Canyon
Road

SAN FRANCISCO MOUNTAIN

KACHINA PEAKS WILDERNESS

✗
11,474 ft.

✗
11,838 ft.

✚
11,783 ft.

N

(Area closed
to
cross-country
travel)

Humphreys Peak
12,633 ft.

0   0.5   1
Miles

The north ridge of Humphreys Peak from the Abineau Trail.

The lack of trees in the valley is due to numerous snow avalanches that roar down the northeast slopes of Humphreys Peak. Some of these slides reach the bottom of the canyon with such power that they continue below the road, crossing back and forth several times before the snow finally loses its momentum. Such a large avalanche will destroy any small trees attempting to grow in the avalanche path.

Hikers desiring a moderate hike can turn around at this point and return to the trailhead via the Abineau Trail. To continue on the loop hike, cross the valley to the west and ascend the avalanche path directly across from the end of the trail. By staying along the tree line, it is possible to avoid the worst of the loose scree and rock. You will reach the ridge at or below the 11,400-foot level, which is approximately timberline. (The mountain is closed to cross-country travel above 11,400 feet; do not climb higher.) Now turn right (north) and descend the ridge. The ridge forks in several places; stay to the east and remain on the ridge directly above Abineau Canyon. The gnarled and twisted bristlecone pine and Englemann spruce near timberline attest to the difficulty of life in this Arctic environment. At about 8,800 feet, Abineau Canyon turns sharply to the northeast. Again, stay on the ridge just above the canyon. Below 8,400 feet, Abineau Canyon becomes much shallower. Turn right and descend into the canyon bottom, rejoin the Abineau Trail, and return to the trailhead.

28 Bear Jaw–Abineau Canyon Loop

See Map on Page 79

Description: This is a hike on the north side of San Francisco Mountain in the Kachina Peaks Wilderness. It's a cool hike on a hot summer day and is a great display of fall aspen color.

Location: 23 miles north of Flagstaff.

Type of trail: Loop.

Type of trip: Day hike.

Difficulty: Moderate.

Total distance: 7.4 miles.

Elevation change: 2,000 feet.

Time required: 5 hours.

Water: None.

Best season: Summer through fall.

Maps: White Horse Hills, Humphreys Peak USGS quads; Coconino National Forest.

Permits and restrictions: Cross-country hiking is prohibited above 11,400 feet (the approximate level of timberline).

For more information: Peaks Ranger District, Coconino National Forest.

Finding the trailhead: From Flagstaff, drive north on U.S. Highway 180 for about 18 miles and then turn right on the north end of Hart Prairie Road (Forest Road 151), a maintained dirt road. Continue 1.6 miles and turn left on the Hostetter Tank Road (FR 418), also maintained dirt. Drive 3.1 miles to the signed Abineau Trail turnoff, turn right, and go 0.3 mile to the trailhead.

Key points:
0.0   Abineau Trailhead.
0.5   Bear Jaw Trail; turn left.
0.9   Cross Reese Canyon.
2.1   Cross Bear Jaw Canyon.
2.5   Turn right on Abineau Canyon Road.
2.8   Cross Bear Jaw Canyon.
3.7   Cross Reese Canyon.
4.7   Abineau Trail.
6.9   Junction with Bear Jaw Trail; stay left.
7.4   Abineau Trailhead.

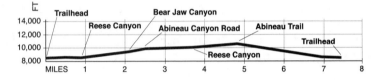

The hike: Start off on the Abineau Trail, which soon drops into Abineau Canyon. A short distance up the canyon, turn left onto the Bear Jaw Trail, which traverses east through open ponderosa pine forest to cross Reese Canyon. Now, you'll start to climb as the trail ascends the north slopes of the mountain. The pure pine forest gradually gives way to a pleasing mix of pine, quaking aspen, Douglas-fir, and white fir. After the trail crosses Bear Jaw Canyon, it's only a short climb to the Abineau Canyon Road, where you'll turn right.

The road, part of the Flagstaff watershed project, was built in an attempt to tap a spring in Abineau Canyon. Parts of the abandoned pipeline can still be seen in the roadbed. Although the road is in a narrow, non-wilderness corridor, it is open only to official vehicles and is rarely used. It makes a pleasant, easy hike along the north side of the mountain. Shortly, you'll cross Bear Jaw Canyon; the road then swings around into Reese Canyon, climbing gradually. The fir and aspen forest is a riot of color during the fall, and the road is often paved with golden aspen leaves for a couple of weeks.

The view opens up as you reach the end of the road in Abineau Canyon. Just before the end of the road, turn right on the Abineau Trail, which descends Abineau Canyon. After a bit over 2 miles, you'll pass the Bear Jaw Trail turnoff; continue on the Abineau Trail to reach the trailhead.

29 Bismarck Lake

Description:	A pleasant hike through alpine meadows on San Francisco Mountain and into the Kachina Peaks Wilderness. There's a good chance of seeing wildlife in this area.
Location:	16.2 miles north of Flagstaff.
Type of trail:	Out and back.
Type of trip:	Day hike.
Difficulty:	Moderate.
Total distance:	4.8 miles.
Elevation change:	1,000 feet.
Time required:	3 hours.
Water:	None.
Best season:	Summer through fall.
Maps:	Humphreys Peak USGS quad; Coconino National Forest.
Permits and restrictions:	Cross-country hiking is prohibited above 11,400 feet (the approximate level of timberline).
For more information:	Peaks Ranger District, Coconino National Forest.

Finding the trailhead: From Flagstaff, drive north on U.S. Highway 180 about 10 miles and turn right (east) on the south end of Hart Prairie Road (Forest Road 151). Continue 5.6 miles on this maintained dirt road and turn right (east) on the unsigned but maintained Bismarck Lake Road (FR 627). Park at the end of the road, 0.6 mile from the turnoff.

Key points:
- 0.0   Trailhead.
- 0.7   Bismarck Lake.
- 1.5   Lew Tank.
- 2.4   East end of meadow.

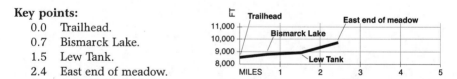

The hike: This area is closed to motor vehicles to protect the wildlife habitat. The closure seems to be having an effect; I have seen more wildlife, including black bear and Merriam's elk, since the old road was closed.

The trail follows the old road, which has been closed by the USDA Forest Service, through ponderosa pine forest. After about 0.2 mile, the trail enters a meadow and skirts a stock tank. This is a good place to see elk, especially around twilight. At the east end of the meadow, the trail climbs a short distance through the forest then enters a much larger meadow. As you continue, you'll have an excellent view of the ridges and canyons on the northwest slopes of Humphreys Peak.

Soon, a spur trail branches left (north) to Bismarck Lake. Only a muddy pond most of the year, Bismarck Lake was long ago enlarged with an earthen dam. This is also a good place to view wildlife, as the bear claw marks on the aspens attest.

Bismarck Lake

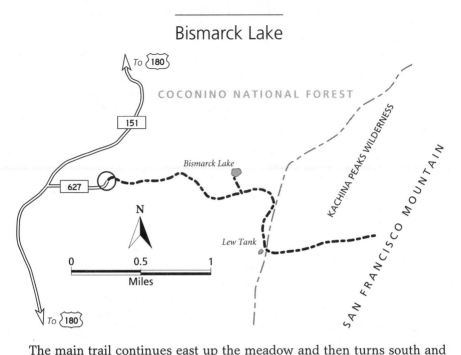

The main trail continues east up the meadow and then turns south and contours through a short section of forest. The trail passes Lew Tank, another stock tank, turns left, and continues into another alpine meadow. The

Alpine meadow near Lew Tank.

trail fades out at the east end of the meadow at about the 9,600 foot level. It's a fine spot to relax and enjoy the sweeping view to the west.

30 Humphreys Peak Trail

Description:	This popular hike takes you to the highest summit in Arizona, which is in the Kachina Peaks Wilderness. On a clear day the views are, well, incredible.
Location:	13.5 miles northwest of Flagstaff.
Type of trail:	Out and back.
Type of trip:	Day hike.
Difficulty:	Difficult.
Total distance:	8.8 miles.
Elevation change:	3,330 feet.
Time required:	6 hours.
Water:	None.
Best season:	Summer through fall.
Maps:	Humphreys Peak USGS quad; Coconino National Forest.
Permits and restrictions:	Cross-country hiking is prohibited above 11,400 feet (the approximate level of timberline). Camping is not allowed in the Interior Valley above Lockett Meadow.
For more information:	Peaks Ranger District, Coconino National Forest.

Finding the trailhead: From Flagstaff, drive 7 miles north on U.S. Highway 180 and turn right (north) on Arizona Snow Bowl Road. Continue 6.5 miles to the ski area lodge, and turn left into the parking lot below the lodge. Park at the north end, where you will see the signed trailhead.

Key points:
  0.0   Trailhead.
  3.4   Agassiz Saddle.
  4.4   Summit, Humphreys Peak.

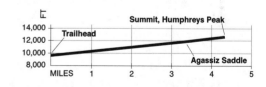

The hike: Note that cross-country hiking is prohibited by the USDA Forest Service above 11,400 feet on San Francisco Mountain. Above timberline, you must stay on the trail. This trail was built in 1985 and is not shown on the topographic map.

The trail starts near the base of a chair lift in upper Hart Prairie and crosses into the forest on the north side of the meadow. The trail ascends in a series of long but well-graded switchbacks through the dense forest. At first, the forest is a mixture of ponderosa pine, Douglas-fir, and quaking aspen trees associated with the Canadian life zone. These give way to limber pine and Englemann spruce in the higher sections of the forest. Near timberline, the forest is mostly subalpine fir, Arizona corkbark fir, and bristlecone pine,

Humphreys Peak Trail • Humphreys–Kachina Loop
Kachina Trail

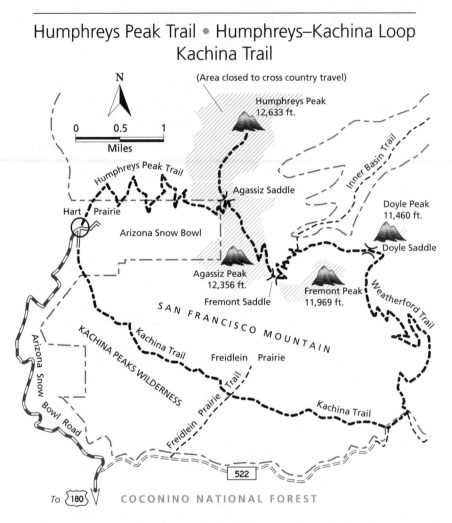

which represents the classic subalpine life zone. Near timberline, the trail crosses the west-facing ridge and climbs up to Agassiz Saddle at 11,800 feet. The few trees in this area show the effect of the harsh Arctic climate. They grow in low mats to conserve heat and protect themselves from wind. In winter, snow collects around the dense foliage, forming drifts that further protect the trees. The climate in this Arctic life zone is similar to that in the far northern regions of Canada and Alaska.

From Agassiz Saddle, the Weatherford Trail branches south along the ridge (see the Humphreys–Kachina Loop). The Humphreys Peak Trail turns north and skirts the west side of the ridge. The next mile of the trail is above timberline with no shelter and should not be attempted if thunderstorms, high wind, or snowstorms threaten. After about 0.2 mile the last struggling trees are left behind as the trail continues to climb along the ridge toward the invisible summit. You'll pass several false summits, each one appearing to be

Humphreys Peak.

the final summit. There are choice views of the Interior Valley to the east along the way, a good excuse to stop to catch your breath in the thin air.

The summit itself is marked by low, stone shelter-walls. A large portion of northern Arizona is visible from this lofty perch. If the air is clear, you can see Utah's 10,300-foot Navajo Mountain to the north-northeast, in Utah, and the 11,400-foot White Mountains in east central Arizona near the New Mexico border. The Mogollon Rim and some of its canyons can be seen to the south, as well as the rugged mountain ranges of central Arizona.

31 Humphreys–Kachina Loop

See Map on Page 86

Description: This is a long but spectacular hike through rugged, alpine terrain on San Francisco Mountain in the Kachina Peaks Wilderness. You can do a shorter, easier hike on this trail system by starting at the Kachina Trailhead and hiking the last 2.7 miles of this loop in reverse, turning around at Freidlein Prairie. This option is a delightful walk through beautiful forest, with an elevation change of 400 feet.

Location: 13.5 miles northwest of Flagstaff.

Type of trail: Loop.

Type of trip: Day hike or overnight backpack.

Difficulty: Difficult.

Total distance: 15.7 miles.

Elevation change: 3,200 feet.

Time required: 11 hours.

Water: Snow in early summer, otherwise none.

Best season: Summer through fall.

Maps: Humphreys Peak USGS quad; Coconino National Forest.

Permits and restrictions: Cross-country hiking is prohibited above 11,400 feet (the approximate level of timberline). Camping is not allowed in the Interior Valley above Lockett Meadow.

For more information: Peaks Ranger District, Coconino National Forest.

Finding the trailhead: From Flagstaff, drive northwest on U.S. Highway 180 about 7 miles and then turn right (north) on the paved and signed Arizona Snowbowl Road. Continue 6.5 miles to the ski area lodge, and turn left into the first parking lot. Drive to the far end of the parking lot and park at the signed trailhead for the Humphreys Peak Trail, near the ski lift.

Key points:

0.0 Trailhead.

3.4 Agassiz Saddle; go right on Weatherford Trail.

3.6 Old Weatherford Road.

5.0 Fremont Saddle.

5.8	Inner Basin Trail junction.
6.8	Doyle Saddle.
10.8	Kachina Trail; turn right.
12.6	Freidlein Prairie Trail junction.
15.3	Kachina Trailhead.
15.7	Humphreys Peak Trailhead.

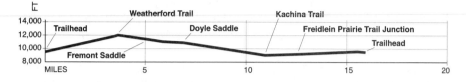

The hike: Follow the Humphreys Peak Trail under the ski lift and across Hart Prairie into the forest. (See the Humphreys Peak Trail for a detailed description.) Please note that the US Forest Service requires hikers to stay on trails on San Francisco Mountain above the 11,400-foot level.

At Agassiz Saddle, the Humphreys Peak Trail meets the Weatherford Trail at a signed junction. Go right and follow the Weatherford Trail as it climbs south along the ridge about 0.2 mile to a flat spot on the ridge crest. This scenic spot at 12,000 feet was the parking area for the Weatherford Road, a scenic drive built in the 1920s and abandoned a few years later. The present Weatherford Trail follows the old road as it switchbacks down the east face of Agassiz Peak. The trail enters an open forest of Englemann spruce and bristlecone pine as it drops to Fremont Saddle, between Agassiz and

Fremont Peak from the upper Weatherford Trail.

Fremont Peaks. (This saddle is named correctly on the Coconino National Forest map but incorrectly on the Humphreys Peak quad.) Trees grow very slowly at this altitude, and some of the trees are 1,200 years old. There are still a few boards lying around, all that remains of Doyle's Camp. Doyle was an early settler and a guide, and his name marks Doyle Saddle as well as Doyle Peak, the fourth highest summit of San Francisco Mountain.

The trail descends the northeast slopes below the saddle in a series of broad switchbacks. At the lowest switchback, you'll pass the turnoff for Inner Basin Trail, which is not shown on the topo map. Now the Weatherford Trail leaves the thicker part of the forest behind as it traverses east onto the rugged north slopes of Fremont Peak. This very alpine section offers expansive views of the Interior Valley in the foreground, and the Painted Desert in the far distance. The old road crosses several major avalanche paths before reaching Doyle Saddle at 10,800 feet, about 2 miles from Fremont Saddle. These avalanche paths are very active during the winter, which is why there are few or no trees. The saddle is open and windswept, the result of a wild fire that burned the saddle and part of the valley to the north around 1900.

Below Doyle Saddle, the trail becomes wider as it descends the southeast slopes of Fremont Peak. Three more avalanche paths are crossed before the trail starts down a series of switchbacks into Weatherford Canyon. Four miles from Doyle Saddle, the trail passes the signed wilderness boundary and comes out into a broad, gentle meadow on the south slopes of Fremont Peak. Here the present Weatherford Trail turns left and descends to the southeast, but our route continues on the old road which crosses the meadow to the southwest. At the west edge of this meadow, you'll see the signed Kachina Trail on the right. Follow it to the west.

A major avalanche path on the north side of Fremont Peak.

The Kachina Trail was one of several trails built during the mid-1980s as part of a recreational trail system on the mountain, and it is not shown on the topographic map. It climbs gradually westward across the slopes of Fremont Peak, traversing several beautiful, aspen-lined meadows. Watch for elk; at times there are more elk tracks than human tracks on the trail. At the junction with Freidlein Prairie Trail, continue straight across Freidlein Prairie, the largest meadow on the south side of the mountain. The meadow is much larger than depicted on the topographic map, extending all the way down to the Freidlein Prairie Road. The trail crosses the canyon that comes down from Fremont Saddle. The trail then continues across the lower slopes of Agassiz Peak. In another 2 miles it crosses a fairly deep, rocky canyon and comes out onto a gentle slope. The forest here is primarily aspen, Douglas-fir, and limber pine. Several small meadows are encountered, and then the trail passes under a powerline, which marks the wilderness boundary. Soon after the paved Snowbowl Road is visible through the trees to the left, you'll reach the trailhead. Walk north, cross the road, and continue to the north end of the parking lot to reach your car at the Humphreys Peak trailhead.

If you wish to do this loop as a backpack trip, note that there are no permanent water sources along the trail. An overnight hike is most practical in early summer when a few patches of snow still linger on the north slopes. You can then melt snow for water with a good backpacking stove. In late season when there is no snow, it's best to do this loop as a long day hike.

32 Kachina Trail

See Map on Page 86

Description: This trail offers an easy hike through fine alpine forest, ending at a scenic meadow. The hike is on the southwest slopes of San Francisco Mountain in the Kachina Peaks Wilderness.

Location: 13.5 miles northwest of Flagstaff.

Type of trail: Out and back.

Type of trip: Day hike.

Difficulty: Easy.

Total distance: 5.4 miles.

Elevation change: 400 feet.

Time required: 3 hours.

Water: None.

Best season: Summer through fall.

Maps: Humphreys Peak USGS quad; Coconino National Forest.

Permits and restrictions: Cross-country hiking is prohibited above 11,400 feet (the approximate level of timberline). Camping is not allowed in the Interior Valley above Lockett Meadow.

For more information: Peaks Ranger District, Coconino National Forest.

Finding the trailhead: From Flagstaff, drive northwest on U.S. Highway 180 about 7 miles and turn right (north) on the paved and signed Arizona Snowbowl Road. Continue 6.5 miles to the ski area lodge, and turn right into the first parking lot. Drive to the far end of the parking lot and park at the signed trailhead for the Kachina Trail.

Key points:

0.0   Trailhead.
2.7   Freidlein Prairie.

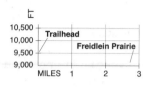

The hike: After a short distance, you'll cross under a powerline and enter Kachina Peaks Wilderness. The trail winds in and out of small canyons and through meadows as it traverses the southwest slopes of Mount Agassiz. The forest is an attractive mixture of quaking aspen, Douglas-fir, and limber pine. In fall, the aspen change to beautiful shades of yellow, orange, and red. This is a good hike to view those colors. After about a mile you'll cross a rocky canyon, and the trail beyond this point crosses a steeper, more rugged slope. After crossing several small draws, the trail crosses the deeper canyon coming down from Fremont Saddle and traverses into Freidlein Prairie, an alpine meadow on the southwest slopes of Fremont Peak. The junction with Freidlein Prairie Trail is in this meadow and marks the end of this hike.

An option for a hike of moderate difficulty is to continue to the east end of the Kachina Trail, which adds 3.6 miles to the total distance but only 200 feet of additional elevation change. Allow an extra two hours for this option. See the Humphreys–Kachina Loop for a description of this section.

Agassiz Peak from the Kachina Trail.

33 Weatherford Canyon

Description:	An enjoyable hike through a scenic alpine canyon in the Kachina Peaks Wilderness on San Francisco Mountain.
Location:	8.5 miles north of Flagstaff.
Type of trail:	Trail and cross-country loop.
Type of trip:	Day hike.
Difficulty:	Moderate.
Total distance:	6.1 miles.
Elevation change:	1,500 feet.
Time required:	4 hours.
Water:	None.
Best season:	Summer through fall.
Maps:	Humphreys Peak USGS quad; Coconino National Forest.
Permits and restrictions:	Cross-country hiking is prohibited above 11,400 feet (the approximate level of timberline). Camping is not allowed in the Interior Valley above Lockett Meadow.
For more information:	Peaks Ranger District, Coconino National Forest.

Finding the trailhead: From Flagstaff, drive northwest about 3 miles on U.S. Highway 180 and turn right (north) on the Schultz Pass Road (Forest Road 420). Continue past the end of the pavement on a maintained dirt road to the signed Weatherford Trail at Schultz Pass, about 5.5 miles from US 180. Park on the right (south) in the parking area next to Schultz Tank.

Key points:
    0.0   Schultz Tank Trailhead.
    0.8   Turn right onto an unmarked trail.
    1.6   Go right, leaving the trail, to remain in Weatherford Canyon.
    2.8   Join the Weatherford Trail and turn left.
    4.2   Kachina Trail junction.
    5.3   Complete the loop; continue straight ahead.
    6.1   Schultz Tank Trailhead.

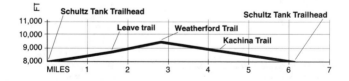

The hike: The walk begins across the road from the east end of the parking area, and follows the Weatherford Trail, an old road. The trail crosses a cleared pipeline corridor and continues to climb gradually north on a ponderosa pine-covered slope. After 0.8 mile, turn right at an unsigned fork onto the Aspen Spring Trail, another old road. The trail descends slightly into Weatherford Canyon and continues up the canyon through a dense stand of young

Weatherford Canyon • Schultz Peak

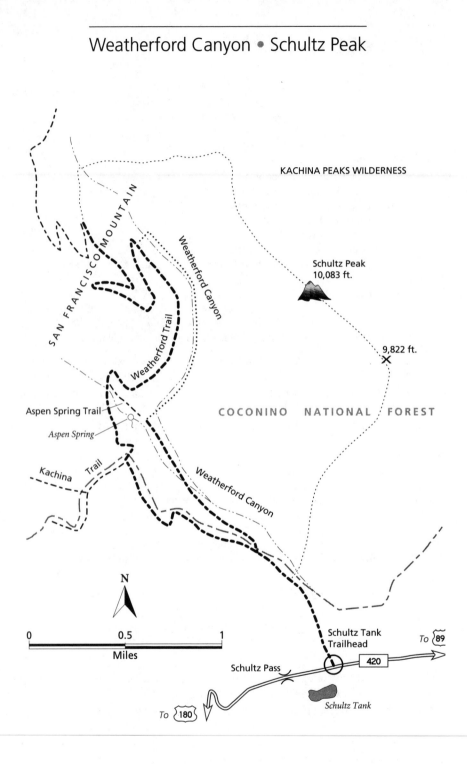

KACHINA PEAKS WILDERNESS

SAN FRANCISCO MOUNTAIN

Weatherford Canyon

Weatherford Trail

Schultz Peak
10,083 ft.

9,822 ft.

COCONINO NATIONAL FOREST

Aspen Spring Trail

Aspen Spring

Kachina Trail

Weatherford Canyon

N

0   0.5   1
Miles

Schultz Tank
Trailhead

To 89

420

Schultz Pass

To 180

Schultz Tank

Old growth ponderosa pine, Weatherford Canyon.

aspen. The old road forms a tunnel through the thick trees for about 0.5 mile, and then the forest becomes more open. Now, watch for an open, grassy slope to the right. Here, the Aspen Spring Trail continues up the unnamed side canyon to the northwest, while Weatherford Canyon, the main canyon, turns northeast. Leave the trail here and hike cross-country along the foot of this slope, staying on the left (north) side of Weatherford Canyon. (If you miss this turnoff and continue on the Aspen Spring trail, you will rejoin the Weatherford Trail in about 0.2 mile. You can turn left and join the return portion of the hike, described below.)

Although there is no official trail, there are elk trails and the walking is easy through the open meadow. There are views of forested Schultz Peak to the east. After about 0.5 mile of open terrain, the meadow ends, and there is a short section of deadfall to negotiate. Many of the fallen trees were destroyed by the exceptionally heavy, wet snowfall of 1992–1993. Stay to the left side of the canyon as it turns northwest and the forest opens up again. You will soon get a glimpse of the bald summit of Fremont Peak and several of its avalanche paths, which follow gullies down into upper Weatherford Canyon. At this point turn left and climb directly up the west slope of the canyon to the Weatherford Trail, a distance of about 100 yards. The old road is impossible to miss, unless you continue too far up Weatherford Canyon. In this case you will still intercept the trail, but at the 10,600-foot level!

Turn left on the Weatherford Trail and follow it south along the slopes of Fremont Peak. You can look down into Weatherford Canyon at several points. One mile from the point at which you intercepted the trail, it turns sharply right around a ridge and enters a meadow. The Weatherford Trail enters the forest again, only to emerge into a larger meadow in 0.3 mile. The old road descends the meadow in several badly eroded switchbacks and descends gradually into Weatherford Canyon. You'll pass the unmarked Aspen Spring Trail junction, closing the loop. Now continue south to the trailhead.

34 Schultz Peak

See Map on Page 94

Description: A cross-country walk along a fine alpine ridge, on San Francisco Mountain in the Kachina Peaks Wilderness.

Location: 8.5 miles north of Flagstaff.

Type of trail: Cross-country loop.

Type of trip: Day hike.

Difficulty: Moderate.

Total distance: 9.6 miles.

Elevation change: 2,200 feet.

Time required: 6.5 hours.

Water: None.

Best season: Summer through fall.

Maps: Humphreys Peak, Sunset Crater West USGS quads; Coconino National Forest.

Permits and restrictions: Cross-country hiking is prohibited above 11,400 feet (the approximate level of timberline). Camping is not allowed in the Interior Valley above Lockett Meadow.

For more information: Peaks Ranger District, Coconino National Forest.

Finding the trailhead: From Flagstaff, drive northwest about 3 miles on U.S. Highway 180 and turn right (north) on the Schultz Pass road (Forest Road 420). Continue past the end of the pavement on a maintained dirt road to the signed Weatherford Trail at Schultz Pass, about 5.5 miles from US 180. Park on the right (south) in the parking area next to Schultz Tank.

Key points:

0.0	Trailhead at Schultz Tank Trailhead.
0.4	Leave Weatherford Trail.
2.0	Peak 9,822.
3.2	Schultz Peak.
4.7	Turn left on Weatherford Trail.
7.7	Kachina Trail.
9.6	Schultz Tank Trailhead.

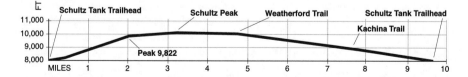

The hike: Start across the road from the east end of the parking area, and follow the Weatherford Trail, an old road, for about 0.4 mile. Leave the road and go cross-country northeast, directly up the gentle slope. About 0.5 mile from the Weatherford Trail, the slope becomes much steeper as you ascend Schultz Peak. About 2 miles from the trailhead, the ridge levels out at Peak

97

9,822, which is the southernmost point along the southeast ridge of Schultz Peak. Now turn northwest and walk the ridge to Schultz Peak. This is probably one of the least climbed peaks in the area, yet the views of San Francisco Mountain and the Dry Lake Hills are excellent. The beautiful alpine meadows, lined with aspen, limber pine, and ponderosa pine are a pleasure to walk through.

From Schultz Peak, continue northwest a couple of hundred yards to a shallow saddle. Contour left along the slopes of Doyle Peak, and maintain the same elevation around to the west to intercept the Weatherford Trail. As you cross several avalanche paths, you will see the trail crossing high above. It is possible to climb up to meet it, but it is much easier to contour. You will meet the old road at one of its switchbacks. Turn left and proceed downhill. The Weatherford Trail descends the southeast slopes of Fremont Peak in several long switchbacks and then emerges from the forest onto a southward sloping meadow at the base of Fremont Peak. The trail stays on the left (east) side of this meadow, passing the Kachina Trail turnoff (stay left), and returns to the trailhead. For more details on the Weatherford Trail, see Hikes 31 and 33.

35 Lockett Meadow–Waterline Loop

Description:	This unique hike features glacial valleys and quaking aspen groves. It's a fine sample of San Francisco Mountain.
Location:	About 22 miles northeast of Flagstaff.
Type of trail:	Loop.
Type of trip:	Day hike.
Difficulty:	Moderate.
Total distance:	4.4 miles.
Elevation change:	800 feet.
Time required:	3 hours.
Water:	Watershed cabins during the summer only.
Best season:	Summer through fall.
Maps:	Sunset Crater West, Humphreys Peak USGS quads; Coconino National Forest.
Permits and restrictions:	Cross-country hiking is prohibited above 11,400 feet (the approximate level of timberline). Camping is not allowed in the Interior Valley above Lockett Meadow.
For more information:	Peaks Ranger District, Coconino National Forest.

Finding the trailhead: From Flagstaff, drive north on U.S. Highway 89, the main street through town, and continue about 18 miles to Lockett Meadow Road (Forest Road 522), and turn left (west). This maintained dirt road is 0.8 mile north of the Sunset Crater National Monument turnoff. About 1.1 miles from the highway, the Lockett Meadow Road turns sharply right and begins climbing. (The road that continues straight ahead dead ends at

Lockett Meadow–Waterline Loop • Flagstaff Spring

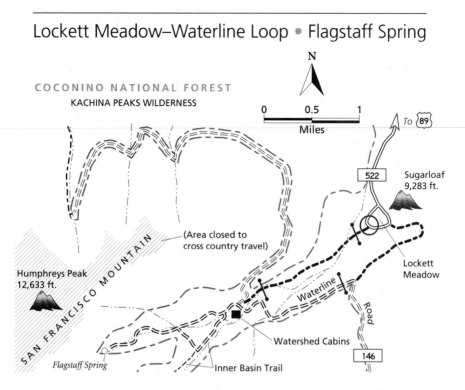

COCONINO NATIONAL FOREST
KACHINA PEAKS WILDERNESS

N

0   0.5   1
Miles

To 89

522

Sugarloaf
9,283 ft.

(Area closed to
cross country travel)

Lockett
Meadow

Humphreys Peak
12,633 ft.

SAN FRANCISCO MOUNTAIN

Waterline

Road

Watershed Cabins

146

Flagstaff Spring

Inner Basin Trail

a private cinder pit.) Continue 2.8 more miles to Lockett Trailhead at the southwest corner of the loop road around Lockett Meadow.

Key points:
- 0.0   Lockett Trailhead.
- 1.5   Watershed cabins, turn left on FR 146.
- 2.8   Turn left and follow old road northeast down ridge.
- 4.0   Lockett Meadow.
- 4.4   Lockett Trailhead.

The hike: The area of this hike, the Interior Valley of San Francisco Mountain, is closed to all overnight camping to protect the Flagstaff city watershed. For details on this closure contact the

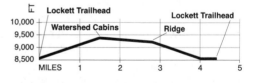

Lockett Trailhead

10,000

Watershed Cabins

9,500

9,000

8,500

MILES   1   2   3   4   5

Lockett Trailhead

Ridge

Peaks Ranger District (see Appendix D). Maps of the closure area are posted at the trailhead.

The trail, which is not shown on the topographic map, climbs gradually southwest through fine stands of quaking aspen, ponderosa pine and the occasional limber pine. The valley floor is broad and fairly flat, though cut by numerous small gullies. If you take the time to walk to either side of the valley, you'll notice that the bordering slopes are very steep. This is characteristic of valleys carved by glaciers. The moving ice shapes the entire valley into a broad U-shape. Valleys carved entirely by water have a V-shaped cross section. Another glacial characteristic is the unsorted debris composing the valley floor. Rocks and boulders of all sizes are randomly scattered around, instead of being sorted by size as they are when carried and deposited by running water. As a glacier moves down hill, it scours rock from its bed. More rock falls from the slopes above and is carried by the glacier. When the ice melts, the sand, gravel, rocks, and boulders are dropped in an unsorted heap, called "glacial till."

After 1.5 miles, the trail reaches a small group of cabins at the junction of several roads. During the summer, untreated spring water is available at a tap by the largest cabin. Take the leftmost road, FR 146, which is also called Waterline Road. The main cabin serves as an emergency shelter for snow surveyors from the U.S. Soil Conservation Service. Snow surveys are conducted throughout the mountains of the West in order to predict the amount of snow runoff that will occur in the spring. Since much of the drinking and irrigation water used in the West comes from mountain watersheds, such predictions are important. The smaller cabins protect the pipelines that collect water from springs and wells higher in the Interior Valley. The pipelines merge here into one pipe that follows the Waterline Road.

The Waterline Road contours through an especially fine aspen stand as it heads east-northeast along the lower slopes of Doyle Peak. Used for access to the watershed project in the Interior Valley, the road is closed to all motor vehicles except those on official business. Generally the only traffic is on weekdays when an occasional maintenance truck passes by, so this road makes a very pleasant and cool hike. You may also encounter mountain bikes and horses. Mountain bikes are allowed on San Francisco Mountain except in the Kachina Peaks Wilderness, and horses are allowed everywhere except in the watershed above the cabins.

After 1.3 miles, the road passes through a gate and turns sharply right as it crosses the east ridge of Doyle Peak. Leave the road to the east-northeast and follow an old, closed road down the ridge. Here the forest is an open stand of ponderosa pine. About 1 mile after leaving the Waterline Road, the old road turns left (northwest) into a saddle next to Sugarloaf, the large cinder cone blocking the lower end of the Interior Valley. Lockett Meadow is visible below to the northwest. Follow the old road through the saddle and west another 0.2 mile into Lockett Meadow. As you descend into the meadow, there are excellent views of the Interior Valley. Then follow the Lockett Meadow loop road west to the trailhead.

36 Flagstaff Spring

See Map on Page 99

Description: A hike through an alpine forest to a large avalanche path on the southeast face of Humphreys Peak on San Francisco Mountain.

Location: About 22 miles northeast of Flagstaff.

Type of trail: Loop.

Type of trip: Day hike.

Difficulty: Moderate.

Total distance: 6.7 miles.

Elevation change: 1,900 feet.

Time required: 5 hours.

Water: Watershed cabins during the summer only.

Best season: Summer through fall.

Maps: Sunset Crater West, Humphreys Peak USGS quads; Coconino National Forest.

Permits and restrictions: Cross-country hiking is prohibited above 11,400 feet (the approximate level of timberline). Camping is not allowed in the Interior Valley above Lockett Meadow.

For more information: Peaks Ranger District, Coconino National Forest.

Finding the trailhead: From Flagstaff, drive north on U.S. Highway 89, the main street through town, and continue about 18 miles to Lockett Meadow Road (Forest Road 522), and turn left (west). This maintained dirt road is 0.8 mile north of the Sunset Crater National Monument turnoff. About 1.1 miles from the highway, Lockett Meadow Road turns sharply right and begins climbing. (The road that continues straight ahead dead ends at a private cinder pit.) Continue 2.8 more miles to Lockett Trailhead at the southwest corner of the loop road around Lockett Meadow.

Key points:

0.0	Lockett Trailhead.
1.5	Watershed cabins; continue straight on Inner Basin Trail.
1.6	Go right on the Flagstaff Spring Road.
2.3	Stay right.
3.1	Flagstaff Spring.
3.9	Turn right.
4.4	Turn left on Inner Basin Trail.
5.2	Watershed cabins.
6.7	Lockett Trailhead.

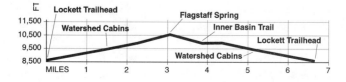

City of Flagstaff well in the Inner Basin.

The hike: Start on Inner Basin Trail, and hike southwest up the Interior Valley to the watershed cabins. See Hike 35 for a detailed description. There is untreated spring water at a tap near the largest cabin.

From the cabins, take Inner Basin Trail, the road that continues west-southwest up the Interior Valley. This road is not open to private vehicles; the City of Flagstaff uses the road only to maintain its water system, so there is very little traffic. One hundred yards beyond the cabins, the road forks. Take the right fork, which goes to Bear Paw and Flagstaff Springs. The road climbs steadily through the dense alpine forest, which sometimes opens up for glimpses of the high peaks. Along the way, you will see old signs of construction dating from the beginnings of the watershed project.

Flagstaff has outgrown its water supply many times. In the early part of the twentieth century, only a couple of decades after the city's founding, someone had an idea: tap the springs in the Interior Valley of San Francisco Mountain. In an area with very few springs, this water was worth considerable effort to reach. A pipeline was built up Schultz Creek, west of the Dry Lake Hills, to Schultz Pass, around the east slopes of Doyle Peak, and into the Interior Valley. From the present site of the watershed cabins, branch pipelines were built to all of the springs in the valley. An attempt was even made to tap a spring in Abineau Canyon on the northeast side of Humphreys Peak.

In the 1950s, in an effort to find more water, the city drilled a number of exploratory wells in the Interior Valley. A few were successful, and diesel-powered pumps were installed. Most of the old roads dating from the exploration period are overgrown now, but the valley still lacks a wilderness feeling. Until the mid-1970s, the entire watershed was closed to all public access, including hiking. Increasing public interest in outdoor activities finally caused the Forest Service to open the area to day hiking, skiing, and snowshoeing. The springs are protected by locked, steel covers—so there are no water sources in the Interior Valley except for the tap at the watershed cabins.

About 0.8 mile from the watershed cabins, a road forks left. This will be the return loop, but for now continue on the main road (right), which ends in another 0.8 mile, just below Flagstaff Spring. The most notable feature here is the incredible swath of destruction in the two-hundred-year-old fir and spruce. The winter of 1972–1973 was an unusually snowy one, and sometime during that winter a large avalanche came down the southeast face of Humphreys Peak and destroyed the trees.

An optional cross-country hike to the glacial cirque south of Humphreys Peak is worth doing. Continue up the forested slope, proceeding southwest from Flagstaff Spring, to reach the rim of the cirque at 11,200 feet. This bowl-shaped basin is a classic glacial cirque, which once contained the last remnants of a glacier that reached to Lockett Meadow at its maximum. You are near timberline, and there are excellent views of the stark alpine ridges above. Return to Flagstaff Spring the way you came.

To continue on the main hike, retrace your steps east down the road 0.8 mile to the junction mentioned above, and then turn right. This road goes south 0.5 mile to the south branch of the Interior Valley, passing through some fine aspen stands before reaching a broad, open meadow at one of the city well sites. This meadow has the best views in the Interior Valley. Facing uphill, from left to right the summits are Doyle Peak, Fremont Peak, Agassiz Peak, and when visible, Humphreys Peak. From this vantage point the pyramidal north face of Fremont Peak is most striking.

Turn left at the road junction in the meadow and descend to the east-northeast, following the road back to the watershed cabins. Then return to the trailhead via the Inner Basin Trail, the way you came.

The Interior Valley of the San Francisco Peaks from near Lockett Meadow.

Elden Mountain and the Dry Lake Hills

Elden Mountain is the 9,299-foot mountain rising dramatically above east Flagstaff, between the city and San Francisco Mountain. The Dry Lake Hills are somewhat lower—the highest point is 8,819 feet. These mountains lie to the west of Elden Mountain, almost directly north of west Flagstaff. They are connected to Elden Mountain by an 8,400-foot pass. Schultz Pass, to the north, separates the Dry Lake Hills from San Francisco Mountain. The USDA Forest Service has developed an extensive network of trails on the Dry Lake Hills and Elden Mountain. Open to all non-motorized uses, these trails are popular with hikers and mountain bikers alike. We are very lucky to have such a fine trail system right next to town. The trails interconnect, which makes it possible to do many different loop hikes. In this section, I present hikes that cover the entire trail system in an enjoyable manner, but you can combine the trails in other ways. I mention some of the possibilities as options after the main hike descriptions.

37 Upper Oldham Trail

Description:	A hike through cool Douglas-fir forest that climbs the west slopes of Elden Mountain to an alpine meadow and a viewpoint overlooking volcanic peaks and the Painted Desert.
Location:	About 7 miles northwest of Flagstaff.
Type of trail:	Out and back.
Type of trip:	Day hike.
Difficulty:	Moderate.
Total distance:	2.4 miles.
Elevation change:	1,070 feet.
Time required:	2 hours.
Water:	None.
Best season:	Summer through fall.
Maps:	Sunset Crater West USGS quad; Coconino National Forest.
For more information:	Peaks Ranger District, Coconino National Forest.

Finding the trailhead: From Flagstaff, drive 3 miles north on U.S. Highway 180 and turn right on the Schultz Pass Road (Forest Road 420). Drive 0.5 mile and go straight onto the Elden Mountain Road (FR 557), which is maintained dirt. Continue past a few houses and through a gate (this gate is closed in winter and spring when the road is muddy). The road becomes rougher, but if care is used it is passable to most vehicles. Watch for the

Upper Oldham Trail • Brookbank Trail

upper Oldham Trail on the right, 3.4 miles after leaving the Schultz Pass Road. Parking is limited; there are several spots on the left before you reach the trailhead.

Key points:

0.0   Trailhead.
1.0   Oldham Park.
1.2   Upper trailhead at Elden Mountain Road.

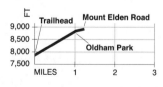

The hike: The trail, which is not shown on the topographic map, starts up a northwest-facing canyon through a cool, dense Douglas-fir and quaking aspen forest. Soon it switchbacks to the left and ascends the slope via several more switchbacks. You'll have occasional views of the beautiful forest on the north slopes of Elden Mountain. The climb ends abruptly when the trail emerges into Oldham Park, an alpine meadow on the summit ridge of the mountain. Follow the trail to the east end of the meadow, where our hike ends at the upper trailhead on the Elden Mountain Road.

A short spur trail on the east side of the road connects to the Sunset Trail. You can hike either direction on this trail to create a loop hike using other trails in the system. All the possible loop hikes from here are long ones.

38 Brookbank Trail

See Map on Page 105

Description:	A short hike up a historic wagon road on the Dry Lake Hills. The hike ends at a seasonal lake and meadow with nice views of San Francisco Mountain.
Location:	6.5 miles northwest of Flagstaff.
Type of trail:	Out and back.
Type of trip:	Day hike.
Difficulty:	Moderate.
Total distance:	2.2 miles.
Elevation change:	710 feet.
Time required:	2 hours.
Water:	None.
Best season:	Summer through fall.
Maps:	Sunset Crater West, Humphreys Peak USGS quads; Coconino National Forest.
Permits and restrictions:	None.
For more information:	Peaks Ranger District, Coconino National Forest.

Finding the trailhead: From Flagstaff, drive 3.0 miles north on U.S. Highway 180 and turn right on the Schultz Pass Road (Forest Road 420). Drive 0.5 mile and then go straight onto the Elden Mountain Road (FR 557), which is maintained dirt. Continue past a few houses and through a gate (this gate is closed in winter and spring when the road is muddy). The road becomes rougher but is passable to most vehicles with care. Watch for the Brookbank Trail on the left, 3.0 miles after leaving the Schultz Pass Road. Parking is very limited here; there are several spots on the right, just before reaching the trailhead, and a couple more on the left beyond the trailhead.

Key points:

0.0   Trailhead.
1.1   Dry Lake and meadow.

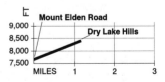

The hike: The present trail follows an old wagon road up an unnamed canyon and climbs the south-facing slopes via several switchbacks. Apparently, an early settler built the old road in order to reach the meadows that enhance the top of the Dry Lake Hills. After a moderate but sustained climb through mixed ponderosa pine, Douglas-fir, aspen, and Gambel oak forest with few views, the trail reaches a junction where the Brookbank Trail goes right. An unsigned trail continues straight ahead. Take this to reach a broad, open meadow. Graceful Mount Agassiz, the second highest summit of San Francisco Mountain

Along the Brookbank Trail.

at 12,356 feet, looms above the meadow. The Dry Lake Hills get their name from the several meadows that lie on the summit plateau. Early in the season, after snow melt, the meadows become seasonal lakes. As the lakes dry up, the meadows become a riot of wildflowers.

This meadow is private land. Although there are no restrictions on hiking at present, this could change in the future. Always respect private property and obey all signs, if posted.

See Hike 41 for options to continue the hike on the trail system.

39 Rocky Ridge Trail

Description:	An easy hike along the base of the Dry Lake Hills. This trail faces south and dries out earlier in the spring than the other trails in the Dry Lake Hills–Elden Mountain trail system. Access is quick from Flagstaff; this is a good hike when you don't have much time.
Location:	About 4 miles northwest of Flagstaff.
Type of trail:	Out and back.
Type of trip:	Day hike.
Difficulty:	Easy.
Total distance:	6.0 miles.
Elevation change:	440 feet.
Time required:	3.5 hours.
Water:	None.
Best season:	Late spring through fall.
Maps:	Flagstaff West, Humphreys Peak, Sunset Crater West USGS quads; Coconino National Forest.
Permits and restrictions:	None.
For more information:	Peaks Ranger District, Coconino National Forest.

Finding the trailhead: From Flagstaff, drive northwest about 3 miles on U.S. Highway 180 and turn right (north) on the Schultz Pass road (Forest Road 420). Continue 0.8 mile to the end of the pavement and park near the gate. (The gate may be closed during winter and early spring, when the Schultz Pass Road is muddy.)

Key points:
- 0.0 Trailhead.
- 1.2 Bearing tree.
- 3.0 Elden Mountain Road.

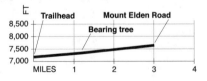

The hike: Walk through the gate and down an unmaintained dirt road to the right (northeast) about 0.1 mile to the signed trailhead. Go right (east) on the Rocky Ridge Trail and follow it up a gentle slope. The trail stays below the steep south slope of the Dry Lake Hills. (It is not shown on the topographic map.) It climbs gradually through

Rocky Ridge Trail • Schultz Creek Trail

COCONINO NATIONAL FOREST

Schultz Pass

To 89

P
Sunset
Trailhead

Schultz Pass Road

8,503 ft.
✗

8,747 ft.
✗

Dry Lake Hills

Schultz Creek Trail

8,460 ft.
✗

8,549 ft.
✗

8,549 ft.
✗

420

Dry Lake Hills

8,504 ft.
✗

8,403 ft.
✗

spur trail

Rocky Ridge Trail

Oldham Trail

420   557   Elden Mountain Road

N

180

To Flagstaff

0   0.5   1
Miles

open ponderosa pine and oak forest and eventually turns more to the north as it enters the canyon between the Dry Lake Hills and Elden Mountain.

The trail continues to contour along the slopes, gradually getting closer to the Elden Mountain Road (FR 557). About the time the road first becomes visible below, a spur trail branches right, descends to the Elden Mountain Road, and connects to the Lower Oldham Trail. The Rocky Ridge Trail stays above the road and swings east and then north as the canyon narrows, before ending at the road.

Optionally, you could continue the hike onto any of three other trails from this point. See Hikes 37, 38, and 48 for more details.

40 Schultz Creek Trail

See Map on Page 109

Description:	A hike along Schultz Creek, a seasonal stream that skirts the northwest slopes of the Dry Lake Hills.
Location:	About 4 miles northwest of Flagstaff.
Type of trail:	Out and back.
Type of trip:	Day hike.
Difficulty:	Moderate.
Total distance:	7.6 miles.
Elevation change:	880 feet.
Time required:	4 hours.
Water:	None.
Best season:	Spring through fall.
Maps:	Flagstaff West, Humphreys Peak USGS quads; Coconino National Forest.
Permits and restrictions:	None.
For more information:	Peaks Ranger District, Coconino National Forest.

Finding the trailhead: From Flagstaff, drive northwest about 3 miles on U.S. Highway 180 and turn right (north) on the Schultz Pass Road (Forest Road 420). Continue 0.8 mile to the end of the pavement and park near the gate. (The gate may be closed during winter and early spring, when the Schultz Pass Road is muddy.)

Key points:
0.0 Trailhead.
3.4 Schultz Loop Trail.
3.8 Schultz Pass and Sunset Trailhead.

The hike: Walk through the gate and down an unmaintained dirt road to the right (northeast) about 0.1 mile to the signed trailhead. The Schultz Creek Trail continues north from the trailhead, following the route of the original wagon road to Schultz Pass. It is not shown on the topographic map. The present Schultz Pass Road (FR 420) parallels this trail closely, so don't expect a wilderness experience. Still, it's a pleasant hike, and the trail can be used with the Little Elden, Pipeline, Oldham, and Rocky Ridge Trails to form a complete loop around the base of the Dry Lake Hills and Elden Mountain. Other loops are possible; see the trail maps and other hike descriptions for ideas.

You'll pass the Schultz Loop Trail just before Schultz Pass. Continue on the Schultz Creek Trail; it veers right, away from the creek, and goes directly to Sunset Trailhead.

41 Sunset–Brookbank Trails

Description:	This hike features easy access and cool, alpine forest and meadows in the Dry Lake Hills.
Location:	8.3 miles northwest of Flagstaff.
Type of trail:	Loop.
Type of trip:	Day hike.
Difficulty:	Moderate.
Total distance:	5.6 miles.
Elevation change:	900 feet.
Time required:	3.5 hours.
Water:	None.
Best season:	Summer through fall.
Maps:	Humphreys Peak, Sunset Crater West USGS quads; Coconino National Forest.
Permits and restrictions:	None.
For more information:	Peaks Ranger District, Coconino National Forest.

Finding the trailhead: From Flagstaff, drive northwest about 3 miles on U.S. Highway 180 and turn right (north) on the Schultz Pass Road (Forest Road 420). Continue past the end of the pavement on maintained dirt road to the Sunset Trailhead at Schultz Pass, 5.3 miles from the highway.

Key points:

0.0	Sunset Trailhead.
0.2	Stay right at Little Elden Trail junction.
1.7	Cross the crest of the Dry Lake Hills.
2.0	Go straight ahead onto Brookbank Trail.
3.8	Turn right, uphill, onto an unsigned trail.
4.2	Join an old road below the stock tank, and turn right downhill.
4.9	Go right at the junction with Schultz Loop Trail.
5.6	Sunset Trailhead.

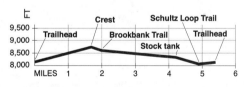

The hike: None of the trails on this hike are shown on the topographic maps. From the trailhead, the Sunset Trail first crosses the gentle slope above Schultz Tank through beautiful ponderosa pine and aspen forest. The Little Elden Trail goes left; continue straight ahead. Now the trail enters a small drainage and turns uphill. Climbing steadily but at a moderate grade, the trail stays on the right side of the drainage for more than a mile. It then crosses

Sunset–Brookbank Trails

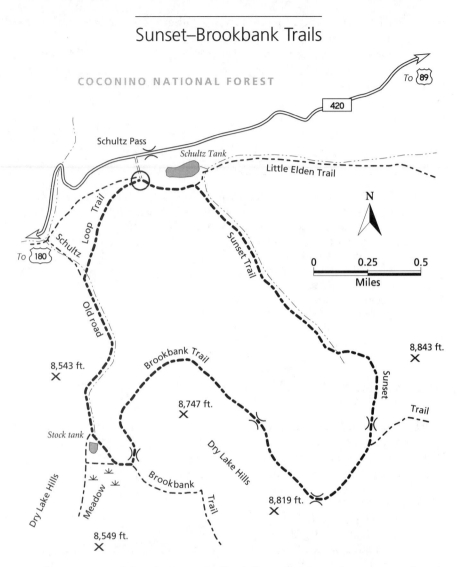

COCONINO NATIONAL FOREST

To 89

420

Schultz Pass

Schultz Tank

Little Elden Trail

N

Schultz Loop Trail

To 180

Sunset Trail

0   0.25   0.5
Miles

Old road

8,843 ft.
X

Brookbank Trail

8,543 ft.
X

Sunset

8,747 ft.
X

Trail

Stock tank

Dry Lake Hills

Brookbank

Meadow

Trail

8,819 ft.
X

Dry Lake Hills

8,549 ft.
X

a road, veers out of the drainage to the left, and enters a more open forest. The openness is due to the fact that the area was once logged. The trail reaches the crest of the Dry Lake Hills, where there are good views of San Francisco Mountain to the north, and descends west on the south side of the ridge to meet the Brookbank Trail.

From this junction, continue straight ahead on the Brookbank Trail as it contours the slope westward. Here the forest is a pleasing mixture of ponderosa pine, Douglas-fir, and aspen. Soon the trail crosses over a broad saddle and turns north. It descends though a small meadow and then heads northwest via several switchbacks through dense fir forest. The trail passes through another saddle and meadow and then contours around a hill to the north. The forest is so thick here that there are very few views. Continuing around the hill, the trail heads south through a saddle. Turn right here, on

San Francisco Mountain from the Brookbank Trail.

an unmarked trail that drops down a short, steep hill, then levels out into a large meadow. (This section of trail crosses private land. It is open to hikers at present. Please respect private property and all posted signs.)

A trail merges from the left as you turn right, directly toward San Francisco Mountain. Now skirt a small stock tank on the east, and then join an old road just below the stock tank. Follow the road down the canyon to the north. At the junction with Schultz Loop Trail, turn right and continue to Sunset Trailhead.

42 Little Bear Trail

Description:	A day hike through cool fir forest up the shadiest trail in the Dry Lake Hills–Mount Elden Mountain trail system.
Location:	8.3 miles northwest of Flagstaff.
Type of trail:	Loop.
Type of trip:	Day hike.
Difficulty:	Moderate.
Total distance:	5.9 miles.
Elevation change:	1,150 feet.
Time required:	4 hours.
Water:	None.
Best season:	Summer through fall.
Maps:	Humphreys Peak, Sunset Crater West, Flagstaff East USGS quads; Coconino National Forest.
Permits and restrictions:	None.
For more information:	Peaks Ranger District, Coconino National Forest.

Finding the trailhead: From Flagstaff, drive northwest about 3 miles on U.S. Highway 180 and turn right (north) on the Schultz Pass Road (Forest Road 420). Continue past the end of the pavement on maintained dirt road to the Sunset Trailhead at Schultz Pass, 5.3 miles from the highway.

Key points:
- 0.0   Sunset Trailhead.
- 0.3   Go left on the Little Elden Trail.
- 1.9   Turn right onto the Little Bear Trail.
- 3.5   Turn right onto the Sunset Trail.
- 4.1   At the Brookbank Trail, turn right to remain on the Sunset Trail.
- 4.3   Cross the crest of the Dry Lake Hills.
- 5.9   Sunset Trailhead.

The hike: Start on the Sunset Trail and turn left onto the Little Elden Trail. See Hike 43 for more details on this section. When the trail enters the open stand of ponderosa pine about 2 miles from the trailhead, watch for the Little Bear Trail. Turn right and follow the trail as it climbs the north slopes of

Little Bear Trail • Little Elden Trail

To (89)

Schultz Pass

Schultz Tank

420

To (180)

N

556

0   0.5   1
Miles

Little Bear Trail

Little Elden Trail

To (89)

P

Little Elden Spring

Sunset Trail

8,843 ft.
×

8,639 ft.
×

Little Elden Trail

8,747 ft.
×

Little Elden Mountain
9,018 ft.

Dry Lake Hills

8,549 ft.
×

8,819 ft.
×

Sunset Trail

E L D E N

Heart Trail

557

9,058 ft.
×

M O U N T A I N

Elden Mountain in a series of well-graded switchbacks. The dense fir forest here is a delight on hot summer days. Little Bear Trail ends at the saddle between the Dry Lake Hills and Elden Mountain. Here, you'll turn right on the Sunset Trail and follow it over the crest of the Dry Lake Hills and back to Sunset Trailhead. Again, see Hike 43 for more details on this section.

43 Little Elden Trail

See Map on Page 115

Description: An enjoyable hike on the Dry Lake Hills and Elden Mountain, featuring a variety of scenery, from cool fir forest to open, scenic views.

Location: About 7 miles northeast of Flagstaff.

Type of trail: Loop.

Type of trip: Day hike.

Difficulty: Moderate.

Total distance: 6.9 miles.

Elevation change: 1,600 feet.

Time required: 5 hours.

Water: None.

Best season: Summer through fall.

Maps: Humphreys Peak, Sunset Crater West, Flagstaff East USGS quads; Coconino National Forest.

Permits and restrictions: None.

For more information: Peaks Ranger District, Coconino National Forest.

Finding the trailhead: From east Flagstaff at the junction of Interstate 40 and U.S. Highway 89, drive north 4.7 miles on US 89 and turn left on Forest Road 556. Continue 2.1 miles to the Little Elden Spring Trailhead.

Key points:
- 0.0   Little Elden Spring Trailhead.
- 1.3   Turn right onto the Heart Trail.
- 3.2   Turn right onto Sunset Trail.
- 3.9   Turn right again, onto Little Bear Trail.
- 5.5   One more right turn, onto Little Elden Trail.
- 6.9   Little Elden Spring Trailhead.

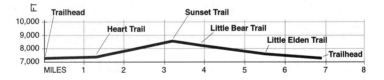

The hike: Hike south on the Little Elden Trail as it skirts the northeast ridge of Elden Mountain. Almost immediately, the trail enters the old Radio Burn. This human-caused forest fire started at the south base of the mountain in June 1977. High winds and hot weather fanned the fire into an inferno that rapidly climbed the south face, threatening the fire lookout and radio sites on the summit, as well as the beautiful pine and fir forest. Heavy application of aerial retardant saved most of the summit facilities, but the forest on the summit and northeast slopes of Elden Mountain was totally destroyed. Eventually, the fire was finally contained along the ridge now traversed by the Sunset Trail and along US 89, several miles east of

Fremont Peak from the Little Elden Trail.

the foot of the mountain. Twenty years after the devastating fire, a few young ponderosa pine and juniper trees dot the landscape.

The stark eastern slopes of Elden Mountain come into view ahead as the trail climbs gradually toward a small hill. Winding in and out of gullies, the trail skirts the hill on the right (west) and enters an open stand of tall ponderosa pine that survived the fire. As the trail passes west of two more hills, turn right (west) on the Heart Trail. Follow the trail as it climbs through the middle of the burn. At first the climb is gentle, but then the trail begins to switchback up a steep ridge. The view expands rapidly as elevation is gained. The fire burned very hot in this area, killing every tree, and there seems to be little new growth as yet. Finally, the Heart Trail reaches the ridge crest and ends at the Sunset Trail.

Turn right (north) on the Sunset Trail and follow it into the unburned pine and fir forest as it descends away from the ridge. The trail traverses an open section of ponderosa pine forest and comes out into a fine alpine meadow in the saddle between Elden Mountain and the Dry Lake Hills. Turn right on the Little Bear Trail, which descends northeast via several well-graded switchbacks through dense fir forest. When the trail comes out into the open ponderosa glade at the foot of the mountain, turn right to rejoin the Little Elden Trail. This trail skirts the foot of the mountain and reaches the Little Elden Spring Trailhead at the base of the northeast ridge.

Optional, longer loops can be hiked using the Elden Mountain Trail and the Sunset Trail. See those hike descriptions and maps (Hikes 46 and 41) for more information.

44 Sandy Seep Trail

Description:	An easy-to-reach, short, easy hike on the eastern slopes of Elden Mountain. This hike is lower in elevation than any other trail in the Elden Mountain–Dry Lake Hills trail system and is a good hike early in the season when the other trails are still muddy.
Location:	2.5 miles northeast of Flagstaff.
Type of trail:	Out and back.
Type of trip:	Day hike.
Difficulty:	Easy.
Total distance:	2.8 miles.
Elevation change:	400 feet.
Time required:	2 hours.
Water:	None.
Best season:	Late spring though fall.
Maps:	Sunset Crater West USGS quad; Coconino National Forest.
Permits and restrictions:	None.
For more information:	Peaks Ranger District, Coconino National Forest.

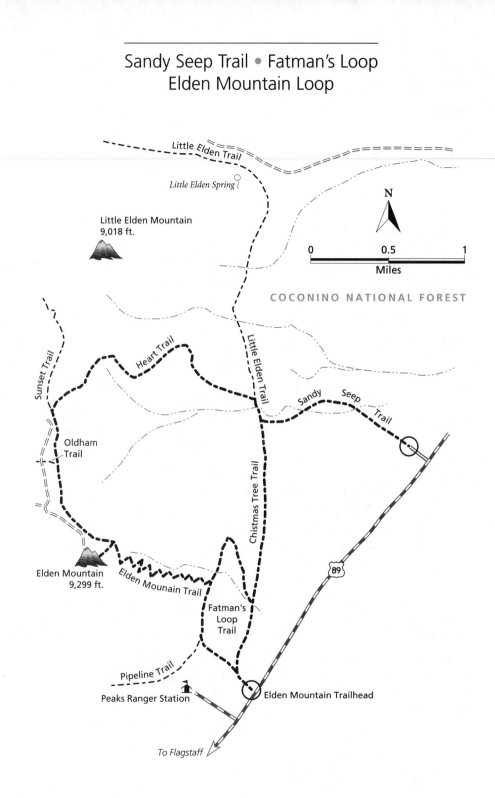

Sandy Seep Trail • Fatman's Loop
Elden Mountain Loop

Little Elden Trail

Little Elden Spring

N

Little Elden Mountain
9,018 ft.

0   0.5   1
Miles

COCONINO NATIONAL FOREST

Sunset Trail

Heart Trail

Little Elden Trail

Sandy   Seep   Trail

Oldham
Trail

Chistmas Tree Trail

Elden Mountain
9,299 ft.

Elden Mounain Trail

89

Fatman's
Loop
Trail

Pipeline Trail

Peaks Ranger Station

Elden Mountain Trailhead

To Flagstaff

Finding the trailhead: From east Flagstaff at the junction of Interstate 40 and U.S. Highway 89, drive north 2.5 miles on US 89 and turn left into the Sandy Seep Trailhead.

Key points:

0.0   Trailhead.
1.4   Junction with Christmas Tree and Little
       Elden Trails.

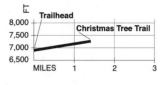

The hike: This easy hike follows the Sandy Seep Trail west toward the base of Elden Mountain, climbing gradually but steadily through open, ponderosa pine forest. It then swings around the south side of a low hill; our hike ends at the junction with the Christmas Tree and Little Elden Trails. These trails can be used for longer hikes, including several loop hikes, using the Elden Mountain–Dry Lake Hills trail system. See Hikes 43, 45, and 46 for information.

45 Fatman's Loop

See Map on Page 119

Description:	A scenic hike through rugged terrain on the east slopes of Elden Mountain. This loop trail is accessible via paved roads. Because of its southeast exposure it dries out earlier than other trails at the same elevation.
Location:	Northeast Flagstaff.
Type of trail:	Loop.
Type of trip:	Day hike.
Difficulty:	Easy.
Total distance:	2.2 miles.
Elevation change:	570 feet.
Time required:	2 hours.
Water:	None.
Best season:	All year.
Maps:	Flagstaff East USGS quad; Coconino National Forest.
Permits and restrictions:	None.
For more information:	Peaks Ranger District, Coconino National Forest.

Finding the trailhead: From east Flagstaff at the junction of Interstate 40 and U.S. Highway 89, drive north about 0.6 mile and turn left into the Elden Mountain Trailhead parking area. This trailhead is just north of the Peaks Ranger Station.

Key points:

0.0   Elden Mountain Trailhead.
0.2   Turn left at the start of the Fatman's Loop.
0.4   Pipeline Trail; stay right.

Fatman's Loop on the southeast slopes of Mount Elden is an easy hike with fine views from the rugged, boulder-covered terrain.

0.8	Elden Mountain Trail; stay right.
1.6	Christmas Tree Trail; stay right again.
2.0	Fatman's Loop; turn left.
2.2	Elden Mountain Trailhead.

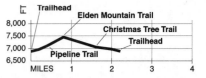

The hike: This is not a wilderness trail, but it traverses some rugged volcanic terrain with some nice views. Follow the trail past the information sign. Turn left at the first signed junction. This is the start of Fatman's Loop; you'll return on the trail that forked right. The trail climbs west toward the 2,000-foot east face of Elden Mountain. It passes through another gate where an unsigned trail joins from the right. Next, you'll pass the Pipeline Trail, which goes left. The Fatman's Trail turns north and climbs the lower slopes of the mountain through Gambel oak and ponderosa pine forest. At the high point of the loop, the Elden Mountain Trail goes left. Our trail continues north for a while and then abruptly turns southeast and starts to descend. As it comes out onto the lower, more gentle slopes, it meets Christmas Tree Trail, which joins on the left. Continue to the right (south) to the Fatman's Loop junction and then turn left to return to the trailhead.

46 Elden Mountain Loop

See Map on Page 119

Description:	This hike takes you to the summit of Elden Mountain and along a scenic ridge, where you'll enjoy 100-mile views.
Location:	Northeast Flagstaff.
Type of trail:	Loop.
Type of trip:	Day hike.
Difficulty:	Difficult.
Total distance:	7.6 miles.
Elevation change:	2,420 feet.
Time required:	5.5 hours.
Water:	None.
Best season:	Summer through fall.
Maps:	Flagstaff East USGS quad; Coconino National Forest.
Permits and restrictions:	None.
For more information:	Peaks Ranger District, Coconino National Forest.

Finding the trailhead: From east Flagstaff at the junction of Interstate 40 and U.S. Highway 89, drive north about 0.6 mile and turn left into the Elden Mountain Trailhead parking area. This trailhead is just north of the Peaks Ranger Station.

Key points:

| 0.0 | Elden Mountain Trailhead. |
| 0.2 | Fatman's Loop junction; stay left. |

0.4	Pipeline Trail; stay right.
0.8	Elden Mountain Trail; turn left, uphill.
1.8	Sunset Trail junction; turn left.
2.0	Elden Mountain summit.
2.2	Turn left onto the Sunset Trail.
3.2	Upper Oldham Trailhead.
3.7	Turn right onto the Heart Trail.
5.6	Turn right onto the Christmas Tree Trail.
5.8	Pass the Sandy Seep Trail junction.
7.0	Fatman's Loop joins from the right.
7.4	Fatman's Loop junction, bear left.
7.6	Elden Mountain Trailhead.

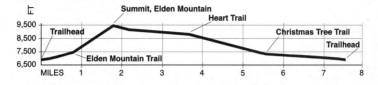

The hike: Follow the Elden Mountain Trail northwest past the information sign and through a gate. After several hundred yards, turn north on the left branch of Fatman's Loop Trail. (The right fork will be our return.) The trail passes through a second gate and then meets the Pipeline Trail at the base of the mountain. Stay right and follow Fatman's Loop Trail as it climbs north along the lower slopes of the mountain. At the high point of Fatman's Trail, turn left on the Elden Mountain Trail. This steep and rocky trail climbs up a minor ridge directly west toward the summit ridge. Although this area was burned in the 1977 Radio Fire, many of the trees survived. The view becomes more expansive as you climb the 2,000-foot east face. Once on the summit ridge, turn left at the junction with the Sunset Trail (you'll return here shortly to continue the loop). The 9,299-foot summit is dotted with radio towers and crowned with a fire lookout. The lookout personnel welcome visitors if not too busy; please ask permission before climbing the tower. This fire tower is one of the busiest in the southwest, both because of the vast area it surveys, and because of the forest/urban interface surrounding Flagstaff. The view is open in all directions, and mountain ranges 100 miles distant are often visible. The city of Flagstaff seems to lie right at your feet, even though it is 2,300 feet below.

To continue the hike, descend the Elden Mountain Trail and turn left onto the Sunset Trail. This trail descends gradually as it crosses the northeast slopes of the mountain, just below the ridge crest. A thick forest of quaking aspen saplings is springing up to replace the fir forest consumed by the Radio Fire. Gradually, shade-loving, young fir trees will become established under the aspen. As the fir grow, they will replace the fast-growing but short-lived aspen. Eventually a mature fir forest will return.

The Sunset Trail meets the ridge crest and Elden Mountain Road (Forest Road 557) at the upper Oldham Trailhead and then continues north along the east-side ridge. Because of the Radio Burn, the view to the east is great.

The Radio Burn along the upper Sunset Trail on Elden Mountain.

Even the Painted Desert far to the northeast is usually visible. When the trail climbs back to the ridge crest, turn right (east) onto the Heart Trail. The Heart Trail descends the eastern slopes of Elden Mountain through gentler terrain than the Elden Mountain Trail. The upper slopes are exceptionally barren, evidence that the fire burned very hot in this area. As the trail descends a minor ridge, more vegetation begins to appear. The trail ends in a meadow spotted with a few surviving ponderosa pines.

Turn right on the Christmas Tree Trail. After a short time, you'll pass the Sandy Seep Trail as the trail descends gradually to the south into pine and oak forest. Fatman's Loop Trail merges from the right, and in another 0.4 mile, you'll complete the loop at Fatman's Loop junction. Stay left to return to the trailhead.

47 Pipeline Trail

Description: A hike along the south slopes of Elden Mountain. This trail faces south and dries out more quickly in the spring than other trails in the area.

Location: Northeast Flagstaff.

Type of trail: Out and back.

Type of trip: Day hike.

Difficulty: Easy.

Total distance: 5.6 miles.

Elevation change: 320 feet.

Time required: 3 hours.

Water: None.

Best season: All year.

Maps: Flagstaff East USGS quad; Coconino National Forest.

Permits and restrictions: None.

For more information: Peaks Ranger District, Coconino National Forest.

Finding the trailhead: From east Flagstaff at the junction of Interstate 40 and U.S. Highway 89, drive north about 0.6 mile, and then turn left into the Elden Mountain Trailhead parking area. This trailhead is just north of the Peaks Ranger Station.

Key points:

0.0   Elden Mountain Trailhead.

2.8   Junction with the Oldham Trail.

The hike: Follow the Elden Mountain Trail northwest through a gate. After several hundred yards, turn left at the Fatman's Loop junction. The trail passes through a second gate then meets the Pipeline Trail at the base of Elden Mountain. Turn left here and follow the trail as it winds through the rough, rocky, volcanic terrain at the base of the southeast ridge. The trail alternates between the pipeline cut and the ponderosa pine–Gambel oak forest between the

125

Pipeline Trail

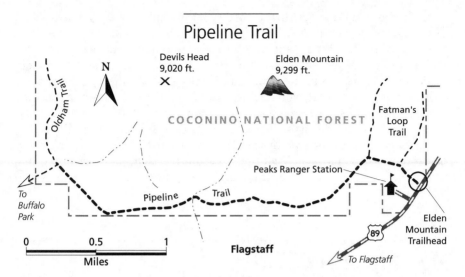

pipeline and the base of the mountain. This is the area where the Radio Fire started on a hot, windy day in June 1977. Driven by the wind and creating its own "chimney effect," it roared uncontrollably up the steep slopes above you.

Eventually the trail swings northwest, and ends at the junction with the lower Oldham Trail. This is the goal of our hike, but it's possible to continue left to Buffalo Park, or right toward the upper Oldham Trail and the Brookbank and Rocky Ridge Trails. See Hikes 37, 38, and 39 for more information.

Flagstaff

The present site of Flagstaff received attention from early American explorers because of several good springs. These were a vital water source in an otherwise dry landscape. In 1851, a party under U.S. Army Captain Lorenzo Sitgreaves passed through the area south of San Francisco Mountain, and in 1859 construction started on the Beale Wagon Road. Intended as an immigrant route to California, the Beale Road was also used to reach Prescott after the discovery of gold there in 1863. In 1876, a migrant party camped a few miles southeast of San Francisco Mountain. They celebrated the one-hundredth anniversary of the signing of the Declaration of Independence by stripping a large ponderosa pine to use as a flagstaff, which gave the tiny settlement its name. When the transcontinental railroad was completed in 1883, Flagstaff began to grow, primarily as a lumbering and ranching town. Later, America's first transcontinental highway, Route 66, was built across northern Arizona and through Flagstaff. Today, Flagstaff is a busy commercial center at the junction of five major highways and the railroad. It depends primarily on tourism, Northern Arizona University, and light industry. At 7,000 feet, Flagstaff is the highest city of its size in the country and is surrounded by the Coconino National Forest. The city is developing an extensive urban trail system, which is open to hiking, bicycling, and other non-motorized uses. You can use these trails for short, easy hikes around town or to connect to the Forest Service trail system for longer hikes or backpack trips.

48 Lower Oldham Trail

Description:	This is a trail along the base of Elden Mountain that provides access to the Elden Mountain–Dry Lake Hills trail system from Flagstaff.
Location:	North Flagstaff.
Type of trail:	Out and back.
Type of trip:	Day hike.
Difficulty:	Moderate.
Total distance:	6.2 miles.
Elevation change:	490 feet.
Time required:	4 hours.
Water:	None.
Best season:	Summer and fall.
Maps:	Flagstaff West, Humphreys Peak USGS quads; Coconino National Forest.
Permits and restrictions:	None.
For more information:	Peaks Ranger District, Coconino National Forest.

Lower Oldham Trail • Buffalo Park

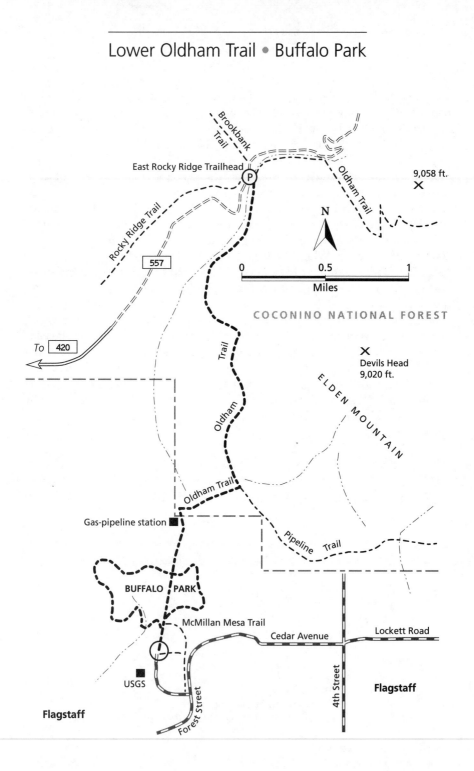

Finding the trailhead: This hike is located in the north-central section of the city, adjacent to the Coconino National Forest. From the junction of U.S. Highway 180 and Business Interstate 40 (Route 66), drive north on US 180 (Humphreys Street) to Columbus. Turn right, go one block and turn left on Beaver Street. Continue to Forest Street and turn right. Continue 0.8 mile and turn left at the sign for Buffalo Park and the U.S. Geological Survey. Follow the road 0.2 mile to its end at the Buffalo Park Trailhead.

Key points:

0.0	Buffalo Park Trailhead.
0.6	Start of the Oldham Trail at the park boundary.
1.5	Pipeline Trail junction; stay left.
3.1	East Rocky Ridge Trailhead.

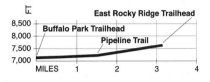

The hike: Go through the old gate into Buffalo Park and continue north on the straight road that goes to the gas-pipeline station at the north side of the park. The signed Oldham Trail starts just to the right (east) of the buildings, at a gap in the fence. The trail, now a footpath, descends the slopes of the mesa and heads northeast across the shallow valley below, directly toward Elden Mountain. The Oldham Trail meets the signed Pipeline Trail on the north side of the cleared gas-pipeline right-of-way and turns north to climb gradually along the west slopes of Elden Mountain. The Dry Lake Hills are visible to the northwest, and soon it is obvious that the trail is heading into the canyon between the Dry Lake Hills and Elden Mountain. After a short descent, you'll pass an unmarked trail coming in from the right. Make note of this junction and avoid taking this false trail by mistake on the return. Though the views are limited, the pine and oak forest and the volcanic boulders make this an interesting hike. Fir and aspen begin to mix with the pine as you near the northern end of the trail about 3 miles from the start, and the slopes to the right become a rock cliff. The signed trailhead on the Elden Mountain Road (FR 557) is also the parking area for a very popular spot for rock climbing. Our hike ends here, but optionally you can continue the hike on any of the three trails that start at this trailhead. See Hikes 37, 38, and 39 for details.

49 Buffalo Park

See Map on Page 128

Description:	This popular, easy walk is part of the Flagstaff Urban Trail System and is located on Switzer Mesa. The scattered pine forest and open meadows give this place an open, airy feeling. The spaciousness is enhanced by the great views of San Francisco Mountain, the Dry Lake Hills, and Elden Mountain.
Location:	In Flagstaff.
Type of trail:	Loop.
Type of trip:	Day hike.
Difficulty:	Easy.
Total distance:	2.0 miles.
Elevation change:	None.
Time required:	1 hour.
Water:	At entrance during the summer.
Best season:	All year.
Maps:	Flagstaff West USGS quad.
Permits and restrictions:	None.
For more information:	Flagstaff Parks and Recreation.

Finding the trailhead: From the junction of U.S. Highway 180 and Business Interstate 40 (Route 66), drive north on US 180 (Humphreys Street) to Columbus. Turn right, go one block, and turn left on Beaver Street. Continue to Forest Street and turn right. Continue 0.8 mile and turn left at the sign for Buffalo Park and the US Geological Survey. Follow the road 0.2 mile to its end at the Buffalo Park Trailhead.

Key points:
0.0   Trailhead.
0.8   Pipeline access road.
2.0   Trailhead.

The hike: The park, but not the trail, is shown on the topographic map. Walk through the entrance gate and continue north. Pass the McMillan Mesa Trail and turn right at the next fork. Stay on the outer trail as it does a loop around the park. There are several left turns that you can use as shortcuts, if desired. Part way through the loop, you'll cross the pipeline access road that runs north through the park. An optional right turn here takes you to the Forest Service trail system on the Dry Lake Hills and Elden Mountain.

Buffalo Park was originally developed to hold a small herd of bison. The high fences, roads, and entrance station were built so that people could drive through the park and see the bison. In the late 1960s the bison were moved to a state bison range, and the facilities were abandoned. Since then, the park has become popular with hikers, walkers, mountain bikers, and runners. In the late 1980s it narrowly escaped having a major road built through it, but

Along the loop trail in Buffalo Park.

that proposal was soundly rejected by a citizen's initiative. It appears the people of Flagstaff appreciate the remarkable views and serenity of this elevated mesa within the city more than they desire a shortcut to the Grand Canyon.

50 Observatory Mesa Trail

Description:	A day hike on the Flagstaff Urban Trail System, with access to national forest trails.
Location:	In west Flagstaff.
Type of trail:	Out and back.
Type of trip:	Day hike.
Difficulty:	Easy.
Total distance:	3.2 miles.
Elevation change:	450 feet.
Time required:	2 hours.
Water:	None.
Best season:	Summer through fall.
Maps:	West Flagstaff USGS quad; Coconino National Forest.
Permits and restrictions:	Much of the trail crosses land owned by Lowell Observatory; hiking off trail is not permitted.
For more information:	Flagstaff Parks and Recreation.

Finding the trailhead: From the intersection of Business Interstate 40 (Route 66) and U.S. Highway 180 (Humphreys Street), drive west on Route

Observatory Mesa Trail • Fort Tuthill Trail
Sinclair Wash Trail

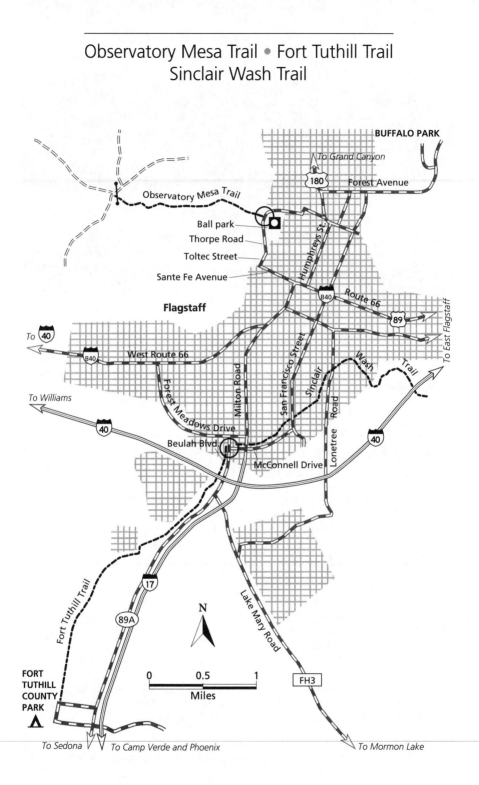

BUFFALO PARK

To Grand Canyon

180

Forest Avenue

Observatory Mesa Trail

Ball park

Thorpe Road

Toltec Street

Sante Fe Avenue

Humphreys St.

Flagstaff

B40

Route 66

89

To East Flagstaff

To 40

B40

West Route 66

San Francisco Street

Milton Road

Sinclair

Wash

Trail

Road

To Williams

Forest Meadows Drive

40

Beulah Blvd.

McConnell Drive

Lonetree

40

17

89A

Fort Tuthill Trail

N

Lake Mary Road

FH3

**FORT
TUTHILL
COUNTY
PARK**

0   0.5   1
Miles

To Sedona   To Camp Verde and Phoenix   To Mormon Lake

66. Continue straight ahead onto Santa Fe Avenue; do not turn left at the underpass. Continue several blocks and turn right on Toltec Street, which becomes Thorpe Road. You'll pass the Adult Center building on the left; watch for the ballpark on the right. The best parking for the trail is the ballpark parking lot.

Key points:
- 0.0   Ball park.
- 0.4   Trail leaves the canyon.
- 1.6   Trail ends at a gate.

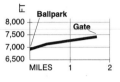

The hike: The trail actually crosses through the ballpark area from the east, but this hike picks up the trail on the west side of Thorpe Road, where a sign and map mark the trailhead. The Observatory Mesa Trail goes west through the city park and follows a gully west about 0.4 mile. Watch for bicycles, especially on the steep downhill sections. The trail turns left and climbs steeply out of the gully to reach the top of Observatory Mesa in another 0.2 mile. From here the trail turns west again through the pine forest. It ends at a gate and a junction with several forest roads. It is possible to use these roads for an extended hike. Refer to the topographic map and the Coconino National Forest map for more information.

Observatory Mesa is named for Lowell Observatory, which is located on its southeast edge. The observatory was established in 1894, just a few years after the settlement of Flagstaff. An influx of astronomers and other researchers began that changed the character of the small logging town

Snow-capped San Francisco Mountain seen from near the Observatory Mesa Trail.

forever. Flagstaff is still a scientific center, hosting the U.S. Naval Observatory, the U.S. Geological Survey Astrogeology Center, a USDA Forest Service Experimental Station, and other facilities.

51 Fort Tuthill Trail

See Map on Page 132

Description:	This is another hike on the Flagstaff Urban Trail System. It provides access to the Fort Tuthill County Park and the adjacent Coconino National Forest.
Location:	In southwest Flagstaff.
Type of trail:	Out and back.
Type of trip:	Day hike.
Difficulty:	Easy.
Total distance:	6.6 miles.
Elevation change:	100 feet.
Time required:	3.5 hours.
Water:	None.
Best season:	Spring through fall.
Maps:	Flagstaff West USGS quad; Coconino National Forest.
Permits and restrictions:	None.
For more information:	Flagstaff Parks and Recreation.

Finding the trailhead: Go south on Milton Road in west Flagstaff and turn right (west) on Forest Meadows Drive. Go one block to Beulah Boulevard. The trail starts here and follows the west side of Beulah Boulevard. Because this trail is part of the Flagstaff Urban Trail System, there is no trailhead; however, there is public parking on several side streets nearby.

Key points:
- 0.0 Intersection of Beulah Boulevard and Forest Meadows Drive.
- 0.4 Cross under Interstate 40.
- 1.6 Cross Mountain Dell Road.
- 2.1 Cross a dirt road.
- 3.3 Fort Tuthill County Park.

The hike: The Flagstaff Urban Trail System is intended for use by pedestrians and cyclists and is closed to all motor vehicles. These trails are most useful for those living or staying in Flagstaff and are especially useful for

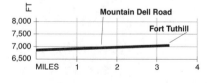

those who do not have a car. Three of the trails offer access to the Coconino National Forest surrounding the city. Eventually, the urban trail system will provide multiple access points to the Forest Service trail system on the city's boundaries.

134

A small bridge crosses Sinclair Wash on the Fort Tuthill Trail.

The Fort Tuthill Trail skirts the east edge of the Wal-Mart parking lot, below street level, as it follows Sinclair Wash to the south. It then joins an old logging railroad grade as it continues south under I-40. After passing the University Heights development, there is more open, undeveloped forest. Soon, the trail crosses Mountain Dell Road and skirts the west edge of Mountain Dell subdivision. Beyond this the trail is in undeveloped forest. It passes through several meadows with views of San Francisco Mountain to the north and finally ends at Fort Tuthill County Park. Plans are to build another segment of trail east of I-17, making it possible to do a loop back to Flagstaff. Check with Flagstaff Parks and Recreation for the current status of the trail system.

Milton Road, in southwest Flagstaff, was originally called Milltown Road because it connected Flagstaff to Milltown. Old Flagstaff was located in the present downtown area, and Milltown was to the southwest along the foot of Observatory Mesa. As the name implies, Milltown was the site of a lumber mill, in this case owned by Tim Riordan. After reading Milton's *Paradise Lost*, Riordan decided to rename the street leading to his mill in honor of one of his favorite authors.

52 Sinclair Wash Trail

See Map on Page 132

Description:	A day hike on a Flagstaff Urban Trail, with easy access for walkers without a vehicle.
Location:	In southwest Flagstaff near Northern Arizona University.
Type of trail:	Out and back.
Type of trip:	Day hike.
Difficulty:	Easy.
Total distance:	4.2 miles.
Elevation change:	100 feet.
Time required:	2.5 hours.
Water:	None.
Best season:	Spring through fall.
Maps:	Flagstaff West USGS quad.
Permits and restrictions:	None.
For more information:	Flagstaff Parks and Recreation.

Finding the trailhead: Go south on Milton Road in west Flagstaff and turn right (west) on Forest Meadows Drive. Go one block to Beulah Boulevard, turn left, and go one more block to McConnell Drive. The trail starts here and goes east along the north side of McConnell Drive. Because this trail is part of the Flagstaff Urban Trail System, there is no trailhead; however, there is public parking on several side streets nearby.

Sinclair Wash Trail along the Rio de Flag.

Key points:
  0.0 Intersection of Beulah Boulevard and McConnell Drive.
  1.0 Cross Lonetree Road.
  2.1 Interstate 40.

The hike: This is another trail in the Flagstaff Urban Trail System. The trail crosses Milton Road and stays on the north side of McConnell Drive as it follows Sinclair Wash downstream onto the university campus. After a couple of

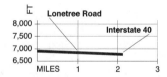

blocks the trail moves farther away from the street as it winds in and out of small drainages. After crossing south San Francisco Street, it continues down Sinclair Wash around a subdivision. The Lonetree Road crossing is somewhat confusing; just remember that the trail follows the wash. A few yards downstream, Sinclair Wash ends as it joins the Rio de Flag. The trail continues another mile downstream before ending at the I-40 overpass. This is the least urban and most enjoyable portion of the trail. Another trail is planned that will connect this point to Lake Mary Road to the southwest and the Foxglenn–Continental area to the northeast. Meanwhile, the hiker without a car can use the Sinclair Wash Trail to reach undeveloped forest south of I-40.

137

Lake Country

Because of the abundance of porous limestone and volcanic rock, most of the Coconino Plateau lacks surface water, despite 25 inches of moisture the region receives each year. The area southeast of Flagstaff is an exception and is locally known as Lake Country because of its numerous small lakes. Most are shallow, while others have been augmented with manmade dams. The lakes are remnants of the wet period at the end of the last glaciation, about 10,000 years ago. Many of the natural meadows that occur throughout the forest are dry lake beds, some of which hold water briefly after wet winters. These meadows have dense soil, formed from silt deposited in the former lake, which makes it difficult for ponderosa pine to take root. The forest very slowly reclaims the meadows, spreading inward from the edges. Three of the hikes in this section are near Mormon Lake, the largest natural lake in Arizona and a haven for wildlife.

53 Sandy's Canyon Trail

Description:	A hike near Lower Lake Mary, offering interesting geology, views, and a connection to the Arizona Trail.
Location:	7 miles southeast of Flagstaff.
Type of trail:	Out and back.
Type of trip:	Day hike.
Difficulty:	Easy.
Total distance:	2.8 miles.
Elevation change:	200 feet.
Time required:	2 hours.
Water:	None.
Best season:	Spring through fall.
Maps:	Flagstaff East USGS quad; Coconino National Forest.
Permits and restrictions:	None.
For more information:	Mormon Lake Ranger District, Coconino National Forest.

Finding the trailhead: From Flagstaff, drive south on Milton Road and turn right on Woodlands Village Drive (this junction is signed for Lake Mary). Go a block and turn left on Beulah Boulevard. Continue 0.6 mile and turn left on Lake Mary Road (Forest Highway 3). Drive 5.7 miles and turn left (east) just after crossing a cattleguard. The unsigned gravel road leads into a campground; bear left and continue to the signed trailhead at the northeast corner of the campground.

Sandy's Canyon Trail • Anderson Mesa

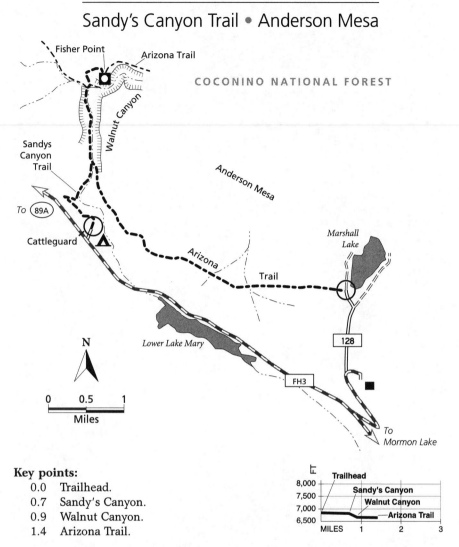

COCONINO NATIONAL FOREST

Key points:
- 0.0   Trailhead.
- 0.7   Sandy's Canyon.
- 0.9   Walnut Canyon.
- 1.4   Arizona Trail.

The hike: The first section of the trail follows an old road directly toward the rim of Walnut Canyon, visible ahead. (The trail is not shown on the topographic map.) At the rim it turns left (north) and skirts the edge. The ponderosa pine forest here is open and spacious, and views of Walnut Canyon are only a few steps to the east. At one point, there is an outcrop of volcanic rock on the rim and a massive boulder field. On the opposite wall of the canyon, the horizontal strata of the Kaibab limestone form white cliffs. The Kaibab limestone forms much of the surface of the Coconino Plateau but is covered with lava flows in the Flagstaff area.

The trail crosses a shallow drainage, turns sharply right (east), and descends Sandy's Canyon. A sign marks this spot. A few aspen trees, wild

A volcanic rock slide on the rim of Walnut Canyon.

grapevines and poison ivy can be found along this short descent to the floor of Walnut Canyon. Poison ivy is a small plant that has shiny green leaves growing three to a bunch. It is usually found near or in streambeds, but not necessarily with flowing water. Many people suffer a serious rash and even blisters from contact with poison ivy. Fortunately it is easy to spot, since it grows in association with wild grape. The grapevines here are a tangled mass of low growing vines and leaves, and the poison ivy grows as single plants.

After the trail crosses the (normally dry) bed of Walnut Creek it turns left (north) and follows the canyon bottom. The canyon is broad and has an open feeling. After about 0.5 mile, the trail emerges into a meadow and ends at the signed junction with the Arizona Trail. It is worth turning right (south) and walking a few steps to another fine meadow and an impressive cliff of Coconino sandstone. Also found in the Grand Canyon, the Coconino was formed from wind drifted sand dunes, and the cross-bedded layers of sand are still visible in the rock today.

You can optionally continue the hike either north or south on the Arizona Trail. See Hikes 26 and 54 for details.

54 Anderson Mesa

See Map on Page 139

Description: This hike starts in a good wildlife-viewing area and traverses a section of the Arizona Trail across Anderson Mesa to a scenic viewpoint overlooking Walnut Canyon.
Location: About 12 miles southeast of Flagstaff.
Type of trail: Out and back.
Type of trip: Day hike.
Difficulty: Moderate.
Total distance: 11.6 miles.
Elevation change: 590 feet.
Time required: 6 hours.
Water: None.
Best season: Spring through fall.
Maps: Lower Lake Mary, Flagstaff East USGS quads; Coconino National Forest.
Permits and restrictions: None.
For more information: Mormon Lake Ranger District, Coconino National Forest.

Finding the trailhead: From Flagstaff, drive south on Milton Road and turn right on Woodlands Village Drive (this junction is signed for Lake Mary). Go a block and turn left on Beulah Boulevard. Continue 0.6 mile and turn left on Lake Mary Road (Forest Highway 3). Drive 9.9 miles and turn left (east) on the paved, signed Marshall Lake Road. After about a mile, the paved road turns sharply right; continue straight ahead on the signed, maintained dirt road (Forest Road 128) to Marshall Lake. When the meadow containing the lake comes into view, turn left at a fork and watch for the small sign marking the Arizona Trail at a parking area on the left.

Key points:

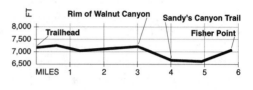

- 0.0 Trailhead.
- 1.3 Shallow canyon.
- 3.0 Rim of Walnut Canyon.
- 4.0 Sandy's Canyon Trail; stay right.
- 4.9 Turn right and then almost immediately left, to stay on the Arizona Trail.
- 5.8 Fisher Point.

The hike: You'll start near the shore of Marshall Lake, which is usually more of a marsh than a lake. Because of the excellent cover, it is a good area to view waterfowl and other wildlife. The best times are before sunrise and after sunset. The trail, which is not shown on the topographic maps, starts from the small sign and heads west through an open forest of pine, oak, and juniper. The trail climbs gradually and then crosses a small canyon, one of the many tributaries of Walnut Canyon. You'll cross several smaller drainages before reaching the rim of Walnut Canyon. The trail then gradually descends into Walnut Canyon. There are good views of San Francisco Mountain to the northwest and occasional glimpses into Walnut Canyon. A single switch-back leads to the bottom of the canyon, where you'll reach the junction with the Sandy's Canyon Trail; turn right and continue north down Walnut Canyon. Here the walking is especially pleasant through a series of mead-ows. Abruptly, the canyon makes a sharp right turn. A trail leaves the canyon to the northwest; turn right to stay on the Arizona Trail. After a hundred yards, the Arizona Trail turns left and goes up a small side-canyon to the north (don't continue on the unnamed trail down Walnut Canyon by mistake). The Arizona Trail climbs out of the side canyon on the east and then swings south-east to Fisher Point. This fine viewpoint overlooking Walnut Canyon is the destination for our hike.

Options: With a car shuttle, you could use the Sandy's Canyon Trail to make this a one-way hike. See the Sandy's Canyon Trail description for informa-tion. Or, you could continue on the Arizona Trail past Fisher Point to the Walnut Canyon Trailhead. See the Walnut Canyon Rim description for de-tails. The unnamed trail leaving the canyon to the northwest below Fisher Point goes to Lonetree Road in south Flagstaff.

55 Mormon Lake

Description:	A hike along the shore of Mormon Lake, Arizona's largest natural lake. This is a great place to view wildlife.
Location:	27 miles southeast of Flagstaff.
Type of trail:	Out and back.
Type of trip:	Day hike.
Difficulty:	Easy.
Total distance:	6.4 miles.
Elevation change:	None.
Time required:	3.5 hours.
Water:	Mormon Lake; however, it may be muddy and difficult to reach.
Best season:	Spring through fall.
Maps:	Mormon Lake USGS quad; Coconino National Forest.
Permits and restrictions:	None.
For more information:	Mormon Lake Ranger District, Coconino National Forest.

Finding the trailhead: From Flagstaff, drive 27 miles southeast on Lake Mary Road (Forest Highway 3). The highway skirts the east side of Mormon Lake then descends through a cut. Watch for the turnoff to Kinnikinick Lake on the left and turn right (east) onto an unmarked, unmaintained dirt road

Quaking aspen frames the view of Mormon Lake and San Francisco Mountain.

Mormon Lake • Ledges Trail • Lake View Trail

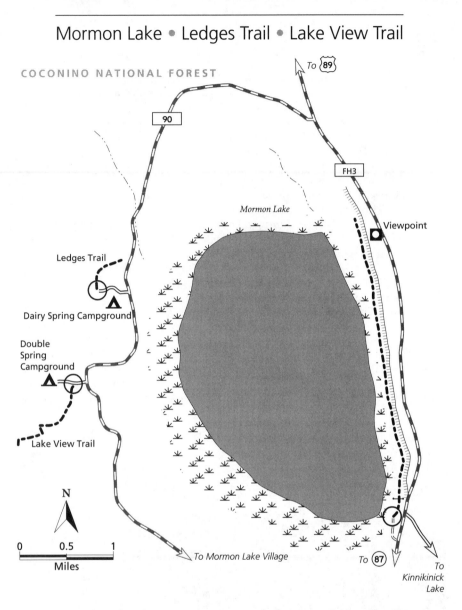

To (89)

90

FH3

Mormon Lake

Viewpoint

Ledges Trail

Dairy Spring Campground

Double
Spring
Campground

Lake View Trail

N

0   0.5   1
Miles

To Mormon Lake Village

To (87)

To
Kinnikinick
Lake

that descends toward the lake and turns right. Go through the gate (low clearance cars should be parked here) and drive a short distance to a fork; turn right, uphill, and drive a few yards to a second gate and park. This gate is normally locked to protect the area's wildlife.

Key points:
  0.0   Trailhead.
  3.2   North end of old highway.

The hike: The walk follows the old road along the shore of the lake. (The topographic map shows this old road but not the present highway, which is

144

to the east, above the lakeside cliffs.) The old road is nearly level and is about 20 feet higher than the lake, so there is a good view. This hike is best done at sunrise or sunset, which are good times for wildlife viewing. The old road can be followed more than 3 miles along the eastern shore to a point just past the viewpoint on the present highway. Cottonwood and aspen trees grow here in an unusual association, and there are fine views of the distant peaks of San Francisco Mountain. Most of the year, Mormon Lake is more a marsh than a lake. When full, after the spring snow melt, it is the largest "natural" lake in Arizona. Although there is no dam (in contrast with Upper and Lower Lake Mary), humans have still influenced the lake. The area was first settled by Mormons who started dairy farming here. In the pioneer days, the lake area was never more than a marsh, so the settlers ran cattle on the rich forage. Eventually, the hooves of the cattle compacted the soil and made it less porous, so that the marsh flooded and became a lake in wet years. Today, the lake and its marshes are important havens for wildlife.

56 Ledges Trail

		See Map on Page 144
Description:	A very easy hike to a vantagepoint near Mormon Lake. This is a good place for wildlife viewing.	
Location:	30.6 miles southeast of Flagstaff.	
Type of trail:	Out and back.	
Type of trip:	Day hike.	
Difficulty:	Easy.	
Total distance:	1.2 miles.	
Elevation change:	100 feet.	
Time required:	1 hour.	
Water:	None.	
Best season:	Spring through fall.	
Maps:	Mormon Lake USGS quad; Coconino National Forest.	
Permits and restrictions:	None.	
For more information:	Mormon Lake Ranger District, Coconino National Forest.	

Finding the trailhead: From Flagstaff, drive about 27 miles south on Lake Mary Road (Forest Highway 3) and turn right (west) on the Mormon Lake Road (Forest Road 90). Continue 3.6 miles and turn right (west) into Dairy Spring Campground. Drive through the campground to site 26 and the signed trailhead.

Key points:
  0.0   Trailhead at site 26.
  0.6   Viewpoint.

The hike: The well-defined trail traverses the hillside above a row of summer homes,

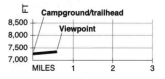

Mormon Lake from the Ledges Trail.

climbing gradually for about a half-mile. It then descends to a small ledge with a close view of the north end of Mormon Lake. Although the paved Mormon Lake Road is only about 0.2 mile away, the road is nicely hidden in the trees, and the view of the lake from this vantagepoint is nearly unspoiled. The ledge is about 100 feet above the lake, so this is a great place to watch wildlife. Bring binoculars, and plan to arrive around sunrise or before sunset for the best viewing. The trail continues to a private camp; it's best to return the way you came.

57 Lake View Trail

See Map on Page 144

Description:	A pleasant hike through pine and oak forest with expansive views of Mormon Lake and the ponderosa pine forest.
Location:	32 miles southeast of Flagstaff.
Type of trail:	Out and back.
Type of trip:	Day hike.
Difficulty:	Easy.
Total distance:	2.8 miles out and back.
Elevation change:	500 feet.
Time required:	2 hours.
Water:	None.
Best season:	Spring through fall.
Maps:	Mormon Lake, Mormon Mountain USGS quads; Coconino National Forest.
Permits and restrictions:	None.
For more information:	Mormon Lake Ranger District, Coconino National Forest.

Finding the trailhead: From Flagstaff, drive about 27 miles south on Lake Mary Road (Forest Highway 3) and turn right (west) on the Mormon Lake Road (Forest Road 90). Continue 5.0 miles and turn right (west) into Double Spring Campground. The signed trailhead is on the left at the south side of the campground.

Key points:

0.0   Trailhead at Double Spring Campground.
1.4   Viewpoint.

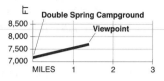

The hike: The Lake View Trail is not shown on the topographic map. It climbs gradually along a shallow drainage through pine and oak forest for about a mile and then switchbacks up a hill to the rim of a rock outcrop. It works its way along the outcrop about 0.2 mile to a point with a commanding view of the forest and the south end of Mormon Lake. The lake is about a mile away so the view is not as intimate as the view from the Ledges Trail.

A panoramic view of Mormon Lake from Lake View Trail.

147

Secret Canyons

Along the Mogollon Rim, between Flagstaff and Sedona, a series of deep canyons cuts deep into the southern edge of the Coconino Plateau. Sycamore Canyon is the westernmost of these. Protected in the Sycamore Canyon Wilderness, the forty-mile-long canyon offers some outstanding hiking and backpacking. To the east of Sycamore Canyon, a series of sandstone canyons and cliff-bound mesas are protected in the Red Rock–Secret Mountain, Munds Mountain Wilderness, Wet Beaver Creek, and Clear Creek Wildernesses. There are a large number of shorter trails in the area, offering excellent day hiking and easy overnight hiking. The first three hikes are reached from the Flagstaff area and the remainder from Sedona and Cottonwood.

58 Kelsey–Dorsey Loop

Description:	A scenic, remote hike in the Sycamore Canyon Wilderness.
Location:	23 miles southwest of Flagstaff.
Type of trail:	Loop.
Type of trip:	Day hike.
Difficulty:	Moderate.
Total distance:	6.4 miles.
Elevation change:	1,080 feet.
Time required:	4 hours.
Water:	Kelsey, Babes Hole, and Dorsey Springs.
Best season:	Spring through fall.
Maps:	Sycamore Point USGS quad; Coconino National Forest.
Permits and restrictions:	None.
For more information:	Peaks Ranger District, Coconino National Forest.

Finding the trailhead: From Flagstaff, drive west on West Route 66 (Business Interstate 40) about 2 miles and turn left (south) on the Woody Mountain Road (Forest Road 231). This road starts out as paved but soon becomes maintained dirt. Continue 13.7 miles and turn right (west) at Phone Booth Tank onto a narrower, maintained dirt road (FR 538). Continue on the main road for 5.3 miles and turn right (northwest) onto an unmaintained road (FR 538G) that is signed for the Kelsey Trail. Go 0.6 mile and turn right at a junction to continue on FR 538G for 1.3 miles to the end of the road at the Kelsey Trailhead.

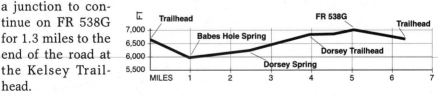

Kelsey–Dorsey Loop • Winter Cabin–Kelsey Loop

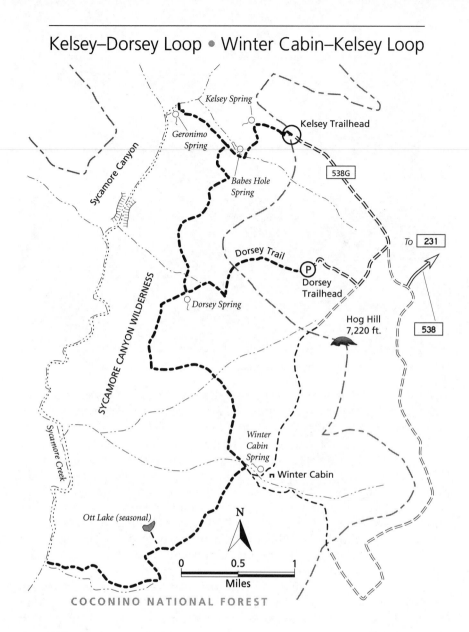

Key points:
- 0.0 Kelsey Trailhead.
- 0.4 Kelsey Spring.
- 1.0 Babes Hole Spring; turn left onto the Dorsey Trail.
- 2.5 Dorsey Spring; turn left onto the Dorsey Spring Trail.
- 4.0 Dorsey Trailhead.
- 4.6 Road junction; turn left.
- 5.1 FR 538G; turn left.
- 6.4 Kelsey Trailhead.

Overlooking Sycamore Canyon from the Mogollon Rim.

The hike: The Kelsey Trail drops over the upper rim of Sycamore Canyon and descends steeply for a couple of switchbacks; it then reaches gentler terrain as it swings west through the pine and oak forest. In 0.5 mile, the trail reaches Kelsey Spring, where it turns sharply left (south) to cross a drainage. The trail follows this drainage to the northwest to Babes Hole Spring. Just past the spring, go left, uphill, on the Dorsey Trail, at a junction marked by a huge, ancient ponderosa pine. There are good views as the trail contours along the inner rim of rugged Sycamore Canyon. At Dorsey Spring, turn left (east) onto the Dorsey Spring Trail. The trail climbs over a low ridge and drops into a drainage, which it follows nearly to the outer rim before swinging north. The trail goes through a low saddle in the forest before turning east again and climbing gradually to the trailhead.

Continue along the seldom-traveled dirt road for 0.6 mile and turn left (northeast) at the junction. In another 0.5 mile you will reach FR 538G. Turn left (north) and walk 1.3 miles to where the road ends and your car is parked. It is possible to do a car shuttle to avoid the hike on the road, but it's not really necessary since there is almost no traffic on these roads and they form a pleasant loop hike.

59 Winter Cabin–Kelsey Loop

See Map on Page 149

Description: This is a rugged trail and cross-country hike through a rugged portion of the Sycamore Canyon Wilderness.

Location: About 23 miles southwest of Flagstaff.

Type of trail: Trail and cross-country loop.

Type of trip: Backpack.

Difficulty: Difficult.

Total distance: 4.1 miles.

Elevation change: 2,240 feet.

Time required: 2 days.

Water: Kelsey, Babes Hole, Dorsey, Winter Cabin, and Geronimo Springs, and seasonally in Sycamore Canyon.

Best season: Spring through fall.

Maps: Sycamore Point USGS quad; Coconino National Forest.

Permits and restrictions: None.

For more information: Peaks Ranger District, Coconino National Forest.

Finding the trailhead: From Flagstaff, drive west on West Route 66 (Business Interstate 40) about 2 miles and turn left (south) on the Woody Mountain Road (Forest Road 231). This road starts out as paved but soon becomes maintained dirt. Continue 13.7 miles and turn right (west) at Phone Booth Tank onto a narrower, maintained dirt road (FR 538). Continue on the main road for 5.3 miles and turn right (northwest) onto an unmaintained road (FR 538G) that is signed for the Kelsey Trail. Go 0.6 mile and turn right at a junction to continue on FR 538G for 1.3 miles to the end of the road at the Kelsey Trailhead.

Key points:

0.0	Kelsey Trailhead.
0.4	Kelsey Spring.
1.0	Babes Hole Spring; turn left on the Dorsey Trail.
2.5	Dorsey Spring.
4.8	Winter Cabin Spring; turn right on the Winter Cabin Trail.
5.8	Ott Lake junction.
7.4	Sycamore Canyon; turn right.
11.2	Sandstone narrows.
12.1	Geronimo Spring; turn right onto the Kelsey Trail.
13.1	Babes Hole Spring.
14.1	Kelsey Trailhead.

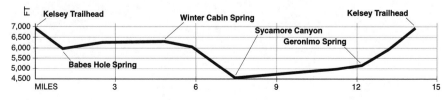

Sycamore Canyon.

The hike: Follow the Kelsey Trail to Babes Hole Spring (the right fork is our return trail) and turn left and hike the Dorsey Trail to Dorsey Spring. (See Hike 58 for more details on this section.) Continue south on the trail to Winter Cabin Spring. The trail continues to contour and after about a mile it climbs through a saddle and turns more to the east as the outer canyon widens. Note the change in vegetation as the trail passes onto this drier, south-facing slope. The trail swings around a broad basin and then ends at the ruins of Winter Cabin. Winter Cabin Spring is in the drainage next to the ruin.

The Hog Hill Trail comes from the northeast, and the Winter Cabin Trail joins from the southeast. Our route turns right (west) onto the Winter Cabin Trail and follows it as it descends a gentle slope. The trail crosses through a saddle and the view becomes more open as the tall ponderosa pine forest changes to pinyon-juniper woodland. An unsigned spur trail leads to Ott Lake, which is dry most of the time. Now the trail turns more to the south and works its way into a drainage, which it follows to the bed of Sycamore Canyon.

Turn right (north) and hike cross-country up Sycamore Canyon. Normally, easy boulder-hopping takes you up the broad, dry streambed. However, a major storm or spring snow melt can send large amounts of water down Sycamore Canyon. Even after the creek has stopped running, large pools can make progress difficult. The best time to do this hike is late spring when the pools are nearly, but not completely, dried up. In the summer and fall the only water source along the canyon bottom is Geronimo Spring. In this case, plan to carry enough water for an overnight camp. If you reach Sycamore Canyon and there is too much water for safe hiking, you will have to retrace your steps.

After about 3.8 miles you'll pass through a short but interesting narrows carved through the Coconino sandstone. Continue another 0.9 mile to Little LO Spring Canyon, a side canyon entering from the right (east). Walk a few yards up Little LO Spring Canyon to reach Geronimo Spring. Beyond the spring, follow the Kelsey Trail, which climbs steeply up the southeast slope just above the spring. Note the stand of Douglas-fir on this cool, shady slope. There are also a few small Arizona cypress, distinguished by reddish, curling bark. When the

Setting up camp under the open sky.

grade starts to become easier, you'll reach Babes Hole Spring and the junction with the Dorsey Trail. Continue on the Kelsey Trail another mile to the rim and the trailhead.

60 Secret Mountain Trail

Description:	This trail wanders out onto Secret Mountain, an isolated mesa in the Red Rock–Secret Mountain Wilderness. It features a historic cabin and some good views of the canyons in the wilderness area.
Location:	35.6 miles southwest of Flagstaff.
Type of trail:	Out and back.
Type of trip:	Day hike or backpack.
Difficulty:	Moderate.
Total distance:	9.8 miles.
Elevation change:	240 feet.
Time required:	5 hours.
Water:	None.
Best season:	Late spring through fall.
Maps:	Loy Butte, Wilson Mountain USGS quads; Coconino National Forest.
Permits and restrictions:	None.
For more information:	Sedona Ranger District, Coconino National Forest.

Finding the trailhead: From Flagstaff, drive west on West Route 66 (Business Interstate 40) about 2 miles and turn left (south) on the Woody Mountain Road (Forest Road 231). This road starts out as paved but soon becomes maintained dirt. Continue 13.7 miles and turn right (west) at Phone Booth Tank onto a narrower, maintained dirt road (FR 538). Continue on this road 6.8 miles, passing the turnoff to Turkey Butte Lookout. The road is unmaintained after this point but with care it is passable to low-clearance vehicles when it is dry. After a storm or during snow melt, the mud will be impassable. In another 1.5 miles the road passes just west of a power line then passes a stock tank. About 8.9 miles from Phone Booth Tank, FR 538 turns left (southeast) at the junction with FR 538B and crosses under the power line. Continue 2.7 miles to the end of the road.

Key points:

0.0	Trailhead.
0.4	Loy Canyon Trail at saddle.
0.6	Side trails.
1.4	Secret Cabin.
4.9	Viewpoint.

The hike: The trailhead is on the edge of the Mogollon Rim, but the view is mostly blocked by the bulk of Secret Mountain rising to the south. Start by following the Secret Mountain Trail along the ridge to the southeast. It

Secret Mountain Trail

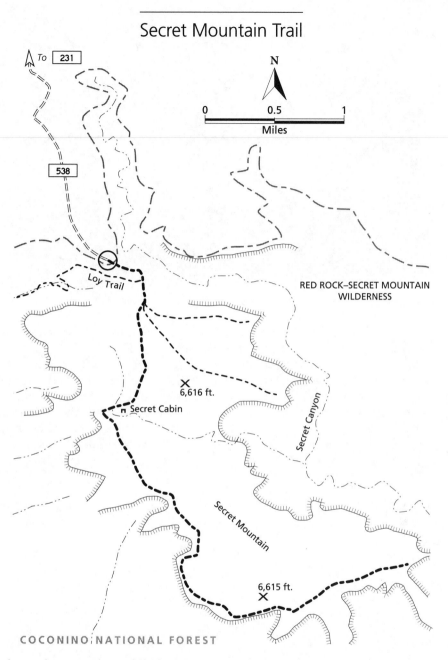

To 231

538

Loy Trail

RED ROCK–SECRET MOUNTAIN
WILDERNESS

X
6,616 ft.

⌂ Secret Cabin

Secret Canyon

Secret Mountain

6,615 ft.
X

COCONINO NATIONAL FOREST

drops down to the saddle between the rim and Secret Mountain, meeting
the Loy Canyon Trail. (See Hike 65 for information.)

The Secret Mountain Trail climbs about 200 feet onto Secret Mountain,
where there is a trail junction. These two side-trails lead east to viewpoints
overlooking Secret Canyon. The main trail continues south across the pine-
and oak-forested plateau to the ruins of Secret Cabin. Most likely, the cabin

Secret Mountain.

was built by ranchers as a line cabin for use during roundups. Water can sometimes be found in the drainage east of the ruin.

From the cabin, continue south. Soon the trail reaches a point on the west rim of Secret Mountain that offers views to the southwest toward the Verde Valley and Mingus Mountain. After this point, the trail heads generally southeast and skirts the southwest rim of Secret Mountain. Much of this area was burned by a large fire in 1996. The trail finally turns east and ends at the eastern tip of Secret Mountain. You're looking down Long Canyon and at the mass of Maroon Mountain, which divides Long and Secret Canyons.

61 Parsons Trail

Description:	A rugged, challenging hike through the remote red-rock canyons of the Sycamore Canyon Wilderness.
Location:	10.2 miles north of Cottonwood.
Type of trail:	Trail and cross-country loop.
Type of trip:	Backpack.
Difficulty:	Difficult.
Total distance:	21.4 miles.
Elevation change:	1200 feet.
Time required:	2 or 3 days.
Water:	Sycamore Creek downstream from Parsons Spring; seasonal pools upstream.
Best season:	Spring and fall.
Maps:	Clarkdale, Sycamore Basin USGS quads; Coconino National Forest.
Permits and restrictions:	A Red Rock Pass is required for vehicle parking. Camping is not allowed in Sycamore Canyon from Parsons Spring downstream to the Verde River.
For more information:	Sedona Ranger District, Coconino National Forest; Chino Valley Ranger District, Prescott National Forest.

Finding the trailhead: From Cottonwood, drive to the north end of town on Arizona Highway 89A and into the town of Clarkdale. Turn right (east) on the road to Tuzigoot National Monument. After 0.2 mile, just after crossing the Verde River bridge, turn left (north) on County Road 139 (it becomes Forest Road 131), a maintained dirt road. Drive 10.0 miles to the end of the road at the Sycamore Canyon trailhead.

Key points:
- 0.0   Sycamore Canyon Trailhead.
- 0.2   Sycamore Creek.
- 1.2   Summers Spring.
- 3.6   Parsons Spring.
- 11.2   Dogie Trail; turn left.
- 11.3   Taylor Cabin Trail; turn left.
- 11.7   Cedar Creek.
- 12.7   Pass into Sycamore Basin.
- 15.8   Pass.
- 19.8   Sycamore Canyon Rim.
- 21.2   Sycamore Creek.
- 21.4   Sycamore Canyon Trailhead.

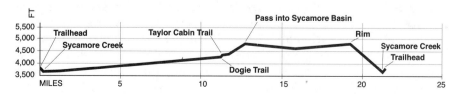

Parsons Trail • Taylor Cabin Loop
Mooney–Casner Loop • Robbers Roost

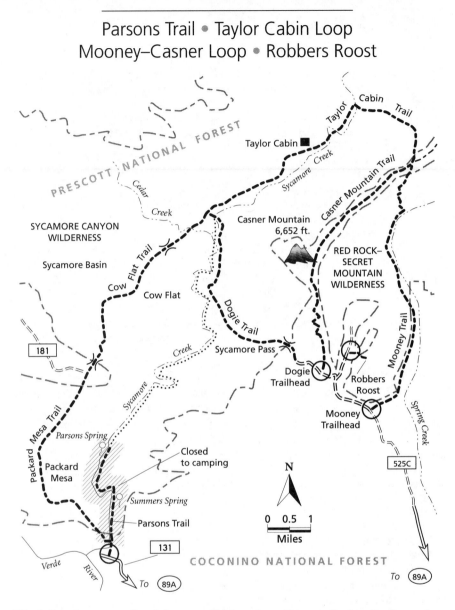

The hike: Sycamore Creek is normally dry above Parsons Spring. In the spring, seasonal pools above this point make it possible to do this loop without carrying water. During summer and fall, you'll have to pick up enough water at Parsons Spring for your camp further up the canyon. The catch is that during early spring, Sycamore Creek may be flooding from snow melt in the high country and this loop trip may be impossible. If the creek is running muddy at the trailhead, content yourself with a short day hike to Summers Spring or Parsons Spring. Do not attempt to cross the creek when it is flooding. In summer, this loop is recommended only for hikers experienced at dry camping in hot weather.

From the trailhead, follow the good trail 0.2 mile north into Sycamore Creek. On the left, the Packard Trail crosses the creek; this is our return trail. Please note that Sycamore Canyon is closed to camping between the trailhead and Parsons Spring due to overuse. Continue following Sycamore Creek on the broad, easy trail along the east bank. Sycamore Creek flows all year and supports a rich variety of riparian trees, including the Arizona sycamore for which the canyon is named. About 1.5 miles from the trailhead, the canyon swings sharply left and then right. During the winters of 1993 and 1994, massive flooding completely rearranged the creek bed. Evidence of the flooding is everywhere: saplings leaning downstream, collapsed stream banks, and piles of driftwood and even huge logs far above normal stream level.

Above Parsons Spring, the source for Sycamore Creek, the creek bed dries up. Continue up Sycamore Canyon by boulder-hopping along the broad, dry wash. You may see seasonal pools of water in the bends of the creek. Also, watch for petroglyphs along the rock walls of the canyon. Although strenuous, progress up the creek bed is relatively fast because the periodic floods keep the bed clear of brush. The gorge becomes shallower after about 6 miles. The Dogie Trail crosses Sycamore Creek 7.6 miles above Parson Spring. Turn left (west) on the Dogie Trail, which joins the Taylor Cabin and Cow Flat Trails above the west bank. Now, turn left (south) on the Cow Flat Trail. There are several good campsites for small groups on the bluffs overlooking the creek to the east. There is no water except for possible seasonal pools in Sycamore Creek.

After the confines of Sycamore Creek and the rugged boulder-hopping, it is a pleasure to walk the easy Cow Flat Trail southwest through the open pinyon-juniper forest. Shortly, the trail crosses Cedar Creek. (This creek is usually dry at the crossing, but water can sometimes be found upstream about a mile.) The trail climbs gradually for another mile and passes through a broad saddle to enter Sycamore Basin. The walking is very easy through this open basin with fine views of the surrounding red rock formations. The trail crosses Cow Flat and skirts the head of a side canyon. It then climbs gradually to another pass. On the far side of the pass, the trail ends at a trailhead at the end of FR 181.

Go south on the Packard Trail. Packard Mesa forms the west rim of lower Sycamore Canyon, and the trail generally stays near the crest as it works its way south through open pinyon pine and juniper stands. About 4 miles from FR 181, the trail turns east and descends into Sycamore Canyon. It crosses the creek and meets the Parsons Trail; turn right to return to the trailhead.

62 Taylor Cabin Loop

See Map on Page 158

Description: This is a fine hike through the remote red-rock canyons of the Sycamore Canyon and Red Rock–Secret Mountain Wildernesses. A bonus is the return trail across the top of Casner Mountain, which gives you outstanding views of Sycamore Canyon.

Location: 19 miles west of Sedona.

Type of trail: Loop.

Type of trip: Backpack.

Difficulty: Difficult.

Total distance: 18.8 miles.

Elevation change: 2,560 feet.

Time required: Two days.

Water: Seasonal in Sycamore Creek.

Best season: Spring through fall.

Maps: Sycamore Point, Sycamore Basin, Loy Butte USGS quads; Coconino National Forest.

Permits and restrictions: A Red Rock Pass is required for vehicle parking.

For more information: Sedona Ranger District, Coconino National Forest.

Finding the trailhead: From Sedona, drive about 8 miles south on Arizona Highway 89A and turn right (northwest) on Forest Road 525, a maintained dirt road. Go 2.2 miles and turn left (west) onto FR 525C. Continue 8.8 miles to the end of the road at the Dogie Trailhead. The last mile or two frequently washes out and may be very rough, but the rest is passable to ordinary cars. The Casner Mountain Trail, which is the return trail for the loop, meets FR 525C at 0.8 mile east of Dogie Trailhead.

Key points:

0.0	Dogie Trailhead.
0.4	Sycamore Pass.
4.9	Sycamore Creek.
5.0	Taylor Cabin Trail; turn right.
7.9	Taylor Cabin.
9.7	Taylor Cabin Trail turns right, up an unnamed side canyon.
12.0	Turn right on Casner Mountain Trail.
15.6	Casner Mountain.
18.0	FR 525C; turn right.
18.8	Dogie Trailhead.

An aerial view of Sycamore Canyon.

The hike: There is usually water in Sycamore Creek during the spring, but it is dry later in the year. Enough water should be carried for a dry camp if the creek is dry. On the other hand, Sycamore Creek may be flooding and be impassable during snow melt or after a major storm. In this case you'll have to make the hike an out and back, which you can do in a day.

The start of the Dogie Trail is shown on the Loy Butte quad, but the trail is missing from the Sycamore Basin quad. You'll climb a short distance to cross Sycamore Pass and then descend gradually to the west. The trail turns north and works its way along a sloping terrace through pinyon-juniper forest. The inner gorge of Sycamore Canyon is visible to the west, and the cliffs of Casner Mountain rise on the east. Finally, the trail descends to Sycamore Creek and crosses it to join the Cow Flat and Taylor Cabin Trails on the west bank. There are several campsites for small groups on the bluff just to the south. (In an emergency, you may be able to find water in Cedar Creek. See Hike 61 for details.)

Turn right (northeast) on the Taylor Cabin Trail, which stays on the bench to the west of Sycamore Creek. After about 2 miles, the trail descends to the creek and becomes harder to find. Watch for Taylor Cabin on the west bank; the trail passes right by this old rancher's line cabin. The trail stays on the west side of the creek after Taylor Cabin. If the trail is lost, boulder-hop directly up the creek bed.

About 1.8 miles from Taylor Cabin, the trail turns right (east) and climbs out of Sycamore Canyon. Watch carefully for the turnoff, which is usually marked by cairns. The topographic maps are essential for finding this trail.

Historic Taylor Cabin in Sycamore Canyon is an old stone line cabin used by the early ranchers.

Most of the trail follows the major drainage south of Buck Ridge, often staying right in the bed of this very pretty canyon. Near the top, the trail turns more to the south and climbs steeply through a fine stand of ponderosa pine and Douglas-fir. A single switchback leads to the top of the ridge, where there are excellent views of Sycamore Canyon and the Taylor Basin. The trail reaches a pass and ends at the junction with the Casner Mountain and Mooney Trails.

Turn right (southwest) on the Casner Mountain Trail, which is an old road built during power line construction. The road is now closed to vehicles and makes a scenic finish to this loop hike. Follow the trail southwest along the narrow ridge leading to Casner Mountain. There are views of Sycamore Canyon on the west and Mooney Canyon on the east. The trail climbs onto Casner Mountain, a broad plateau capped with dark volcanic rocks. A gradual descent leads to the south edge of the plateau, where the trail descends rapidly in a series of switchbacks. Near the bottom of the descent the trail is shown as ending on the topographic map; if you lose it just follow the power line down to FR 525C. Now, turn right and walk 0.8 mile up the road to the Dogie Trailhead.

63 Mooney–Casner Loop

Description: This hike takes you through a little-traveled, red-rock canyon to the scenic Casner Mountain Ridge. Most of the loop is in the Red Rock–Secret Mountain Wilderness.

See Map on Page 158

Location: 19 miles west of Sedona.
Type of trail: Loop.
Type of trip: Day hike or overnight backpack.
Difficulty: Difficult.
Total distance: 14.1 miles.
Elevation change: 2,300 feet.
Time required: 9 hours.
Water: None.
Best season: Spring through fall.
Maps: Loy Butte USGS quad; Coconino National Forest.
Permits and restrictions: A Red Rock Pass is required for vehicle parking.
For more information: Sedona Ranger District, Coconino National Forest.

Finding the trailhead: From Sedona, drive about 8 miles south on Arizona Highway 89A and turn right (northwest) on Forest Road 525, a maintained dirt road. Go 2.2 miles and turn left (west) onto FR 525C. Continue 7.2 miles to the Mooney Trailhead at Black Tank. The Casner Mountain Trail, which is the return trail for the loop, meets FR 525C at 1.6 miles west.

Key points:

- 0.0 Mooney Trailhead.
- 1.7 Ridgetop.
- 2.9 The trail contours into Mooney Canyon.
- 5.0 Leave Spring Creek.
- 6.5 Turn left on the Casner Mountain Trail.
- 10.1 Casner Mountain.
- 12.5 Turn left on FR 525C.
- 14.1 Mooney Trailhead.

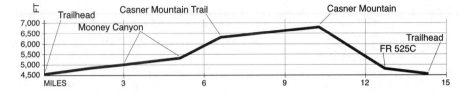

The hike: This scenic loop can be done as a long day-hike or as an overnight backpack if you carry water for a dry camp. The Mooney Trail follows an old road northeast toward a long, low ridge. It climbs east onto the ridge and then follows it north. Where the ridge butts up against the steep slopes of Casner Mountain, the Mooney Trail contours into Mooney Canyon. It follows the normally dry bed of Spring Creek, which drains Mooney Canyon, past some red-rock outcrops, and then climbs the brushy northwest side of the canyon. At the top of the ridge, turn left on the Casner Mountain Trail and follow this scenic old road south over the top of Casner Mountain and down to FR 525C. Turn left and walk 1.6 miles southeast to your vehicle.

64 Robbers Roost

See Map on Page 158

Description: This is a very easy walk to a scenic red-rock overlook and a small cave in the Coconino National Forest. According to local lore, the cave was once an outlaw hideout.

Location: About 19 miles west of Sedona.

Type of trail: Out and back.

Type of trip: Day hike.

Difficulty: Easy.

Total distance: 0.6 mile.

Elevation change: None.

Time required: 30 minutes.

Water: None.

Best season: All year.

Maps: Loy Butte USGS quad; Coconino National Forest.

Permits and restrictions: A Red Rock Pass is required for vehicle parking.

For more information: Sedona Ranger District, Coconino National Forest.

Finding the trailhead: From Sedona, drive west about 8 miles on Arizona Highway 89A and turn right (northwest) on Forest Road 525, a maintained dirt road. Go 2.2 miles and turn left (west) at a sign for FR 525C. Continue 7.5 miles and turn right (north) on an unmaintained road which climbs up a ridge toward the east side of Casner Mountain. (Casner Mountain can be identified by the power line that runs down its south slopes.) Go 1.1 miles up this road until you are directly west of Robbers Roost, a low red-rock mesa across the gully to the east. The trailhead and trail are unmarked.

Key points:
   0.0   Trailhead.
   0.3   Robbers Roost.

The hike: Follow an unmarked trail (not shown on the topographic map) across the shallow gully and up to the north side of Robbers Roost. Then, traverse a red sandstone ledge around to a cave on the east side of the rock, just below the rim. Inside the cave, a small wall was supposedly built by the robbers for defense. The main attraction, however, is the picture-window view of Secret Mountain, Bear Mountain, and the Sedona area from within the cave. A hole though a small fin provides a smaller window. It is also interesting to explore the top of this small mesa. After a rain, there will be temporary water pockets that reflect the sky and the red rocks.

65 Loy Canyon Trail

Description:	A scenic hike up a red-rock canyon to the Mogollon Rim in the Red Rock–Secret Mountain Wilderness.
Location:	11 miles northwest of Sedona.
Type of trail:	Out and back.
Type of trip:	Day hike.
Difficulty:	Moderate.
Total distance:	9.6 miles.
Elevation change:	1,900 feet.
Time required:	6 hours.
Water:	None.
Best season:	All year.
Maps:	Loy Butte USGS quad; Coconino National Forest.
Permits and restrictions:	A Red Rock Pass is required for vehicle parking.
For more information:	Sedona Ranger District, Coconino National Forest.

Finding the trailhead: From Sedona, drive to the west end of town on Arizona Highway 89A and turn right at a traffic light onto the Dry Creek Road. Drive 2.8 miles and turn left onto Boynton Canyon Road. Continue 1.6 miles and turn left onto Forest Road 152C, a maintained dirt road. After 3.0 miles, turn right onto FR 525. Continue 3.7 miles to the Loy Canyon Trailhead. (If you go too far you will see the Hancock Ranch to the right.)

Loy Canyon Trail

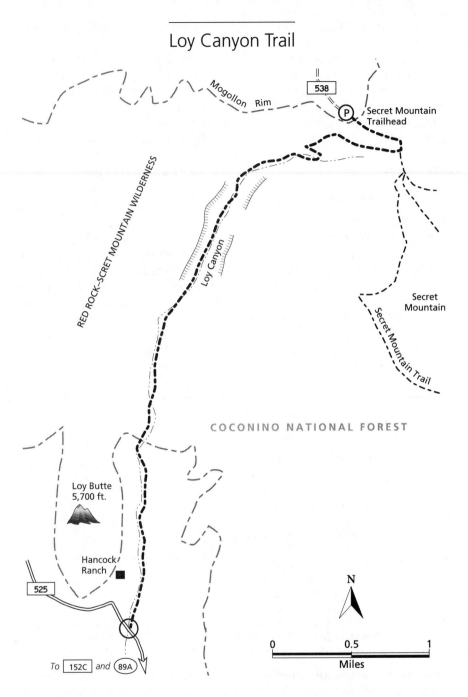

Key points:

0.0 Loy Canyon Trailhead.
2.1 Red-rock narrows.
3.0 End of narrows.
4.4 Junction with Secret Mountain Trail; turn left.
4.8 Secret Mountain Trailhead.

The hike: Initially the trail skirts the Hancock Ranch along its east boundary and joins the dry creek bed which it follows northward through the open pinyon pine, juniper, and Arizona cypress for-

est. Conical Loy Butte looms to the west, and the cliffs of Secret Mountain tower over Loy Canyon on the east. After 2.1 miles, the canyon becomes narrower, and the trail turns slightly toward the northeast. In another mile the trail turns toward the east as the canyon opens up a bit. The buff-colored Coconino sandstone cliffs of the Mogollon Rim tower above the trail to the north, and matching cliffs form the north end of Secret Mountain. Watch carefully for the point where the trail leaves the canyon bottom and begins climbing the north side of the canyon in a series of switchbacks. Though it is a steep climb, the reward is an expanding view of Loy Canyon. Notice the contrast between the brushy vegetation on this dry, south-facing slope and the cool, moist pine and fir forest across the canyon to the south.

The Loy Canyon Trail ends where it joins the Secret Mountain Trail in the saddle between Secret Mountain and the Mogollon Rim. Turn left here and climb the short distance to the rim and the Secret Mountain Trailhead. Views are limited here, but if you walk a few hundred yards along the road there is a great view down Loy Canyon.

As an option, you could combine the Loy Canyon and Secret Mountain Trails for a longer hike. See Hike 60 for information.

Agave, or century plant, is a desert-dwelling relative of the lily.

167

66 Bear Mountain

Description:	This is a less-used trail in the Red Rock–Secret Mountain Wilderness. It features some of the best views in the area.
Location:	5.7 miles northwest of Sedona.
Type of trail:	Out and back.
Type of trip:	Day hike.
Difficulty:	Moderate.
Total distance:	4.2 miles.
Elevation change:	1,800 feet.
Time required:	3 hours.
Water:	None.
Best season:	Fall through spring.
Maps:	Wilson Mountain, Loy Butte USGS quads; Coconino National Forest.
Permits and restrictions:	A Red Rock Pass is required for vehicle parking.
For more information:	Sedona Ranger District, Coconino National Forest.

Finding the trailhead: From Sedona, drive to the west end of town on Arizona Highway 89A and turn right at a traffic light onto the Dry Creek Road. Drive 2.8 miles and turn left onto Boynton Canyon Road. Continue 1.6 miles and turn left onto Forest Road 152C, a maintained dirt road. Go 1.3 miles to the Bear Mountain Trailhead.

Key points:

0.0 Bear Mountain Trailhead.
0.9 Top of second terrace.
2.1 Bear Mountain.

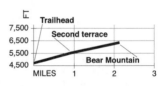

The hike: This trail is dry and exposed to the south for all of its length and is hot in summer. Be sure you carry plenty of water. As you start up the trail, you are looking at massive Bear Mountain directly ahead. The trail crosses several small gulches and is confused by false trails. Keep in mind that you are heading directly to the base of Bear Mountain (the trail is visible as it starts the climb) and you won't have any problems. After a pleasant stroll across the flat, the trail climbs steeply up the talus slopes and surmounts the lowest cliff band via a break to the right. It then starts a gentle climb along the terrace to the left. Already the views are excellent—looking to the southeast you are now level with the top of Doe Mountain. As the trail swings into a bay, you should be able to pick out the break the trail will use to climb the imposing cliffs above. The trail climbs very steeply up the gully then swings right to gain the top of the second terrace. The south summit of Bear Mountain, the end of the hike, is now visible about a mile ahead. Fainter now but marked by a few cairns, the trail crosses the mesa to its west rim and stays along the ridge crest as it crosses through several shallow notches. The trail climbs

Bear Mountain • Doe Mountain • Fay Canyon Arch
Boynton Canyon • Long Canyon

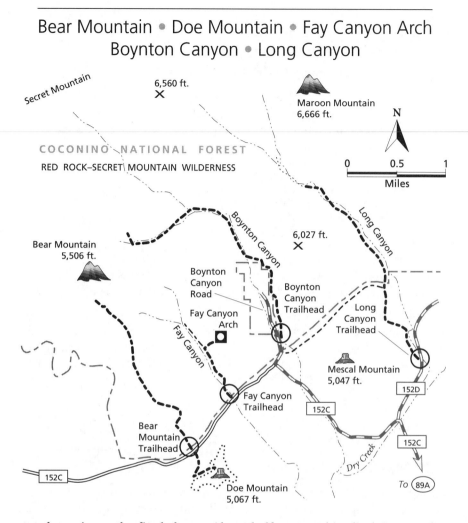

Secret Mountain

6,560 ft.
×

Maroon Mountain
6,666 ft.

N

COCONINO NATIONAL FOREST
RED ROCK–SECRET MOUNTAIN WILDERNESS

0   0.5   1
Miles

Boynton Canyon

6,027 ft.
×

Long Canyon

Bear Mountain
5,506 ft.

Boynton
Canyon
Road

Boynton
Canyon
Trailhead

Fay Canyon
Arch

Long
Canyon
Trailhead

Fay Canyon

Mescal Mountain
5,047 ft.

152D

Fay Canyon
Trailhead

152C

Bear
Mountain
Trailhead

152C

Dry Creek

152C

Doe Mountain
5,067 ft.

To 89A

steeply again on the final slopes. About halfway up this climb it ascends a beautiful section of crossbedded Coconino sandstone, with the route marked by a few cairns. Along the top of this outcrop, a few windblown ponderosa pine grace the stark rock slabs. The eye can sweep over an immense view, from Mingus Mountain to the west to the Mogollon Rim and the Dry Creek basin to the northeast. The section of the trail climbs along the brushy ridge to the northwest. The trail ends at the southernmost summit of Bear Mountain, in a thick pinyon-juniper forest. The views are restricted except for a glimpse of Red Canyon to the northwest. Although our hike ends here, an option is to walk cross-country about 1.5 miles north through the forest to the highest point on Bear Mountain, which is about 120 feet higher than the end of the trail.

67 Doe Mountain

See Map on Page 169

Description: The top of Doe Mountain features fine views of Bear Mountain and the Dry Creek basin.
Location: 5.7 miles northwest of Sedona.
Type of trail: Out-and-back trail and cross-country loop.
Type of trip: Day hike.
Difficulty: Easy.
Total distance: 2.8 miles.
Elevation change: 440 feet.
Time required: 2 hours.
Water: None.
Best season: All year.
Maps: Wilson Mountain USGS quad; Coconino National Forest.
Permits and restrictions: A Red Rock Pass is required for vehicle parking.
For more information: Sedona Ranger District, Coconino National Forest.

Finding the trailhead: From Sedona, drive to the west end of town on Arizona Highway 89A and turn right at a traffic light onto the Dry Creek Road. Drive 2.8 miles and turn left onto Boynton Canyon Road. Continue 1.6 miles and turn left onto Forest Road 152C, a maintained dirt road. Go 1.3 miles to the Bear Mountain Trailhead.

Key points:
0.0 Bear Mountain Trailhead.
0.5 Doe Mountain rim.
2.3 Doe Mountain Trail.
2.8 Bear Mountain Trailhead.

The hike: Doe Mountain is the flat, red mesa to the southwest. Cross the road and walk up the Doe Mountain Trail, which starts by heading directly toward a large ravine splitting the northwest side of the mesa. After a few hundred yards the trail turns right as the slope becomes steeper. A single, long switchback takes the trail back into the ravine, which it climbs to reach the rim of Doe Mountain. The trail ends, but now turn right and follow the rim cross-country all the way around the top of Doe Mountain. The walk is easy and nearly level, and the reward is a series of views in all directions. Rejoin the trail to return to the trailhead.

68 Fay Canyon Arch

See Map on Page 169

Description: A hike to a natural arch in the Red Rock–Secret Mountain Wilderness.

Location: About 5 miles northwest of Sedona.

Type of trail: Out and back.

Type of trip: Day hike.

Difficulty: Easy.

Total distance: 1.6 miles.

Elevation change: 220 feet.

Time required: 1 hour.

Water: None.

Best season: All year.

Maps: Wilson Mountain USGS quad; Coconino National Forest.

Permits and restrictions: A Red Rock Pass is required for vehicle parking.

For more information: Sedona Ranger District, Coconino National Forest.

Finding the trailhead: From Sedona, drive to the west end of town on Arizona Highway 89A and turn right at a traffic light onto the Dry Creek Road. Drive 2.8 miles and turn left onto Boynton Canyon Road. Continue 1.6 miles and turn left onto Forest Road 152C, a maintained dirt road. Go 0.5 mile to the Fay Canyon Trailhead, which is on the right.

Fay Canyon Arch frames a view of Bear Mountain in the Red Rock–Secret Mountain Wilderness.

Key points:

 0.0 Fay Canyon Trailhead.
 0.6 Arch turnoff.
 0.8 Fay Canyon Arch.

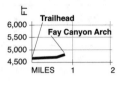

The hike: The Fay Canyon Trail starts out as an easy walk through pinyon-juniper forest. The only difficulty is a few false trails near the beginning. About 0.6 mile from the trailhead, watch for an unmarked trail going right (northeast) toward the canyon wall. This trail climbs steeply about 0.2 mile to Fay Canyon Arch, which is difficult to see until you are very close. The arch was formed from a massive fin in the Schnebly Hill formation and stands close to the cliff behind it, so there is little skylight shining through.

It is also worthwhile to continue on the main trail up Fay Canyon. It fades out at a fork in the canyon about 1.0 mile from the trailhead; this side trip would add 2.0 miles to the hike.

69 Boynton Canyon

See Map on Page 169

Description: This is a very popular hike into a spectacular red-rock canyon that ends below the towering cliffs of Bear Mountain in the Red Rock–Secret Mountain Wilderness.

Location: About 5 miles northwest of Sedona.

Type of trail: Out and back

Type of trip: Day hike.

Difficulty: Easy.

Total distance: 5.0 miles.

Elevation change: 540 feet.

Time required: 3 hours.

Water: None.

Best season: All year.

Maps: Wilson Mountain USGS quad; Coconino National Forest.

Permits and restrictions: A Red Rock Pass is required for vehicle parking.

For more information: Sedona Ranger District, Coconino National Forest.

Finding the trailhead: From Sedona, drive to the west end of town on Arizona Highway 89A and turn right at the traffic light onto the Dry Creek Road. Continue 2.8 miles and turn left onto Boynton Canyon Road. Drive 1.6 miles and turn right, remaining on Boynton Canyon Road. Go 0.3 mile and park at the Boynton Canyon Trailhead on the right. If you go too far you'll reach the entrance to a private resort.

Key points:

- 0.0   Boynton Trailhead.
- 1.0   Spur trail to the resort.
- 2.5   End of the trail below Bear Mountain.

The hike: This is a well-known hike that skirts a large resort for its first mile, so don't expect a wilderness experience. The upper part of Boynton Canyon is spectacular and makes up for the initial section of the hike. The Boynton Canyon Trail climbs along the north side of the canyon to avoid the resort and then drops into the canyon. Here a spur trail to the resort joins from the left. The Boynton Canyon Trail follows the drainage to the northwest. In another half-mile or so, both the canyon and the trail turn toward the southwest, and the noises of the resort are left behind. The head of the canyon is formed by massive walls of Coconino sandstone on the east face of Bear Mountain. The trail becomes fainter near the end as it winds through cool, pine and fir forest. A final short climb leads out of the dense forest to a viewpoint on the brushy slope above. Allow some time to linger at this fine spot.

The head of Boynton Canyon.

70 Long Canyon

See Map on Page 169

Description: A easy hike to a less-visited canyon in the Red Rock–Secret Mountain Wilderness.

Location: 3.4 miles northwest of Sedona.

Type of trail: Out and back.

Type of trip: Day hike.

Difficulty: Easy.

Total distance: 4.8 miles.

Elevation change: 320 feet.

Time required: 3 hours.

Water: None.

Best season: All year.

Maps: Wilson Mountain USGS quad; Coconino National Forest.

Permits and restrictions: A Red Rock Pass is required for vehicle parking.

For more information: Sedona Ranger District, Coconino National Forest.

Finding the trailhead: From Sedona, drive to the west end of town on Arizona Highway 89A and turn right at the traffic light onto the Dry Creek Road. Continue 2.8 miles and turn right onto Long Canyon Road. Drive 0.6 mile to the trailhead parking on the left. (The road continues to a private subdivision.)

Key points:

0.0   Long Canyon Trailhead.

1.0   Deadman Pass Trail.

2.4   End of trail.

The hike: The mouth of Long Canyon is over a mile from the trailhead, so the first section of the hike is through open pinyon-juniper flats, with tantalizing views of the canyon walls ahead, as well as Mescal Mountain to the south. Contrast this quiet area with the first part of the Boynton Canyon Trail. As you pass the north tip of Mescal Mountain, you'll reach the wilderness boundary and the junction with the Deadman Pass Trail.

The canyon walls gradually close in as you continue, and the trail starts to fade out. It's possible to continue the hike cross-country, and also to explore several side canyons. If you end the hike when the trail fades out, you'll be turning back about 2.4 miles from the trailhead.

The yucca was a valuable source of food, fiber, and even soap for the Navajo and Hopi living in northern Arizona.

71 Secent Canyon

Description:	This is an exceptionally fine hike up the longest canyon in the Red Rock–Secret Mountain Wilderness. Its length keeps the crowds away.
Location:	5.2 miles northwest of Sedona.
Type of trail:	Out and back.
Type of trip:	Day hike.
Difficulty:	Moderate.
Total distance:	7.8 miles.
Elevation change:	480 feet.
Time required:	5 hours.
Water:	Upper Secret Canyon.
Best season:	All year.
Maps:	Wilson Mountain USGS quad; Coconino National Forest.
Permits and restrictions:	A Red Rock Pass is required for vehicle parking.
For more information:	Sedona Ranger District, Coconino National Forest.

Finding the trailhead: From Sedona, drive to the west end of town on Arizona Highway 89A and turn right at a traffic light onto the Dry Creek Road. After 2.0 miles, turn right on dirt Forest Road 152 (also called Dry Creek Road). Although this road is maintained, it receives heavy traffic, and its condition varies. Drive 3.2 miles to the Secret Canyon Trailhead on the left side of the road. The parking area is small, but there are other parking spots nearby.

Key points:

0.0   Secret Canyon Trailhead.
1.8   Small clearing.
3.9   End of trail in Secret Canyon.

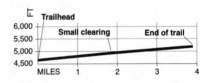

The hike: Secret Canyon is the longest and most remote canyon in the Dry Creek basin, and it is nearly as long as its more famous neighbor, Oak Creek. It also has permanent water in the upper section, a rarity in the red-rock area.

The Secret Canyon Trail crosses Dry Creek and enters the Red Rock–Secret Mountain Wilderness only a few yards from the road. You'll cross Secret Canyon wash several times; if either it or Dry Creek are flooding, this hike will be impossible. Normally, the lower section of Secret Canyon is dry and the hike is easy through the pinyon-juniper-cypress forest. About 0.5 mile from the trailhead, the HS Canyon Trail branches left. Just before the trail enters upper Secret Canyon, it passes through a small clearing that gives you good views. The trail contours along the north side of the drainage for a short distance before dropping back into the bed. The canyon walls become narrower here and are formed by the Mogollon Rim on the north and Maroon Mountain on the south. There is normally water in this section. Watch for poison ivy, a low-growing plant with shiny leaves that grow in groups of

Secret Canyon • Bear Sign Canyon • Dry Creek
Vultee Arch

three. Fall colors in this part of the canyon are a beautiful mix of reds, oranges, and violets, with most of the color provided by Arizona bigtooth maple and poison ivy. About 4 miles from the trailhead, our hike ends as the trail fades out. Only those willing to do difficult cross-country hiking should continue above this point.

72 Bear Sign Canyon

See Map on Page 177

Description: A very easy hike into a red-rock canyon in the Red Rock–Secret Mountain Wilderness.

Location: 6 miles northwest of Sedona.

Type of trail: Out and back.

Type of trip: Day hike.

Difficulty: Easy.

Total distance: 3.2 miles.

Elevation change: 280 feet.

Time required: 2 hours.

Water: Seasonal in Bear Sign Canyon.

Best season: All year.

Maps: Wilson Mountain USGS quad; Coconino National Forest.

Permits and restrictions: A Red Rock Pass is required for vehicle parking.

For more information: Sedona Ranger District, Coconino National Forest.

Finding the trailhead: From Sedona, drive to the west end of town on Arizona Highway 89A and turn right at a traffic light onto the Dry Creek Road. After 2.0 miles, turn right on dirt Forest Road 152 (also called Dry Creek Road). Although this road is maintained, it receives heavy traffic, and its condition varies. Drive 4.0 miles to the end of the road at the Dry Creek Trailhead.

Upper Bear Sign Canyon.

Arizona cypress is easily distinguished by its curly, reddish bark.

0.0 Dry Creek Trailhead.
0.6 Turn left onto Bear Sign Canyon Trail.
1.6 End of the hike as the trail fades out.

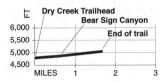

The hike: Start out on the Dry Creek Trail. (There are two trails that begin at this trail-head. The Dry Creek Trail goes north, and the Vultee Arch Trail goes east.) Hike 0.6 mile north and turn left (northwest) at Bear Sign Canyon, the first side canyon on the left. The trail continues about a mile up Bear Sign Canyon before fading out. It is possible to go further, but the canyon becomes much rougher. There are great views of the cliffs of the Mogollon Rim, and after wet periods the creek will be running. The vegetation is the usual, but still delightful, mix of Arizona cypress, pinyon pine, juniper trees, and chaparral brush.

73 Dry Creek

See Map on Page 177

Description: This is a demanding cross-country hike to the Mogollon Rim at the headwaters of Dry Creek, in the Red Rock–Secret Mountain Wilderness. The first 1.1 miles is an easy on-trail hike.
Location: 6 miles northwest of Sedona.
Type of trail: Trail and cross-country out and back.
Type of trip: Day hike.
Difficulty: Difficult.
Total distance: 7.0 miles.
Elevation change: 2,040 feet.
Time required: 6 hours.
Water: Seasonal in Dry Creek.
Best season: All year.
Maps: Wilson Mountain USGS quad; Coconino National Forest.
Permits and restrictions: A Red Rock Pass is required for vehicle parking.
For more information: Sedona Ranger District, Coconino National Forest.

Finding the trailhead: From Sedona, drive to the west end of town on Arizona Highway 89A and turn right at a traffic light onto the Dry Creek Road. After 2.0 miles, turn right on dirt Forest Road 152 (also called Dry Creek Road). Although this road is maintained, it receives heavy traffic, and its condition varies. Drive 4.0 miles to the end of the road at the Dry Creek Trailhead.

Key points:

0.0 Dry Creek Trailhead.
0.6 Bear Sign Canyon Trail.
1.1 Start of cross-country.

2.7   Turn right, up a side canyon.

3.5   Mogollon Rim.

The hike: Follow the Dry Creek Trail
north out of the parking area. After 0.6
mile, Bear Sign Canyon branches left;
continue north on the trail along Dry
Creek. The informal trail fades out after

a while, and this makes a good destination for an easy day hike.

You'll need the topographic map for the remainder of this hike. Continue
cross-country up the bed of Dry Creek. As the canyon heads against the impressive cliffs and ramparts of the Mogollon Rim, the canyon itself opens
up a bit. Looking east, you'll see glimpses of brushy ridges descending from
the rim, which offer the possibility of a route. Turn right (east) up the side
canyon that enters Dry Creek just below the 5,600-foot contour on the topographic map. Follow this side canyon until it becomes difficult to continue.
Turn right (southeast) and continue up the brushy ridge to reach the Mogollon Rim. This is the destination for our hike.

An option that requires a car shuttle links this hike with the AB Young
Trail into Oak Creek Canyon. To do this, walk cross-country north through
the rim forest to FR 231 and then turn right to reach East Pocket Knob. There
is a forest fire lookout tower on the top of this hill. From here, you can follow the AB Young Trail east to the rim and down to Oak Creek. See Hike
92 for details on this trail.

An aerial view of Coffee Pot Rock and Brins Mesa in the Dry Creek basin.

181

74 Vultee Arch

See Map on Page 177

Description: A pleasant walk to a graceful natural arch in the Red Rock–Secret Mountain Wilderness.

Location: 6 miles northwest of Sedona.

Type of trail: Out and back.

Type of trip: Day hike.

Difficulty: Easy.

Total distance: 3.6 miles.

Elevation change: 600 feet.

Time required: 2.5 hours.

Water: None.

Best season: All year.

Maps: Wilson Mountain USGS quad; Coconino National Forest.

Permits and restrictions: A Red Rock Pass is required for vehicle parking.

For more information: Sedona Ranger District, Coconino National Forest.

Finding the trailhead: From Sedona, drive to the west end of town on Arizona Highway 89A and turn right at a traffic light onto the Dry Creek Road. After 2.0 miles, turn right on dirt Forest Road 152 (also called Dry Creek Road). Although this road is maintained, it receives heavy traffic, and its condition varies. Drive 4.0 miles to the end of the road at the Dry Creek Trailhead.

Key points:
- 0.0   Dry Creek Trailhead.
- 1.8   Vultee Arch.

The hike: Hike east on the Vultee Arch Trail, which follows Sterling Canyon. This is an easy walk though pleasant pinyon-juniper-cypress forest, and the

Vultee Arch.

canyon is nearly straight. After about 1.6 miles, right where Sterling Canyon takes a turn to the southeast, follow a trail left (north) out of the bed to reach the arch. It was named after the president of Vultee Aircraft who was killed in a plane crash nearby in the 1930s.

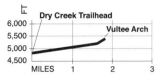

The trail up Sterling Canyon continues to its head, a pass overlooking Oak Creek Canyon. With a car shuttle, you can do a one-way hike to Oak Creek. See Hike 93 for information.

75 Brins Mesa

Description:	This is a mostly on-trail hike—with a short section of easy cross-country—to a very scenic viewpoint overlooking Sedona, Dry Creek, and the high cliffs of Wilson Mountain. It is in the Red Rock–Secret Mountain Wilderness.
Location:	4.2 miles northwest of Sedona.
Type of trail:	Out and back.
Type of trip:	Day hike.
Difficulty:	Easy.
Total distance:	5.8 miles.
Elevation change:	820 feet.
Time required:	3.5 hours.
Water:	None.
Best season:	All year.
Maps:	Wilson Mountain USGS quad; Coconino National Forest.
Permits and restrictions:	A Red Rock Pass is required for vehicle parking.
For more information:	Sedona Ranger District, Coconino National Forest.

Finding the trailhead: From Sedona, drive to the west end of town on Arizona Highway 89A and turn right at a traffic light onto the Dry Creek Road. After 2.0 miles, turn right on dirt Forest Road 152 (also called Dry Creek Road). Although this road is maintained, it receives a great deal of traffic, and its condition varies. Drive 2.2 miles and turn right into the trailhead parking area. Parking is limited, but there are other parking spots nearby.

Key points:

- 0.0   Trailhead.
- 1.1   Soldier Pass Trail; stay left.
- 2.4   Brins Mesa.
- 2.9   Viewpoint.

The hike: A small metal sign at the east side of the parking area marks the start of the Brins Mesa Trail. About 1.1 miles from the trailhead, the unsigned Soldier Pass Trail turns right (south). Stay left, on the Brins Mesa Trail. For

183

Brins Mesa • Devils Bridge

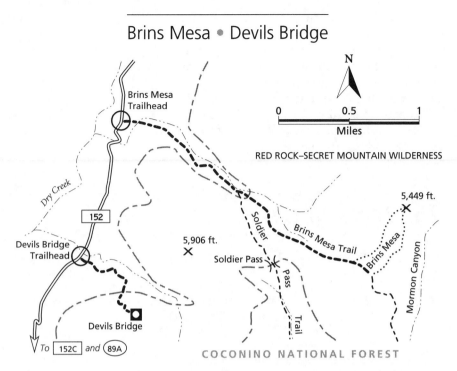

nearly 2 miles, the trail follows a normally dry wash, crossing the bed as necessary. The forest is mixed pinyon pine, juniper, and Arizona cypress, and views are limited until the trail climbs onto Brins Mesa. After crossing the flat mesa, the trail drops abruptly off the southeast side. Leave the trail here and go left, walking cross-country (there is actually a faint trail) along the southeast edge of the mesa. Brins Mesa tilts up to the northeast, and the view gets better as you continue. At the northeast end of the mesa, about 0.5 mile

Coffee Pot Rock from the Brins Mesa Trail.

A hiker enjoys the view from Brins Mesa, with Sedona and Munds Mountain in the background.

from the trail, work your way onto a red outcrop. This is the end of the hike, a point that offers close-up views of Wilson Mountain and the sandstone spires at the head of Mormon Canyon. You're standing on the Schnebly Hill formation, which is responsible for most of the red sandstone cliffs and rock formations in the Sedona area. It was deposited in a coastal tidal-flat environment, and repeated exposure to the air oxidized traces of iron in the rock to create the red color. The buff-colored cliffs above, forming the impressive west face of Wilson Mountain, are Coconino sandstone, which was deposited in a dry, sand dune desert. Gray layers of volcanic basalt rocks laid down in lava flows cap the rim of Wilson Mountain. The hard basalt protects the softer rocks below, so that erosion by water has shaped Wilson Mountain into a flat topped mesa. In contrast, look southwest at Capitol Butte. It lacks a basalt cap and the soft Coconino sandstone has eroded into a dome shape.

Return to the trail by walking directly down the center of the mesa, through the open meadow. You'll intercept the Brins Mesa Trail before you reach the end of the meadow; turn right (northwest) to return to the trailhead.

The Brins Mesa Trail continues from the point where we left it and drops into Mormon Canyon. See Hike 79 for details.

76 Devils Bridge

See Map on Page 184

Description: A short hike to a striking natural arch in the Red Rock–Secret Mountain Wilderness.

Location: 3.2 miles northeast of Sedona.

Type of trail: Out and back.

Type of hike: Day hike.

Difficulty: Easy.

Total distance: 1.4 miles.

Elevation change: 300 feet.

Time required: 1 hour.

Water: None.

Best season: All year.

Maps: Wilson Mountain USGS quad; Coconino National Forest.

Permits and restrictions: A Red Rock Pass is required for vehicle parking.

For more information: Sedona Ranger District, Coconino National Forest.

Finding the trailhead: From Sedona, drive to the west end of town on Arizona Highway 89A and turn right at a traffic light onto the Dry Creek Road. After 2.0 miles, turn right on dirt Forest Road 152 (also called Dry Creek Road). Although this road is maintained, it receives heavy traffic, and its condition varies. Drive 1.2 miles and turn right into the Devils Bridge Trailhead. Parking is limited, but there are other parking spots nearby.

Devils Bridge.

Key points:

    0.0   Trailhead.

    0.4   Trail turns uphill.

    0.7   Devils Bridge.

The hike: On the first section of the walk, you'll parallel a wash. The trail is well-used and easy to follow.

Then the trail turns right and starts to climb the slope toward the imposing mass of Capitol Butte. It soon reaches a red sandstone ledge and works its way to the top via a series of stone steps. Follow the trail a few hundred feet east to the top of the bridge.

Devils Bridge is actually a natural arch, since it doesn't span a stream course. The arch was formed by weathering of both sides of the narrow fin of sandstone. First, water erosion exploited a joint, or crack, in the rock that was parallel to the rim, separating the fin from the main ledge. Then, weathering of the natural cement holding the sand grains together caused the base of the fin to grow thinner. Finally, the fin was eroded completely though, and the arch was formed.

Several natural features in the Sedona area bear names starting with "devil." The common explanation is that the early settlers found travel through the area very difficult before good trails and roads were built.

187

Sedona

The early ranchers and cowboys referred to the Sedona area as Hells Hole because of its color and the difficulty of travel by horse before trails and roads were constructed. Settlers were attracted to Oak Creek because of its permanent water. Originally called Oak Creek Crossing, the tiny settlement changed its name to Sedona after the Post Office balked at the length of the name. Sedona Schnebly, the town's namesake, was the wife of an early rancher. Modern Sedona, easily reached over good highways, is a Mecca for tourism and retirement communities. The town is surrounded by the spectacular Red Rock–Secret Mountain and Munds Mountain Wildernesses of the Coconino National Forest, and there are many excellent hiking trails.

77 Eagles Nest Trail

Description:	A day hike along Oak Creek in Red Rock State Park.
Location:	3 miles southwest of Sedona.
Type of trail:	Loop.
Type of trip:	Day hike.
Difficulty:	Easy.
Total distance:	2.0 miles.
Elevation change:	120 feet.
Time required:	1 hour.
Water:	Visitor center.
Best season:	All year.
Maps:	Sedona USGS quad; Red Rock State Park brochure.
Permits and restrictions:	None.
For more information:	Red Rock State Park.

Finding the trailhead: From Sedona, go west on Arizona Highway 89A to the lower Red Rock Loop Road, which is signed for Red Rock State Park. Turn left (south) and continue 2.9 miles and turn right on the Red Rock State Park Road. Continue past the entrance station to the end of the road at the visitor center.

Key points:

0.0 Visitor Center Trailhead.
0.1 Sentinel Crossing.
0.2 Eagles Nest Trail.
1.8 Kisva Trail.
2.0 Visitor Center Trailhead.

The hike: Red Rock State Park is one of the newest additions to the state park system. In 1986, the state purchased the Smoke Trail Ranch. The ranch was the vacation retreat of Jack Fry, the president of Trans World Airlines.

Eagles Nest Trail • Apache Fire Trail

Purposes of the park include the preservation of the riparian habitat of Oak Creek and environmental education. A number of short hiking trails have been built along Oak Creek and on the red sandstone bluffs overlooking the creek.

From the visitor center, follow the main trail downhill toward Oak Creek. Turn right at a junction, and cross Oak Creek on a low bridge at Sentinel Crossing. Notice the flood debris piled up from the huge flood that roared down the creek in the winter of 1993. On the far side of the creek, turn right (west) on the signed Kisva Trail. Continue a short distance and turn left (south) on the signed Eagles Nest Trail. This trail crosses an irrigation ditch then climbs away from the creek via several short switchbacks. At the signed junction with the Coyote Ridge Trail, turn right (south). The Eagles Nest Trail eventually turns northwest and works its way onto a ridge with a fine view of Oak Creek in the foreground and Cathedral Rock in the distance. Continue north as the trail descends to Oak Creek, crosses the ditch, and turns southeast to follow the creek. At the junction with the Kisva Trail, you've completed the loop. Retrace your steps to return to the visitor center.

78 Apache Fire Trail

See Map on Page 189

Description:	An easy, scenic hike near Oak Creek in Red Rock State Park.
Location:	3 miles southwest of Sedona.
Type of trail:	Loop.
Type of trip:	Day hike.
Difficulty:	Easy.
Total distance:	1.8 miles.
Elevation change:	120 feet.
Time required:	1 hour.
Water:	Visitor center.
Best season:	All year.
Maps:	Sedona USGS quad; Red Rock State Park brochure.
Permits and restrictions:	None.
For more information:	Red Rock State Park.

Finding the trailhead: From Sedona, go west on Arizona Highway 89A to the lower Red Rock Loop Road, which is signed for Red Rock State Park. Turn left (south), continue 2.9 miles, and then turn right on the Red Rock State Park road. Continue past the entrance station to the end of the road at the visitor center.

Key points:

0.0   Trailhead at visitor center.
0.3   Kingfisher Crossing; turn left on the Apache Fire Trail.
0.5   Trail to the House of Apache Fire.
0.9   Javelina Trail.
1.3   Turn right on the Eagles Nest Trail.
1.5   Turn right on the Kisva Trail.
1.6   Turn left at Sentinel Crossing.
1.8   Trailhead at visitor center.

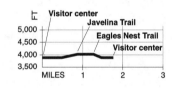

The hike: From the visitor center, follow the main trail downhill toward Oak Creek, and cross Oak Creek on the bridge at Kingfisher Crossing. On the far side of the creek, turn left (east) on the signed Apache Fire Trail. A side trail goes to the House of Apache Fire, which was built by Jack and Helen Fry in 1946. They named their vacation retreat house for the smoke from the campfires of the Yavapai Apache they employed in the construction. Back on the Apache Fire Trail, continue a short distance past the junction with the Javelina Trail. The trail works its way along the foot of the steeper bluffs above and then encounters another signed junction. Turn left (west) on the Coyote Ridge Trail, which continues to contour west. There are good views of Oak Creek and its lush habitat of Fremont cottonwood trees and other riparian vegetation. At the Eagles Nest Trail junction, turn right (north), and follow the trail down toward Oak Creek. After crossing an irrigation ditch, turn right (east) on the Kisva Trail. Next, turn left (north) and cross Oak Creek on the low bridge at Sentinel Crossing. Here there is an excellent view of the House of Apache Fire reflected in the creek. On the north side of Oak Creek, turn left on the main trail to the visitor center.

79 Mormon Canyon

Description:	A trail and cross-country hike to the towering sandstone cliffs and spires on the west side of Wilson Mountain, in the Red Rock–Secret Mountain Wilderness.
Location:	Northeast Sedona.
Type of trail:	Out-and-back trail and cross-country.
Type of trip:	Day hike.
Difficulty:	Moderate.
Total distance:	4.2 miles.
Elevation change:	640 feet.
Time required:	3 hours.
Water:	None.
Best season:	All year.
Maps:	Wilson Mountain USGS quad; Coconino National Forest.
Permits and restrictions:	A Red Rock Pass is required for vehicle parking.
For more information:	Sedona Ranger District, Coconino National Forest.

Looking across Lee and Wilson Mountains in an aerial view.

Mormon Canyon • Jim Thompson Trail

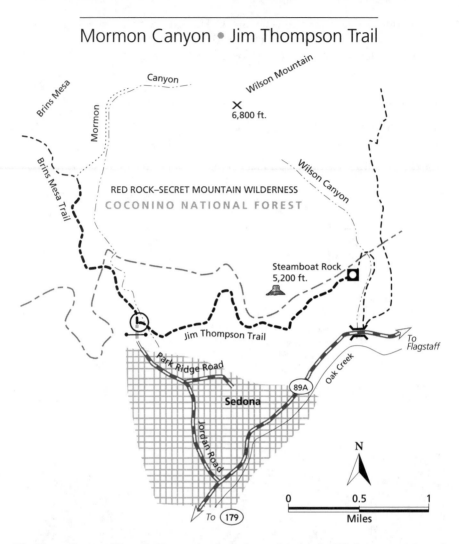

Finding the trailhead: From the junction of Arizona Highways 89A and 179 in Sedona, drive north on AZ 89A about 0.4 mile and turn left onto Jordan Road. After 0.8 mile, turn left on Park Ridge Road and continue to the trailhead at a locked gate (the last 0.2 mile is dirt).

Key points:

- 0.0   Trailhead.
- 1.4   Leave the trail and hike northeast.
- 2.1   Head of Mormon Canyon.

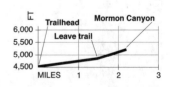

The hike: Go past the gate and continue past the old shooting range on the Brins Mesa Trail.
This trail works its way through the Arizona cypress forest along the west side of Mormon Canyon. Arizona cypress is easily identified by its curling red bark and juniper-like scaly needles. It is a survivor of past climate

change and now grows only in isolated pockets below the western Mogollon Rim and in the central mountains of Arizona. As the trail starts to climb toward Brins Mesa, visible on the skyline to the north, watch for a cairned route that turns off to the right (northeast). Leave the trail and follow the cairns across the red sandstone ledges of the Schnebly Hill formation. The route descends into the bed of Mormon Canyon and follows it upstream. Without much difficulty you can get very close to the beautiful cliffs of Wilson Mountain. The head of Mormon Canyon offers a surprisingly remote feeling, considering its proximity to Sedona.

80 Jim Thompson Trail

See Map on Page 192

Description: A short hike south of Wilson Mountain with spectacular views of Steamboat Rock, lower Oak Creek Canyon, and Mitten Ridge.
Location: Northeast Sedona.
Type of trail: Out and back.
Type of trip: Day hike.
Difficulty: Easy.
Total distance: 4.0 miles.
Elevation change: 200 feet.
Time required: 2.5 hours.
Water: None.
Best season: All year.
Maps: Wilson Mountain, Munds Park USGS quads; Coconino National Forest.
Permits and restrictions: A Red Rock Pass is required for vehicle parking.
For more information: Sedona Ranger District, Coconino National Forest.

Finding the trailhead: From the junction of Arizona Highways 89A and 179 in Sedona, drive north on AZ 89A about 0.4 mile and turn left onto Jordan Road. After 0.8 mile, turn left on Park Ridge Road, and continue to the trailhead at a locked gate (the last 0.2 mile is dirt).

Key points:
0.0   Trailhead.
0.7   Base of Steamboat Rock.
2.0   Wilson Canyon overlook.

The hike: Go through the gate and turn right on the Jim Thompson Trail, which crosses the bed of Mormon Canyon and then swings northeast. You'll be heading directly for Steamboat Rock, the southernmost ridge of Wilson Mountain. When the trail reaches the base of the red sandstone cliffs, it turns east and contours along ledges. After passing the eastern end of Steamboat Rock, the trail reaches a viewpoint overlooking Wilson Canyon and lower Oak Creek. This is a great ending for an easy hike, though the trail does continue to the bottom of Wilson Canyon. You can hike to the Wilson Mountain Trailhead at Midgely Bridge on AZ 89A in Oak Creek Canyon and also connect to the Wilson Mountain Trail. See Hikes 94 and 98 for details.

81 Huckaby Trail

Description:	A fine day hike on a trail on the Coconino National Forest that follows Oak Creek for part of the way.
Location:	2.3 miles east of Sedona.
Type of trail:	Out and back (can be done one way with a car shuttle).
Type of trip:	Day hike.
Difficulty:	Easy.
Total distance:	5.0 miles.
Elevation change:	260 feet.
Time required:	3 hours.
Water:	Oak Creek.
Best season:	All year.
Maps:	Munds Park, Munds Mountain, Sedona USGS quads; Coconino National Forest.
Permits and restrictions:	A Red Rock Pass is required for vehicle parking.
For more information:	Sedona Ranger District, Coconino National Forest.

Finding the trailhead: From the junction of Arizona Highways 89A and 179 in Sedona, go south 0.4 mile on AZ 179, across Oak Creek Bridge and then turn left on Schnebly Hill Road. Drive 1.9 miles and turn left into Margs Draw/Huckaby Trailhead. To reach the north trailhead from the junction of AZ 89A and 179 in Sedona, drive 1.6 miles north on AZ 89A, cross Midgely Bridge, and park on the left at the Wilson Canyon Trailhead and viewpoint.

Key points:
- 0.0   Trailhead.
- 0.3   Bear Wallow Canyon.
- 1.5   Oak Creek.
- 2.1   Cross Oak Creek.
- 2.5   Wilson Mountain Trailhead.

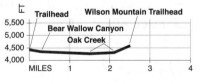

The hike: At first, the Huckaby Trail goes west. After the Margs Draw Trail junction, the trail turns right and follows an old road down into Bear Wallow Canyon. This is the canyon north of the trailhead. Follow the old road across normally dry Bear Wallow Canyon and out the north side. Here the newly constructed foot trail leaves the old road and contours northeast above the canyon. Soon a switchback takes you to the north as the trail begins to work its way toward Oak Creek. This is a delightful traverse through pinyon-juniper forest, though it would be hot on a summer afternoon. Soon you'll start to descend, and the trail finally switchbacks down to Oak Creek.

194

Wilson Mountain towers above lower Oak Creek Canyon.

Huckaby Trail • Munds Mountain

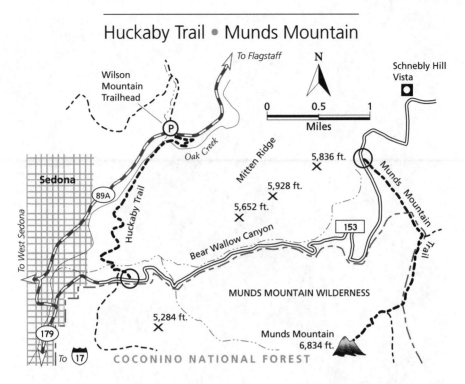

For over half a mile, the trail stays on the east side of the creek and then crosses to the west side below Midgely Bridge, the impressive structure spanning Mormon Canyon on AZ 89A. Now it follows an old wagon road that climbs steeply out of the canyon and switchbacks up to the north end of the bridge. Follow the trail past the viewpoint, under the bridge, and up to the Wilson Mountain Trailhead.

One option is to do this hike one way with a shuttle. Another is to hike further on either the Wilson Mountain or Wilson Canyon Trails. See Hikes 97 and 98 for details.

82 Munds Mountain

See Map on Page 196

Description: This hike in the Munds Mountain Wilderness takes you up a historic road, and offers excellent views of Mitten Ridge, Bear Wallow Canyon, Munds Mountain, and Sedona.

Location: 4.7 miles east of Sedona.

Type of trail: Out and back.

Type of trip: Day hike.

Difficulty: Moderate.

Total distance: 4.2 miles.

Elevation change: 1,200 feet.

Time required: 3 hours.

Water: None.

Best season: Spring, summer, and fall.

Maps: Munds Park, Munds Mountain USGS quads; Coconino National Forest.

Permits and restrictions: A Red Rock Pass is required for vehicle parking.

For more information: Sedona Ranger District, Coconino National Forest.

Finding the trailhead: From the junction of Arizona Highways 89A and 179 in Sedona, go south 0.4 mile on AZ 179, across Oak Creek Bridge and turn left on Schnebly Hill Road. Drive 4.3 miles, and park at the unsigned trailhead where the road passes through a saddle between the red buttes to the west and the brushy slope on the right.

Key points:

0.0   Trailhead.

0.9   Continue south on the foot trail.

1.8   Saddle.

2.1   Munds Mountain.

The hike: From the parking area, look across the road and up. You will see an old road descending the slopes from the left (southeast). It nearly comes down to the present road then does a switchback to the right and parallels the road just above it. Walk south down the main road about 100 yards until you can climb up to reach the old road. Follow the old road back to the left (north), around the switchback, and then southward. This is the old Schnebly Hill Road, which was originally built as a wagon road from Sedona to the Mogollon Rim and on to Flagstaff. It is now closed to motorized vehicles and makes a fine hiking trail with a panoramic view. Because of the west-facing slope, the dominant vegetation is chaparral brush. Near the top, there is a dense stand of Gambel oak, a small slender deciduous tree about 15 to 20 feet high. Gambel oak favor the slopes just below escarpments or rims. The trail reaches the Mogollon Rim after 0.9 mile, and the old road turns sharply north.

197

The view down Bear Wallow Canyon from the Munds Mountain Trail.

Take the foot trail, which continues south along the rim through tall ponderosa pine, climbing gradually. About 0.7 mile from the old road, the trail reaches a high point along the rim and crosses a grassy section with scattered juniper trees where the view opens out to the southeast. The long ridge of Munds Mountain dominates the view ahead to the southwest. The trail drops down a short ridge to a saddle where there is a signed junction with the Hot Loop Trail to the left. Continue straight ahead about 50 yards to another saddle where there is a signed junction with the Jacks Canyon Trail.

Stay right and follow the Munds Mountain Trail as it climbs steeply up the northeast slopes. Several switchbacks lead to a ridge where the grade moderates. This section is interesting for the extreme contrast in vegetation on the two sides of the ridge. Douglas-fir growing on the north slopes meet pinyon, juniper, and Arizona cypress growing on the south slopes. The trail reaches the rim of Munds Mountain about 0.4 mile from the junction at the saddle. According to the map, the actual high point is about 100 yards south along the east edge of the clearing. But it's more rewarding to walk about 200 yards west to the rim for a sweeping view of Sedona and the red-rock country. You can also walk about 100 yards to the north rim for a superb view of lower Oak Creek Canyon and nearly the entire trail you just came up.

83 Little Horse Trail

Description:	An easily reached hike that goes past the dramatic Chapel Rocks to a scenic overlook.
Location:	Southeast Sedona.
Type of trail:	Out and back.
Type of trip:	Day hike.
Difficulty:	Easy.
Total distance:	3.6 miles.
Elevation change:	280 feet.
Time required:	2 hours.
Water:	None.
Best season:	All year.
Maps:	Sedona USGS quad.
Permits and restrictions:	A Red Rock Pass is required for vehicle parking.
For more information:	Sedona Ranger District, Coconino National Forest.

Finding the trailhead: From the junction of Arizona Highways 89A and 179 in Sedona, go 3.5 miles south on AZ 179 and park at the North Bell Rock Pathway Trailhead, on the left.

Key points:
   0.0   North Bell Rock Pathway Trailhead.
   0.3   Turn left onto the Little Horse Trail.
   1.8   Chicken Point.

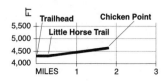

Little Horse Trail

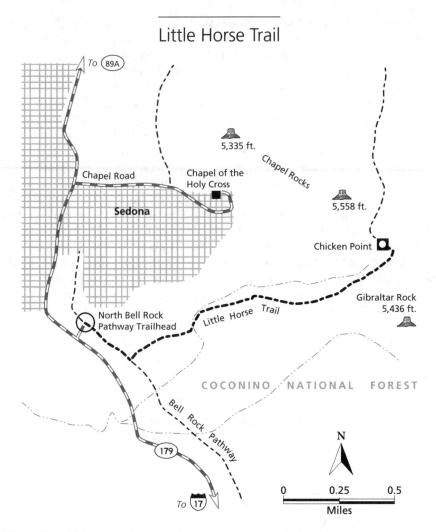

The hike: This short but scenic hike uses part of the urban trail system in Sedona. From the trailhead, turn right on the Bell Rock Pathway. After 0.3 mile, turn left on the Little Horse Trail. This trail is marked with rock cairns in wire cages. Ignore any side trails and follow the cairns to Chicken Point, which is actually the pass between the Chapel Rocks and Gibraltar Rock.

84 Courthouse Butte

Description:	A day hike in and near the Munds Mountain Wilderness, offering close-up views of Bell Rock and Courthouse Butte.
Location:	6 miles south of Sedona.
Type of trail:	Loop.
Type of trip:	Day hike.
Difficulty:	Easy.
Total distance:	4.3 miles.
Elevation change:	200 feet.
Time required:	2.5 hours.
Water:	None.
Best season:	All year.
Maps:	Sedona, Munds Mountain USGS quads; Coconino National Forest.
Permits and restrictions:	A Red Rock Pass is required for vehicle parking.
For more information:	Sedona Ranger District, Coconino National Forest.

Finding the trailhead: From the junction of Arizona Highways 89A and 179 in Sedona, go 6.0 miles south on AZ 179, and turn left into the South Bell Rock Pathway Trailhead.

Key points:
- 0.0 South Bell Rock Pathway Trailhead.
- 1.0 Turn right on an old jeep road.
- 2.1 Pass northeast of Courthouse Butte.
- 2.7 Cross a wash and turn right.
- 3.8 Turn left on the Bell Rock Pathway.
- 4.3 South Bell Rock Pathway Trailhead.

The hike: Don't let the crowds of windshield tourists at the trailhead put you off. You'll soon leave them and the roar of the highway behind. Follow the broad Bell Rock Pathway north toward Bell Rock. The trail squeezes between Bell Rock and the highway. Turn right on an old, closed jeep trail that heads around the north side of Bell Rock. After

Courthouse Butte.

201

Courthouse Butte

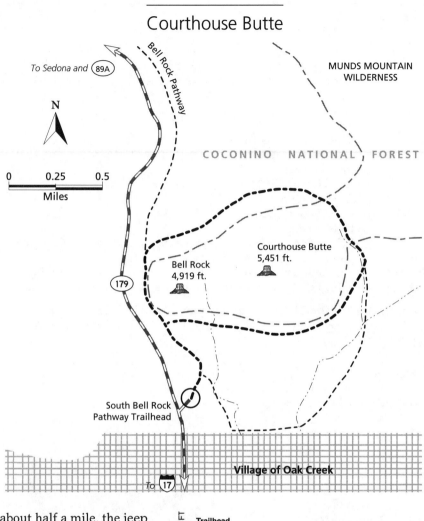

To Sedona and (89A)

Bell Rock Pathway

N

MUNDS MOUNTAIN
WILDERNESS

COCONINO   NATIONAL   FOREST

0   0.25   0.5
Miles

Courthouse Butte
5,451 ft.

Bell Rock
4,919 ft.

179

South Bell Rock
Pathway Trailhead

Village of Oak Creek

To (17)

about half a mile, the jeep trail veers left (northeast), descends into a drainage, and crosses it. At this point, turn right (east) and stay in the drainage, following a

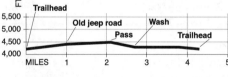

Trailhead
5,500
Old jeep road   Wash
5,000
Pass
4,500   Trailhead
4,000
MILES   1   2   3   4   5

foot trail that climbs gradually toward the pass east of Courthouse Rock, the massive butte east of Bell Rock. From the pass follow the trail as it descends the drainage to the southeast. About half a mile from the pass, the trail meets an unsigned trail that crosses the dry streambed. Turn right (west) on this trail and continue around Courthouse Butte. The trail comes out onto a flat where the view is more open and stays just at the base of Courthouse Butte. Numerous trails branch left; go right at each junction. Back near the highway, you'll pass the cottonwood trees marking Bell Rock Spring (not reliable) and then meet the Bell Rock Pathway. Turn left to return to the trailhead.

Bell Rock.

85 House Mountain

Description:	A hike near lower Oak Creek with unusual views of the red-rock country.
Location:	About 12 miles south of Sedona.
Type of trail:	Trail and cross-country, out and back.
Type of trip:	Day hike.
Difficulty:	Moderate.
Total distance:	6.0 miles.
Elevation change:	1,100 feet.
Time required:	3.5 hours.
Water:	None.
Best season:	All year.
Maps:	Sedona USGS quad, Coconino National Forest.
Permits and restrictions:	A Red Rock Pass is required for vehicle parking.
For more information:	Sedona Ranger District, Coconino National Forest.

Finding the trailhead: From the junction of Arizona Highways 89A and 179 in Sedona, go south 6.8 miles on AZ 179 and turn right at the traffic signal onto the Verde Valley School Road. Continue 4.2 miles (the road turns to maintained gravel after 3.0 miles) and turn left onto Forest Road 9126B, the unmaintained road to the Turkey Creek Trail. Go 0.6 mile and park at the unsigned trailhead on the left, marked by a turnaround circle and small parking area.

Key points:

0.0	Trailhead.
0.4	Stay right at an unsigned junction.
1.4	Turkey Creek Tank.
2.6	House Mountain.
3.0	Summit.

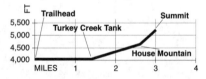

The hike: Follow the unsigned Turkey Creek Trail, which begins as an old jeep road, north through pleasant pinyon-juniper forest. Stay right where a well-used but unmarked trail branches left. The Turkey Creek Trail crosses a wash and turns more to the southwest. It roughly parallels the north rim of House Mountain, visible to the southeast. The trail climbs over a low pass between red-rock formations and descends a long, gentle meadow to reach Turkey Creek Tank. The trail skirts the right (north) side of the tank, where a metal sign marks the Turkey Creek Trail, and continues southwest around the north end of a red-rock ridge. It turns south and follows a drainage through dense pinyon-juniper forest and then climbs steeply to reach a saddle on the north rim of House Mountain. The trail continues 0.3 mile north at a stock tank, but our hike leaves the trail at the saddle.

Hike cross-country directly east up the ridge 0.3 mile to the top of the rocky peak on the skyline. This turns out to be a false summit, and another 0.1 mile of easy walking leads to the end of the hike at the top of a gentle hill. This unnamed rise is the second highest point on House Mountain, at

Agave, House Mountain.

House Mountain

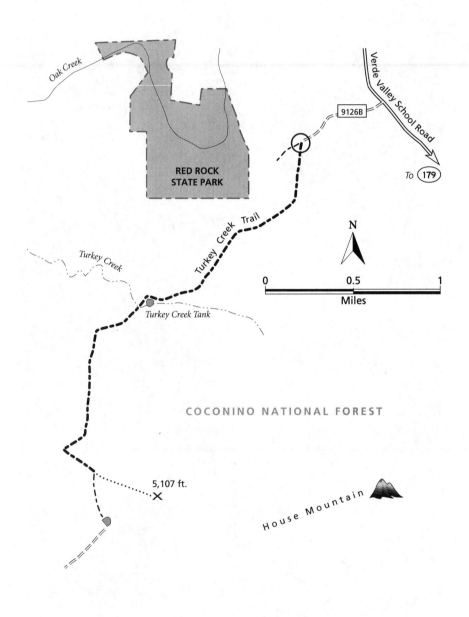

5,107 feet. (The highest point is about 1.5 miles southwest.) It offers panoramic views of House Mountain, which is a large mesa that slopes gradually to the south, the Sedona area, and the red-rock country to the north. In the middle distance, lower Oak Creek winds past Red Rock State Park.

86 Jacks Canyon

Description:	A little-used trail into a remote portion of the Munds Mountain Wilderness. If you want an all-day hike away from the crowds, you'll like this trail.
Location:	9 miles south of Sedona.
Type of trail:	Out and back.
Type of trip:	Day hike.
Difficulty:	Difficult.
Total distance:	13.6 miles.
Elevation change:	2,540 feet.
Time required:	8 hours.
Water:	None.
Best season:	All year.
Maps:	Munds Mountain USGS quad; Coconino National Forest.
Permits and restrictions:	A Red Rock Pass is required for vehicle parking.
For more information:	Sedona Ranger District, Coconino National Forest.

Finding the trailhead: From Sedona, drive about 7 miles south on Arizona Highway 179 to the Village of Oak Creek and turn left at the traffic light onto Jacks Canyon Road. Go 0.9 mile and turn right to remain on Jacks Canyon Road. After another 1.1 miles, turn right into the trailhead.

Key points:

0.0   Trailhead.
2.4   Jacks Canyon Tank.
6.0   Head of Jacks Canyon.
6.4   Saddle.
6.8   Munds Mountain.

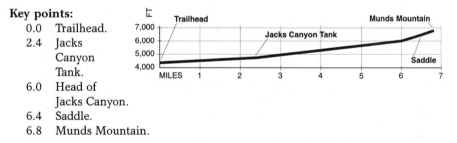

The hike: The first mile or so of trail parallels the Jacks Canyon Road as it heads northeast to skirt a subdivision. As the canyon starts to swing north, you'll pass an old stock tank, Jacks Canyon Tank, about 2.4 miles from the trailhead. Unlike many of the canyons in the Sedona area, Jacks Canyon is

Jacks Canyon

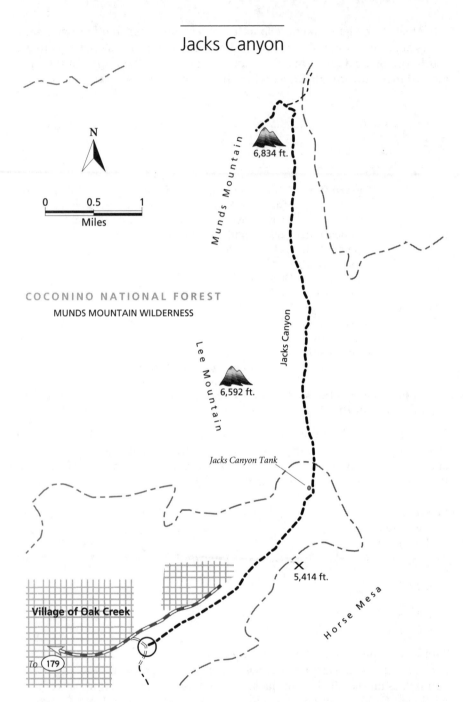

N

0   0.5   1
Miles

COCONINO NATIONAL FOREST
MUNDS MOUNTAIN WILDERNESS

Munds Mountain
6,834 ft.

Lee Mountain
6,592 ft.

Jacks Canyon

Jacks Canyon Tank

5,414 ft.

Horse Mesa

Village of Oak Creek

To 179

open and spacious. It also gets less use than the shorter trails. As you continue north, the canyon gradually narrows. At its head, a short, steep climb leads to the saddle between the Mogollon Rim and Munds Mountain. Turn left on the Munds Mountain Trail and climb another 0.4 mile to the summit. The best views are from the west rim of this broad mesa.

Oak Creek Canyon

Sliced out of the Mogollon Rim, Oak Creek Canyon is very accessible from Arizona Highway 89, which traverses its 20-mile length from Sedona to Flagstaff. The year-round flow of Oak Creek adds to its charm. Numerous Forest Service campgrounds, picnic areas, and private resorts can be found along the highway. In the pioneer days, travel along the canyon was much more difficult. The easiest route to Flagstaff, the nearest source of supplies, was via the canyon rims, so the early settlers built several horse trails up the steep walls of the canyon. Once on the rim, the horse would be hitched to a wagon (left there from the last trip), and the all-day journey would resume. Many of these trails survive today, and provide the hiker with a variety of routes. Other hikes in Oak Creek Canyon explore the side canyons.

87 Pumphouse Wash

Description: A cross-country hike through a narrow sandstone canyon near Oak Creek Canyon.
Location: 15 miles south of Flagstaff.
Type of trail: Cross-country out and back.
Type of trip: Day hike.
Difficulty: Moderate.
Total distance: 6.2 miles.
Elevation change: 60 feet.
Time required: 4 hours.
Water: Seasonal in Pumphouse Wash.
Best season: Spring through fall.
Maps: Mountainaire USGS quad; Coconino National Forest.
Permits and restrictions: A Red Rock Pass is required for vehicle parking.
For more information: Sedona Ranger District, Coconino National Forest.

Finding the trailhead: From Flagstaff, drive south about 15 miles on Arizona Highway 89A. The highway descends into the canyon via a series of switchbacks and then crosses the bridge over Pumphouse Wash. Park just south of the bridge at the pullout on the right.

Key points:
0.0   Pumphouse Wash Bridge.
1.7   First sharp left bend.
3.1   End of the hike at the side canyon near the highway.

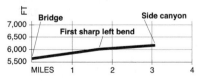

The hike: From the highway pullout, drop down the bank into Oak Creek, turn right, and hike upstream cross-country. In just a few yards, Pumphouse Wash joins from the right. Most of the flow in Oak Creek comes

Pumphouse Wash • Cookstove Trail
Harding Spring Trail • Thomas Point Trail
West Fork Trail • AB Young Trail

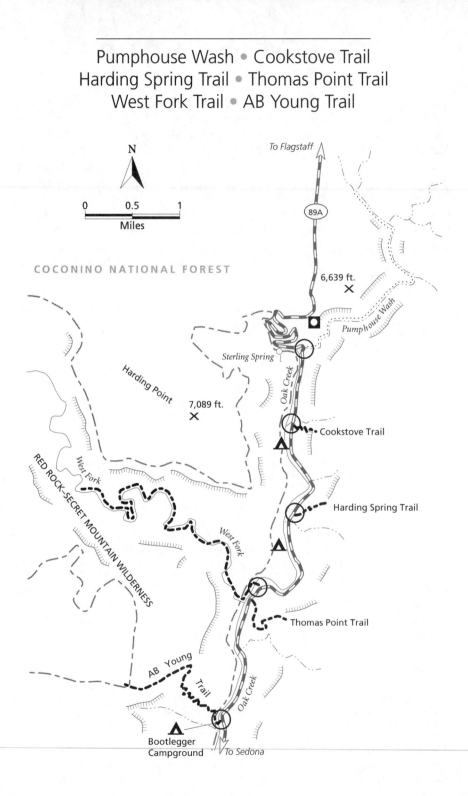

N

0   0.5   1
Miles

To Flagstaff

89A

COCONINO NATIONAL FOREST

6,639 ft.
X

Sterling Spring

Pumphouse Wash

Harding Point

7,089 ft.
X

Oak Creek

Cookstove Trail

RED ROCK–SECRET MOUNTAIN WILDERNESS

West Fork

West Fork

Harding Spring Trail

Thomas Point Trail

AB Young
Trail

Oak Creek

Bootlegger
Campground

To Sedona

from Sterling Spring, which is about 0.3 mile up Oak Creek. During summer and fall, Pumphouse Wash usually has little or no flow, but in spring during snow melt, or after a summer thunderstorm, there may be so much water that this hike is impossible. Follow the wash upstream, under the highway bridge. Soon the canyon meanders around a couple of bends, and the sounds of the highway are left behind. The lower canyon walls here are composed of the buff-colored Coconino sandstone. The rock was deposited as wind-blown sand dunes in a vast, Sahara-like desert. If you look closely at the rock, you can see the crossbedded, sloping surfaces of the petrified sand dunes.

After a gentle curve to the right, followed by a straight section of about 0.5 mile, the canyon swings sharply left and heads northwest. Here the canyon is about 500 feet deep. In the fall, the dark greens of the firs and pine growing in the canyon are supplemented by the bright yellows, oranges, and reds of the deciduous trees. Potholes carved in the sandstone bed of the canyon sometimes hold water. Now the canyon turns gradually north then sharply left again and becomes noticeably shallower. James Canyon enters from the right. Another 0.7 mile of straight canyon heading northwest ends with another sharp turn, this time to the right. This is the end of our hike.

Optionally, from this point you can go northwest 0.6 mile up a side canyon and reach AZ 89A near the Forest Road 237 turnoff. Another option is to continue 4.5 miles up Pumphouse Wash to Kachina Village. Although upper Pumphouse Wash is not as spectacular as the lower section you've just hiked, it is a long, scenic canyon that has its headwaters just south of Flagstaff. In fact, Pumphouse Wash is the true head of Oak Creek Canyon.

88 Cookstove Trail

See Map on Page 210

Description: This short trail offers unique views of upper Oak Creek Canyon.
Location: 13 miles north of Sedona.
Type of trail: Out and back.
Type of trip: Day hike.
Difficulty: Moderate.
Total distance: 1.0 mile.
Elevation change: 940 feet.
Time required: 1 hour.
Water: None.
Best season: Spring through fall.
Maps: Mountainaire USGS quad; Coconino National Forest.
Permits and restrictions: A Red Rock Pass is required for vehicle parking.
For more information: Sedona Ranger District, Coconino National Forest.

Finding the trailhead: From Sedona, drive about 13 miles north on Arizona Highway 89A to the north end of Pine Flat Campground, and park along the highway.

Key points:

   0.0   Pine Flat Campground.
   0.5   East rim of Oak Creek Canyon.

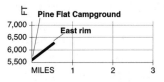

The hike: The trail, which is not shown on the topographic map, starts just north of the campground on the east side of the highway. It climbs directly up the ridge just south of Cookstove Draw. Although the trail is steep, it has been maintained in recent years and is in good shape. There are good views of upper Oak Creek Canyon, which is heavily forested with ponderosa pine, Gambel oak, and Douglas-fir. Alligator junipers are also common and are easily identified by their bark, which is broken into deep squares like an alligator's hide. Some alligator junipers reach massive sizes. The trail, originally built for fire fighting access, reaches the rim just south of Cookstove Draw.

An option is to hike the rim to the south about a mile and descend back into Oak Creek Canyon via the Harding Spring Trail. See Hike 89 for more information. It would be a good idea to have already hiked the Harding Spring Trail so that you will know where to look for the trail on the rim.

89 Harding Spring Trail

See Map on Page 210

Description:	A cool, shady hike through ponderosa pine and Douglas-fir forest to the east rim of Oak Creek canyon.
Location:	12 miles north of Sedona.
Type of trail:	Out and back.
Type of trip:	Day hike.
Difficulty:	Moderate.
Total distance:	1.4 miles.
Elevation change:	750 feet.
Time required:	1.5 hours.
Water:	None.
Best season:	Spring through fall.
Maps:	Mountainaire USGS quad; Coconino National Forest.
Permits and restrictions:	A Red Rock Pass is required for vehicle parking.
For more information:	Sedona Ranger District, Coconino National Forest.

Finding the trailhead: From Sedona, drive about 12 miles north on Arizona Highway 89A to the Cave Springs Campground turnoff. (The campground sign may be missing when the campground is closed for the winter.) The turnoff is on the left (west); park in the pullout just to the north.

Looking down Oak Creek Canyon from the Harding Spring Trail.

Key points:
  0.0   Trailhead.
  0.7   East rim of Oak Creek Canyon.

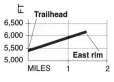

The hike: Although the trail is not shown on the topographic map, the trailhead is signed and is located across the highway to the east. The trail immediately starts to climb. (Ignore the trail that doesn't.) Originally built by the early settlers as a route to move their cattle to and from the plateau above, the Harding Springs Trail is still in good shape. The dense, cool forest offers welcome shade, so this is a good hike for a hot day.

Options are to hike the rim north and descend via the Cookstove Trail, or hike south and descend via the Thomas Point Trail. You should have the topographic map and have hiked your planned descent trail at least once so that you will be able to find its upper end. See Hikes 88 and 90 for more information.

90 Thomas Point Trail

See Map on Page 210

Description: This hike is a great alternative to the crowded West Fork Trail, and it's located right across the highway. There are excellent views of the West Fork of Oak Creek, and of Oak Creek Canyon itself.

Location: 11 miles north of Sedona.

Type of trail: Out and back.

Type of trip: Day hike.

Difficulty: Moderate.

Total distance: 2.0 miles.

Elevation change: 970 feet.

Time required: 1.5 hours.

Water: None.

Best season: Spring through fall.

Maps: Munds Park USGS quad; Coconino National Forest.

Permits and restrictions: A Red Rock Pass is required for vehicle parking.

For more information: Sedona Ranger District, Coconino National Forest.

Finding the trailhead: From Sedona, drive about 11 miles north on Arizona Highway 89A and turn left into the West Fork parking area.

Key points:

0.0 Trailhead.

0.4 The trail emerges onto the south-facing slope.

1.0 East rim of Oak Creek Canyon.

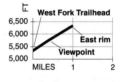

The hike: Like most of the old trails in Oak Creek Canyon, this trail is not shown on the topographic map. From the parking area, follow the trail south through the old orchard for about 100 yards and cross the highway to a trail sign. The trail climbs south through a shady forest of ponderosa pine and Gambel oak and then turns a corner onto a much drier, south-facing slope. Here, because of the increased temperature and evaporation, the chaparral plants dominate: scrub oak, mountain mahogany, and manzanita. There are fine views down the canyon to the flat-topped mesa of Wilson Mountain. A switchback leads to a point overlooking the mouth of the West Fork and then the trail turns east again and climbs into a pine saddle. The trail finishes by following the ridge east 100 yards to the rim, where views are limited because of the thick forest. You'll find a better viewpoint by walking about 100 yards west from the saddle, onto a rock outcrop. Here you're looking up the West Fork of Oak Creek.

91 West Fork Trail

See Map on Page 210

Description: An easy, very popular hike through the spectacular West Fork of Oak Creek, in the Red Rock–Secret Mountain Wilderness.

Location: 11 miles north of Sedona.

Type of trail: Out and back.

Type of trip: Day hike.

Difficulty: Easy.

Total distance: 6.0 miles.

Elevation change: 300 feet.

Time required: 3 hours.

Water: West Fork.

Best season: Spring through fall.

Maps: Dutton Hill, Wilson Mountain, Munds Park USGS quads; Coconino National Forest.

Permits and restrictions: A Red Rock Pass is required for vehicle parking. The lower 6 miles of the West Fork is closed to camping due to heavy use.

For more information: Sedona Ranger District, Coconino National Forest.

Finding the trailhead: From Sedona, drive about 11 miles north on Arizona Highway 89A and turn left into the West Fork Trailhead parking area.

Key points:

0.0 Trailhead.

0.4 Mouth of the West Fork.

3.0 Trail ends.

The hike: The West Fork is an easy but extremely popular hike. It is not the place to go to escape crowds, especially on weekends. For solitude, try the Thomas Point Trail on the opposite side of Oak Creek. Note that the Forest Service prohibits camping in the lower West Fork due to heavy use. Stay on the trail and do not pick flowers or otherwise disturb this fragile environment. Watch for poison ivy, which is common along the trail.

Follow the trail, which is not shown on the topographic map, across Oak Creek. The trail goes south along the creek and then turns right (west) into the West Fork. Soon you'll leave the sounds of the busy highway behind and be able to hear the pleasant murmur of the creek and the whisper of the wind in the trees. Buttresses of Coconino sandstone tower on the left, while the canyon floor is filled with a tall ponderosa pine and Douglas-fir forest. The trail crosses the creek several times, and ends about 3 miles up the canyon. Walking is very easy to this point, which is the end of the hike.

An aerial view looking up the West Fork of Oak Creek. The Thomas Point Trail is visible traversing the chaparral-covered slopes in the foreground.

An option for the experienced canyon hiker is to continue up the West Fork to its head near Forest Road 231. This hike requires wading in the creek and occasional swimming to cross deep pools. There is a serious danger of flash flooding; do not continue unless you have a stable weather forecast and are prepared to handle the deep, often cold pools.

Another possible hike for the adventurous, experienced canyon hiker is to hike cross-country to the south rim of the canyon, hike to East Pocket Knob, and use the AB Young Trail to descend back into Oak Creek Canyon. There is a cross-country route up the nameless canyon that is just west of West Buzzard Point.

92 AB Young Trail

See Map on Page 210

Description: This is a good trail to the west rim of Oak Creek Canyon, in the Red Rock–Secret Mountain Wilderness. It offers the best views of Oak Creek Canyon from any of the rim trails.
Location: 9 miles north of Sedona.
Type of trail: Out and back.
Type of trip: Day hike.
Difficulty: Moderate.
Total distance: 4.4 miles.
Elevation change: 2,000 feet.
Time required: 9 hours.
Water: None.
Best season: Spring through fall.
Maps: Munds Park, Wilson Mountain USGS quads; Coconino National Forest.
Permits and restrictions: A Red Rock Pass is required for vehicle parking.
For more information: Sedona Ranger District, Coconino National Forest.

Finding the trailhead: From Sedona, drive about 9 miles north on Arizona Highway 89A to the Bootlegger Campground. Do not block the campground entrance; park in the highway pullout just to the north.

Key points:
0.0   Trailhead at Bootlegger Campground.
1.4   West Rim of Oak Creek Canyon.
1.8   Trail leaves rim.
2.2   East Pocket Lookout.

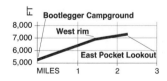

The hike: Walk through the campground and cross Oak Creek. Turn left (south) on the trail that parallels the creek, and watch for the signed junction with the AB Young Trail. It is a good, maintained trail

Oak Creek Canyon from AB Young Trail.

that turns sharply right and starts climbing to the northwest. The broad-leafed trees in the riparian habitat along the creek are soon left behind as the trail climbs through ponderosa pine forest. After a short distance, the trail begins switchbacking directly up the steep slope. The dry southwest exposure supports dense chaparral brush, and the view opens up as you climb. Just below the rim, the trail veers north in a long final switchback. At the rim, the trail enters pine forest again. Turn southwest and follow the cairned trail, which is fainter, along the pine-forested rim to the crest of an east–west ridge. Here the trail turns west and follows the flat-topped ridge to East Pocket Knob and the end of the trail at the USDA Forest Service fire tower. Get permission from the lookout before climbing the tower for a panoramic view of the Mogollon Rim and Oak Creek Canyon.

The AB Young Trail was originally built to move cattle to and from the rim country; it was improved by the Civilian Conservation Corps in the 1930s. The CCC, along with several other conservation agencies, built thousands of miles of trails in the national forests and parks during this period.

93 Sterling Pass Trail

Description: A less-used trail below the impressive cliffs on the north face of Wilson Mountain, in the Red Rock–Secret Mountain Wilderness.
Location: 6 miles north of Sedona.
Type of trail: Out and back.
Type of trip: Day hike.
Difficulty: Moderate.
Total distance: 1.8 miles.
Elevation change: 1,160 feet.
Time required: 1.5 hours.
Water: None.
Best season: Spring through fall.
Maps: Munds Park, Wilson Mountain USGS quads; Coconino National Forest.
Permits and restrictions: A Red Rock Pass is required for vehicle parking.
For more information: Sedona Ranger District, Coconino National Forest.

Finding the trailhead: From Sedona, drive about 6 miles north on Arizona Highway 89A to the Manzanita Campground. The trail starts from the west side of the highway just north of the campground, but parking is very limited. You may have to park at the pullouts south of the campground and walk through the campground to reach the trailhead.

Key points:
- 0.0 Trailhead.
- 0.9 Sterling Pass.

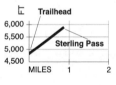

The hike: The Sterling Pass Trail is not shown on the topographic map. After leaving the highway, it climbs steeply up a drainage and through a fine stand of ponderosa pine. It skirts a dry waterfall and begins a series of short, steep switchbacks. There are occasional views of the massive cliffs that form the north side of Wilson Mountain. The hike ends at Sterling Pass, the sharp notch between the Mogollon Rim and Wilson Mountain.

Sterling Pass Trail • North Wilson Mountain Trail
Casner Canyon Trail • Allens Bend Trail
Wilson Mountain • Wilson Canyon

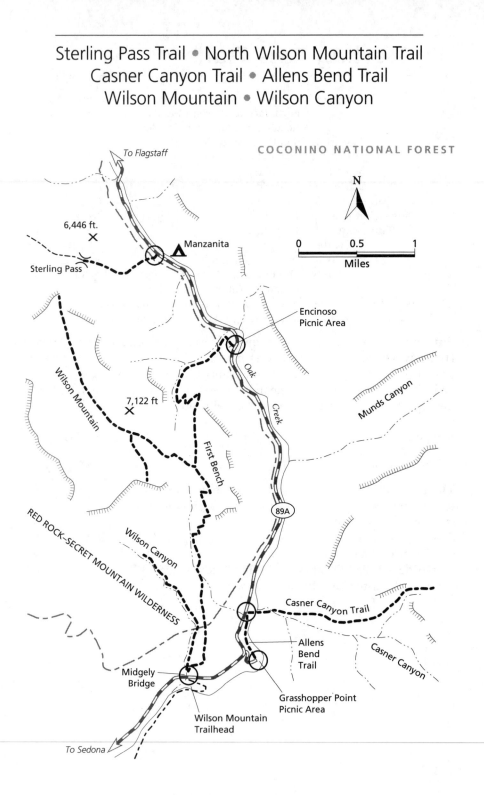

COCONINO NATIONAL FOREST

To Flagstaff

N

6,446 ft.
✗

Sterling Pass

Manzanita

0   0.5   1
Miles

Encinoso
Picnic Area

Wilson Mountain

Oak

Creek

Munds Canyon

7,122 ft
✗

First Bench

89A

RED ROCK–SECRET MOUNTAIN WILDERNESS

Wilson Canyon

Casner Canyon Trail

Allens
Bend
Trail

Casner Canyon

Midgely
Bridge

Grasshopper Point
Picnic Area

Wilson Mountain
Trailhead

To Sedona

An option is to continue this hike by descending west to the Dry Creek trailhead. See Hike 74 for more information. This would require a car shuttle if hiked one-way.

94 North Wilson Mountain Trail

See Map on Page 220

Description: This is a good hike on a hot day since much of the trail is in a north-facing, shady canyon in the Red Rock–Secret Mountain Wilderness. You'll have excellent views of Oak Creek Canyon, the Dry Creek basin, and the Mogollon Rim.

Location: 5 miles north of Sedona.

Type of trail: Out and back.

Type of trip: Day hike.

Difficulty: Difficult.

Total distance: 7.6 miles.

Elevation change: 2,200 feet.

Time required: 5 hours.

Water: None.

Best season: Spring through fall.

Maps: Munds Park, Wilson Mountain USGS quads; Coconino National Forest.

Permits and restrictions: A Red Rock Pass is required for vehicle parking.

For more information: Sedona Ranger District, Coconino National Forest.

Finding the trailhead: From Sedona, drive about 5 miles north on Arizona Highway 89A to the Encinoso Picnic Area. Park in the trailhead parking area at the entrance to the picnic area.

Key points:

0.0	North Wilson Mountain Trailhead.
1.4	First Bench of Wilson Mountain.
1.8	Turn right on the Wilson Mountain Trail.
2.4	Summit trail junction.
3.8	North rim of Wilson Mountain.

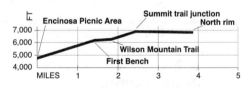

The hike: The trailhead is signed, although the North Wilson Mountain Trail is not shown on the topographic map. The trail starts climbing immediately through mixed chaparral, ponderosa pine, and oak forest. When the trail reaches the ridge above the picnic area, it turns to the south and follows the ridge a short distance, giving you good views of Oak Creek Canyon. After leaving the ridge, the trail climbs southwest up a heavily wooded drainage.

The volcanic rim of Wilson Mountain.

The shade of the large ponderosa pines is a welcome relief on hot days. As the trail nears the base of the massive, buff-colored Coconino sandstone cliffs, it crosses the drainage and begins to switchback up the slope to the east. There are more fine views when the trail reaches the ridge at the top of this slope. The trail turns to the south again and follows the ridge onto the First Bench of Wilson Mountain, a gently sloping volcanic plateau level with the east rim of Oak Creek Canyon.

Near the south end of the bench, the North Wilson Mountain Trail meets the Wilson Mountain Trail at a signed junction. This trail is shown on the topographic map. Turn right (west) here and follow the Wilson Mountain Trail as it climbs Wilson Mountain itself. Several switchbacks lead through the basalt cliffs near the rim. The trail swings left into a drainage that it follows to reach a gentle saddle on the wooded summit plateau. The actual summit is a small knob just to the north of this saddle.

There is a signed trail junction in the saddle. Continue straight ahead and follow the trail northwest about 1.4 miles to the north end of Wilson Mountain. The topographic map shows the trail ending just west of the point marked 7,076 on the map, but actually it continues to the rim. Here you are overlooking Sterling Pass, upper Dry Creek, Oak Creek, the Mogollon Rim, and, in the distance to the north, San Francisco Mountain. The view of the maze of red, buff, and gray cliffs is well worth the long hike.

The actual summit is a small knob with limited views, located 0.2 mile north of the summit trail junction. A better option is to walk 0.4 mile to the south rim of the mountain. See Hike 97 for information.

95 Casner Canyon Trail

See Map on Page 220

Description: A little-used trail to the east rim of Oak Creek Canyon.
Location: 2.4 miles north of Sedona.
Difficulty: Moderate.
Type of trail: Out and back.
Type of trip: Day hike.
Total distance: 3.6 miles.
Elevation change: 1,480 feet.
Time required: 3 hours.
Water: None.
Best season: All year.
Maps: Munds Park USGS quad; Coconino National Forest.
Permits and restrictions: A Red Rock Pass is required for vehicle parking.
For more information: Sedona Ranger District, Coconino National Forest.

Finding the trailhead: From Sedona, drive about 2.4 miles north on Arizona Highway 89A, and park on the right (east) side of the highway at a closed road. This trailhead is 0.3 mile north of Grasshopper Point Picnic Area.

Key points:

0.0   Trailhead.
0.1   Oak Creek.
1.8   East Rim of Oak Creek Canyon.

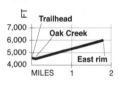

The hike: The trail follows the closed road down to Oak Creek, crosses the creek, and heads up the bed of Casner Canyon. There is no trail across the creek because of the damage from the massive flood in 1993. The key is to locate the mouth of Casner Canyon on the east side of the creek, downstream of the point where you first reach the creek; the topographic map, which shows the trail, may be useful. After following the bed of Casner Canyon for a few hundred yards, the trail climbs out onto the north slope. It turns northwest into an unnamed side canyon below Indian Point and climbs to reach the rim at the head of this side canyon. Most of the trail is on a dry, south-facing slope, and the low chaparral brush allows good views. This is a good trail to hike on weekends and holidays when other trails are crowded.

96 Allens Bend Trail

See Map on Page 220

Description:	This is one of the few trails along Oak Creek itself. Although short, it's an easy, pleasant walk. It's especially fine in the fall when the colors are changing.
Location:	2 miles north of Sedona.
Type of trail:	Out and back.
Type of trip:	Day hike.
Difficulty:	Easy.
Total distance:	0.6 mile.
Elevation change:	None.
Time required:	0.5 hour.
Water:	Oak Creek.
Best season:	All year.
Maps:	Munds Park USGS quad; Coconino National Forest.
Permits and restrictions:	A Red Rock Pass is required for vehicle parking.
For more information:	Sedona Ranger District, Coconino National Forest.

Finding the trailhead: From Sedona, drive about 2.0 miles north on Arizona Highway 89A, and turn right (east) into the Grasshopper Point Picnic Area. This is a fee area.

Key points:
- 0.0   Trailhead.
- 0.3   End of trail.

The hike: The unsigned trail, which is not shown on the topographic map, starts from the north end of the parking lot, and follows the west bank of Oak Creek. There are several sections of elaborate trail construction near the beginning and the trail comes out onto a wider bench. Watch for poison ivy, which is very common along Oak Creek. The trail ends near an old road that comes down from the highway above. Although short, the Allens Bend Trail is a pleasant, shady walk along the rushing waters of Oak Creek. It also provides an alternate access to the Casner Canyon Trail, which crosses the creek at the end of this trail.

In this area, the red rocks near the creek are shales, sandstones and limestones of the Supai formation. The Supai begins to outcrop here and forms the inner gorge of Oak Creek Canyon below this point. These mixed rock formations resulted from a fluctuating near-shore marine environment, in which deep sea limestones were laid down alternately with shallow water shale and sandstones.

97 Wilson Mountain

See Map on Page 220

Description: This popular trail climbs the south slopes of Wilson Mountain in the Red Rock–Secret Mountain Wilderness. Your reward for the effort is one of the best views of the Sedona area.

Location: 1.6 miles north of Sedona.

Type of trail: Out and back.

Type of trip: Day hike.

Difficulty: Difficult.

Total distance: 6.4 miles.

Elevation change: 2,440 feet.

Time required: 5 hours.

Water: None. The trail faces south and is hot in summer; bring plenty of water.

Best season: All year.

Maps: Wilson Mountain, Munds Park USGS quads; Coconino National Forest.

Permits and restrictions: A Red Rock Pass is required for vehicle parking.

For more information: Sedona Ranger District, Coconino National Forest.

Finding the trailhead: From Sedona, drive 1.6 miles north on Arizona Highway 89A, cross Midgely Bridge, and turn left into the Wilson Mountain Trailhead and viewpoint.

Key points:

0.0 Wilson Mountain Trailhead.
2.2 First Bench of Wilson Mountain.
2.8 Summit trail junction in a saddle.
3.2 South rim of Wilson Mountain.

The hike: The Wilson Mountain Trail starts climbing immediately, but then the climb moderates for a bit as the trail goes north through open pinyon-juniper forest. The climb starts in earnest as the trail starts switchbacking up the steep, south-facing slopes. The view opens up as the pigmy forest is replaced by the chaparral brush that favors this sun-baked slope. The trail reaches the First Bench of Wilson Mountain, and continues north to the junction with the North Wilson Mountain Trail. Stay left here, and continue as the trail swings west and climbs onto the summit plateau. At a trail junction in a saddle, turn left and walk 0.4 mile to the south rim of Wilson Mountain. This great spot has a sweeping view of the Sedona area.

The actual summit is a small knob with limited views, located 0.2 mile north of the summit trail junction. Another option is to hike 1.4 miles to the north rim of the mountain. See Hike 94 for information.

98 Wilson Canyon

See Map on Page 220

Description: An easy, popular walk up a red-rock canyon in the Red Rock–Secret Mountain Wilderness.

Location: 1.6 miles north of Sedona.

Type of trail: Out and back.

Type of trip: Day hike.

Difficulty: Easy.

Total distance: 2.0 miles.

Elevation change: 440 feet.

Time required: 1.5 hours.

Water: None.

Best season: All year.

Maps: Munds Park USGS quad; Coconino National Forest.

Permits and restrictions: A Red Rock Pass is required for vehicle parking.

For more information: Sedona Ranger District, Coconino National Forest.

Finding the trailhead: From Sedona, drive 1.6 miles north on Arizona Highway 89A, cross Midgely Bridge, and turn left into the Wilson Mountain Trailhead and viewpoint.

Key points:

0.0   Wilson Mountain Trailhead.

1.0   End of trail.

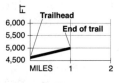

The hike: The Wilson Canyon Trail starts from the north end of the parking area and stays near the rim of the inner canyon. After this gorge ends at a high, dry waterfall, the Jim Thompson Trail branches left. The trail wanders another half-mile up the canyon though fine stands of Arizona cypress before fading out.

Verde Rim

The western boundary of the Verde Valley is formed by the Blac[k]
the Verde Rim. The rim was formed by faulting, which caused it ṭʊ ɾɪ̣ṣe nɪgn
above the Verde Valley. The highest section of the Verde Rim is formed by
flat-topped Mingus and Woodchute Mountains, which both rise to nearly 8,000
feet. There are a number of trails, remnants of the pre-road transportation
system, which ascend the pine-covered slopes of these mountains. All have
superb views of the surrounding mountains and valleys. South of Interstate
17, the Black Hills give way to the Verde Rim, which faces the Mogollon
Rim across the rugged canyon of the Verde River.

99 Woodchute Trail

Description:	This easy trail goes to the north end of Woodchute Mountain in the Woodchute Wilderness. You'll have some panoramic views of the western Mogollon Rim and Sycamore Canyon.
Location:	7.4 miles south of Jerome.
Type of trail:	Out and back.
Type of trip:	Day hike.
Difficulty:	Easy.
Total distance:	7.4 miles.
Elevation change:	640 feet.
Time required:	4 hours.
Water:	None.
Best season:	Summer through fall.
Maps:	Hickey Mountain, Munds Draw USGS quads; Prescott National Forest.
Permits and restrictions:	None.
For more information:	Verde Ranger District, Prescott National Forest.

Finding the trailhead: From Jerome, drive about 7 miles west on Arizona
Highway 89A. At the highway pass on Mingus Mountain, turn right at
Potato Patch Campground. Go about 0.4 mile and turn left into the Wood-
chute Trailhead.

Key points:

- 0.0 Woodchute Trailhead.
- 0.4 Turn right on the Woodchute Trail.
- 1.7 Ridgetop.
- 2.2 Mescal Gulch.
- 2.7 South rim of Woodchute Mountain.
- 3.7 North rim of Woodchute Mountain.

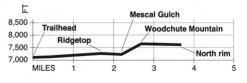

227

Woodchute Trail

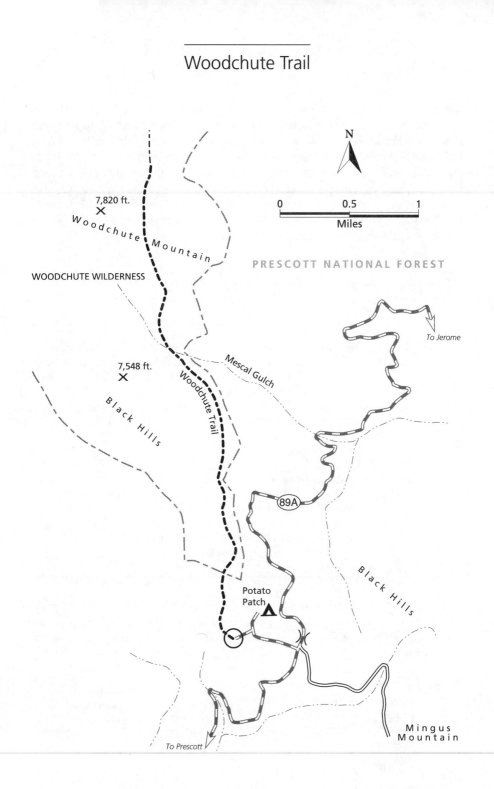

N

0   0.5   1
Miles

7,820 ft.
✕
Woodchute Mountain

WOODCHUTE WILDERNESS

PRESCOTT NATIONAL FOREST

To Jerome

7,548 ft.
✕

Mescal Gulch

Black Hills

Woodchute Trail

89A

Black Hills

Potato
Patch ▲

Mingus
Mountain

To Prescott

The hike: Hike north for 0.4 mile through ponderosa pine woodland. Notice the large alligator junipers—these are the trees with, appropriately enough, bark that looks like alligator hide. The Woodchute Trail forks right and climbs onto the main crest of the mountain. After crossing several dips in the ridge, it contours into the head of Mescal Gulch and climbs to the south rim of Woodchute Mountain. The trail continues north across the flat summit area, and finally reaches the north rim of the flat-topped mountain, which is our destination. (From here, the trail descends the north slopes of Woodchute Mountain and ends at Forest Road 318A. This section of the trail is little used.) From here, you have a panoramic view of the headwaters of the Verde River, the western Mogollon Rim, and Sycamore Canyon Wilderness.

100 North Mingus Trail

Description:	This is a scenic hike through a historic mining district on Mingus Mountain, with views of Verde Valley and Mogollon Rim.
Location:	4.5 miles east of Jerome.
Type of trail:	Out and back.
Type of trip:	Day hike.
Difficulty:	Moderate.
Total distance:	6.0 miles.
Elevation change:	1,660 feet.
Time required:	4 hours.
Water:	Mescal Spring.
Best season:	Spring through fall.
Maps:	Hickey Mountain, Cottonwood USGS quads; Prescott National Forest.
Permits and restrictions:	None.
For more information:	Verde Ranger District, Prescott National Forest.

Finding the trailhead: From Jerome, drive about 4 miles west on Arizona Highway 89A. Watch for a Prescott National Forest sign and turn left on an unsigned, unmaintained dirt road (Forest Road 338) just before this sign. Low clearance vehicles should park at the highway. Go through the gate, continue 0.5 mile to Mescal Spring, and park. Mescal Spring is marked by a large, cement tank that catches water piped down a few feet from the actual spring.

Key points:

- 0.0 Trailhead.
- 1.2 Turn right on the unsigned foot trail.
- 2.6 Junction with Trail 105A; turn right.
- 3.0 Rim.

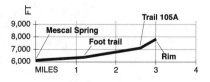

North Mingus Trail • Mingus Rim Loop

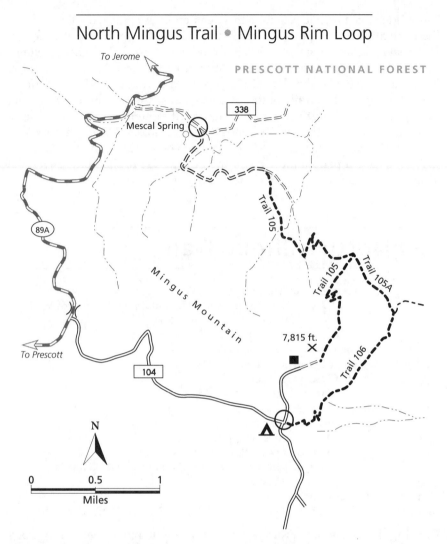

PRESCOTT NATIONAL FOREST

338

Mescal Spring

Trail 105

89A

Mingus Mountain

Trail 105   Trail 105A

7,815 ft.
✕

Trail 106

To Prescott

104

N

0   0.5   1
Miles

The hike: Walk up the jeep road that forks right and climbs steeply (it is shown as a foot trail on the topographic map). The little-used jeep road does a switchback then contours around a basin. This section of the road is very easy, pleasant walking. It crosses a ridge just as it enters another basin. Watch carefully for the cairned but unsigned foot trail that goes up this ridge. This junction is 1.2 miles from Mescal Spring. Although it is possible to reach this point in a high-clearance vehicle, there is no parking. The rocky but well-maintained trail climbs through a fine stand of ponderosa pine and starts switchbacking up the north ridge of Mingus Mountain. The view starts to open up as the trail gains elevation. About 1.4 miles from the jeep road, the trail reaches a shallow saddle and the signed junction with Trail 105A. Continue south, directly up the steep ridge, on Trail 105. The trail soon resumes switchbacking and passes through a small aspen grove near the rim. The trail reaches the rim, our destination, about 0.4 mile from the trail junction.

The forest is thick here, but by walking around, good views
A large section of the Mogollon Rim, the Verde Valley and the
try of Sedona and Sycamore Canyon are visible. A trailhe?
mile south.

101 Mingus Rim Loop

See Map on Page 230

Description:	A scenic hike along and below the rim of Mingus Mountain.
Location:	9.4 miles west of Jerome.
Type of trail:	Loop.
Type of trip:	Day hike.
Difficulty:	Moderate.
Total distance:	3.6 miles.
Elevation change:	900 feet.
Time required:	2.5 hours.
Water:	None.
Best season:	Summer through fall.
Maps:	Cottonwood USGS quad; Prescott National Forest.
Permits and restrictions:	None.
For more information:	Verde Ranger District, Prescott National Forest.

Finding the trailhead: From Jerome, drive about 7 miles west on Arizona Highway 89A to the highway pass on Mingus Mountain and turn left on the maintained Mingus Mountain road (Forest Road 104). Go 2.4 miles to the east end of the Mingus Mountain Campground, and park at the viewpoint. This trailhead is also signed for Trail 106.

Key points:

0.0   Trail 106 trailhead.
1.4   Turn left on Trail 105A.
2.0   Turn left on Trail 105.
2.4   Rim.
2.9   Trailhead.
3.6   Trail 106 trailhead.

The hike: After checking out the view, descend east on Trail 106. The steep trail leaves the cool pine forest behind as it rapidly descends in a series of switchbacks. Soon the trail starts a more gentle descent to the north as it traverses a chaparral slope. The chaparral country is difficult to penetrate without a trail, but it provides vital wildlife cover under the dense brush.

The trail enters a shadier section of pine forest and meets Trail 105A, which is not shown on the topographic map. This junction is signed; turn left on Trail 105A and follow it as it gradually climbs to another saddle, where it meets Trail 105. Turn left and follow this trail as it climbs to the north rim of Mingus in a series of switchbacks. Walk south to the trailhead and then follow the main road to the Mingus Mountain Campground and the start of the hike.

Description:	This is an enjoyable loop hike on Mingus Mountain, with views of Prescott Valley.
Location:	10 miles east of Prescott.
Type of trail:	Loop.
Type of trip:	Day hike.
Difficulty:	Moderate.
Total distance:	6.0 miles.
Elevation change:	1,200 feet.
Time required:	4 hours.
Water:	None.
Best season:	Spring through fall.
Maps:	Hickey Mountain USGS quad; Prescott National Forest.
Permits and restrictions:	None.
For more information:	Verde Ranger District, Prescott National Forest.

Finding the trailhead: From Prescott, drive 10 miles east on Arizona Highway 89A to the unmarked trailhead. (If you miss the trailhead, continue to the Potato Patch Campground turnoff, then backtrack 3.2 miles west.). Turn left onto the dirt road, and park on either side of the normally dry creek.

This variety of mistletoe is a parasite on ponderosa pine.

232

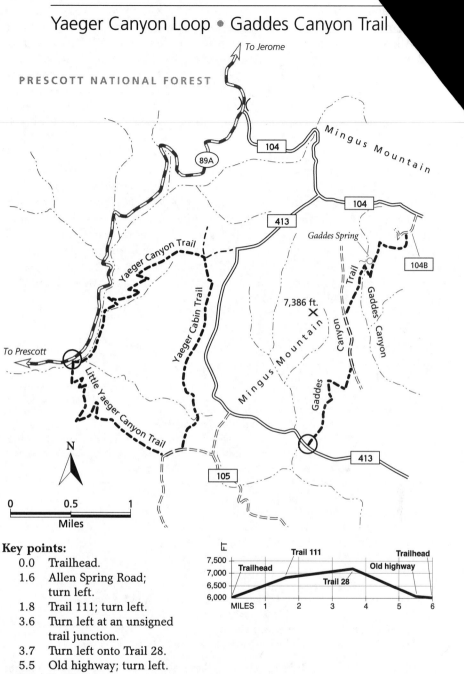

Yaeger Canyon Loop • Gaddes Canyon Trail

To Jerome

PRESCOTT NATIONAL FOREST

Mingus Mountain

104

89A

104

413

Gaddes Spring

Yaeger Canyon Trail

104B

Yaeger Cabin Trail

7,386 ft.
×

Gaddes Canyon Trail

Gaddes Canyon

To Prescott

Mingus Mountain

Little Yaeger Canyon Trail

Gaddes

N

413

105

0   0.5   1
Miles

Key points:

- 0.0   Trailhead.
- 1.6   Allen Spring Road; turn left.
- 1.8   Trail 111; turn left.
- 3.6   Turn left at an unsigned trail junction.
- 3.7   Turn left onto Trail 28.
- 5.5   Old highway; turn left.
- 6.0   Trailhead.

Elevation profile:

7,500 — Trailhead / Trail 111 / Old highway / Trailhead
7,000
6,500 — Trail 28
6,000

MILES 1   2   3   4   5   6

The hike: The hike starts on the Little Yaeger Canyon Trail, which begins from the southeast side of the parking area. Several switchbacks lead through

rest to the top of a gentle ridge, where ponderosa pine begin
rail climbs more gradually through a small saddle and meets
Road from the trailhead. Turn left and walk down the road
ger Cabin Trail (Forest Trail 111) and turn left.
oak forest, the Yaeger Cabin Trail drops slightly as it trav-
of Little Yaeger Canyon and then begins to work its way
canyon. Sometimes there is water in the bed of the canyon
nead. The trail comes out onto a pine flat on the southwest ridge of
Mingus Mountain. Turn left on a signed trail. (This side trail also goes right to
the Allen Spring Road.) Continue 0.1 mile to the end of the Yaeger Cabin Trail
at a junction with three other trails. Forest Trail 530 continues straight ahead,
while the Yaeger Canyon Trail (Forest Trail 28) crosses from right to left.

Turn left (west), and follow the Yaeger Canyon Trail to the rim where there
is a good view of Little Yaeger Canyon and the rim of Mingus Mountain.
The trail descends to the southwest in a series of switchbacks, and the trailhead is visible next to the highway. When the trail reaches the bottom of
Yaeger Canyon it turns left on the old highway road bed. It stays on the left
(east) side of the creek and doesn't cross on the old highway bridge. Continue down the canyon to your vehicle.

103 Gaddes Canyon Trail

See Map on Page 233

Description:	This is an enjoyable hike through ponderosa pine and Gambel oak forest on Mingus Mountain, with some good views.
Location:	About 11 miles west of Jerome.
Type of trail:	Out and back.
Type of trip:	Day hike.
Difficulty:	Moderate.
Total distance:	5.2 miles.
Elevation change:	970 feet.
Time required:	3 hours.
Water:	Gaddes Spring.
Best season:	Spring through fall.
Maps:	Hickey Mountain USGS quad; Prescott National Forest.
Permits and restrictions:	None.
For more information:	Verde Ranger District, Prescott National Forest.

Finding the trailhead: From Jerome, drive about 7.0 miles east on Arizona
Highway 89A to the highway pass on Mingus Mountain. Turn left on the
maintained dirt Mingus Mountain road (Forest Road 104). Continue 1.4
miles and turn right on FR 413, the Allen Spring Road. There is a signed
junction 2.2 miles down this road; stay left and continue 0.7 mile farther to
the trailhead.

Key points:

   0.0   Gaddes Canyon Trailhead.
   0.9   Rim.
   1.9   Gaddes Canyon.
   2.6   Mingus Lookout Road.

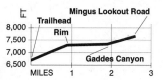

The hike: The well-graded trail climbs gently north through an open stand of ponderosa pine. After about 0.5 mile the slope becomes steeper and the trail switchbacks past several large rock outcrops to reach the rim of Mingus Mountain. There are glimpses of Prescott Valley to the west and Hickey Mountain to the northwest during this ascent. The trail joins a jeep road as it continues north along the top of the broad, flat ridge. After about 0.6 mile, it turns right to leave the jeep road. This junction is signed with the Forest Service trail number 110. Shortly after, the trail veers north-northeast and descends into Gaddes Canyon. At the bottom of the drainage, our trail passes a junction with Trail 535, a faint trail that heads down the canyon. The Gaddes Canyon Trail ascends the east side of the canyon past Gaddes Spring, which appears to be reliable. There was water here in February 1996, one of the driest winters ever recorded in Northern Arizona. The trail reaches the east rim of the canyon and then crosses a flat to end at the Mingus Lookout Road, FR 104B.

104 Coleman Trail

Description:	A hike with excellent views of the east side of Mingus Mountain and the Verde Valley.
Location:	14.7 miles west of Jerome.
Type of trail:	Out and back.
Type of trip:	Day hike.
Difficulty:	Moderate.
Total distance:	4.0 miles.
Elevation change:	1,000 feet.
Time required:	3 hours.
Water:	None.
Best season:	Spring through fall.
Maps:	Cottonwood USGS quad; Prescott National Forest.
Permits and restrictions:	None.
For more information:	Verde Ranger District, Prescott National Forest.

Finding the trailhead: From Jerome, drive about 7 miles west on Arizona Highway 89A to the highway pass at the top of Mingus Mountain and turn left on Forest Road 104, which is maintained dirt. Continue 1.4 miles and turn right on FR 413, the Allen Spring Road. There is a signed junction 2.2 miles down this road; stay left and continue 4.1 miles further to the signed trailhead. Park about 100 yards east of the trailhead.

Coleman Trail • Black Canyon Trail

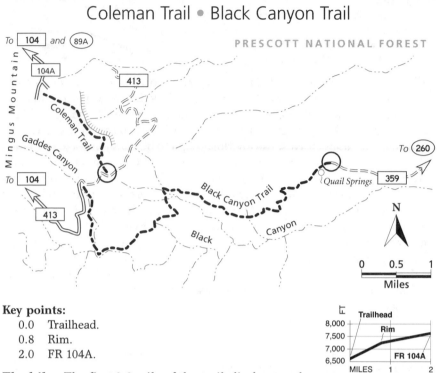

Key points:

0.0	Trailhead.
0.8	Rim.
2.0	FR 104A.

The hike: The first 0.8 mile of the trail climbs steeply up a brushy slope to the rim of Mingus Mountain. There are good views of upper Black Canyon in the foreground, and beyond, the Black Hills. After the trail reaches the rim, it crosses to the north side of the

The rim of Mingus Mountain, along the Coleman Trail.

flat-topped ridge, where the view is superb. The red-rock country around Sedona is visible, as is San Francisco Mountain and most of the western Mogollon Rim. The steep east slopes of Mingus Mountain are in the foreground. The Coleman Trail turns to the northwest along the ridge. After a rocky but short section of trail, the going becomes easier. The last 1.2 miles of trail is a pleasant walk though pinyon-juniper forest that gradually becomes ponderosa pine forest. The trail ends at FR 104A near a cluster of radio towers.

105 Black Canyon Trail

See Map on Page 236

Description: This hike starts on the lower slopes of Mingus Mountain and takes you into a rugged canyon and a pine-forested valley. It can also be done one way with a car shuttle.
Location: About 9.5 miles south of Cottonwood.
Type of trail: Out and back.
Type of trip: Day hike.
Difficulty: Difficult (Moderate with a shuttle).
Total distance: 12.0 miles.
Elevation change: 2,280 feet.
Time required: 7 hours.
Water: None.
Best season: All year.
Maps: Cottonwood USGS quad; Prescott National Forest.
Permits and restrictions: None.
For more information: Verde Ranger District, Prescott National Forest.

Finding the trailhead: From Cottonwood, drive 4 miles south on Arizona Highway 260 and turn right on Forest Road 359. Continue 4.5 miles to the end of the road at Quail Springs.

To reach the upper trailhead from Jerome, drive about 7 miles west on AZ 89A to the highway pass at the top of Mingus Mountain and turn left on FR 104, which is maintained dirt. Continue 1.4 miles and turn right on FR 413, the Allen Spring Road. There is a signed junction 2.2 miles down this road; stay left and continue 3.5 miles further to the trailhead, which is on the right.

Key points:
0.0   Quail Springs.
4.4   Black Canyon.
6.0   Allen Spring Road.

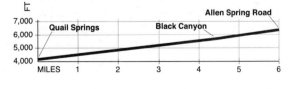

The hike: As an out-and-back hike, this is a long one with significant elevation gain. Optionally, you could leave a vehicle at Quail Springs and hike the trail downhill one way from the Allen Spring Road.

Above Quail Spring, the trail climbs steadily along the brushy slopes above Black Canyon. This chaparral brush becomes thicker as you climb. Although the dense brush is favored wildlife habitat, it's not fun stuff to bash through on a cross-country hike. After nearly 4 miles of steady climbing, the trail swings south, crosses a minor saddle, and drops into Black Canyon.

You can leave the trail temporarily and walk 0.4 mile cross-country down the streambed to the point where the stream plunges over the first of many falls and cascades. There is often a good flow of water here in the spring.

The trail continues up the bed of Black Canyon through a pleasant ponderosa pine forest and then turns right up an unnamed side canyon to end at the Allen Spring Road.

Another option would be to walk 0.6 mile east on the road and then climb to the top of Mingus Mountain via the Coleman Trail. This adds another 4.0 miles round trip distance and 1,000 feet of elevation gain.

106 Chasm Creek Trail

Description:	This is a seldom-used trail that climbs from Chasm Creek to the Verde Rim in the Cedar Bench Wilderness.
Location:	12 miles south of Camp Verde.
Type of trail:	Out and back.
Type of trip:	Day hike.
Difficulty:	Difficult.
Total distance:	6.8 miles.
Elevation change:	2,200 feet.
Time required:	5 hours.
Water:	Spring in Chasm Creek.
Best season:	Spring and fall.
Maps:	Horner Mountain USGS quad; Prescott National Forest.
Permits and restrictions:	None.
For more information:	Verde Ranger District, Prescott National Forest.

Finding the trailhead: From Camp Verde, drive south on the General Crook Trail (Forest Highway 9) and turn right on paved County Road 163. This turnoff is just before the Verde River Bridge. The paved road becomes the maintained dirt FR 574. Continue generally south and east 11.8 miles and turn right (southwest) just before crossing Chasm Creek. This rocky side road is marked with a small hiking-trail symbol. Those with low-clearance vehicles may want to walk 0.25 mile to the unsigned trailhead, which is a turn-around loop at a wire fence.

Key points:
0.0   Trailhead.
2.0   Saddle.
3.4   Verde Rim.

Chasm Creek Trail • Cold Water Spring

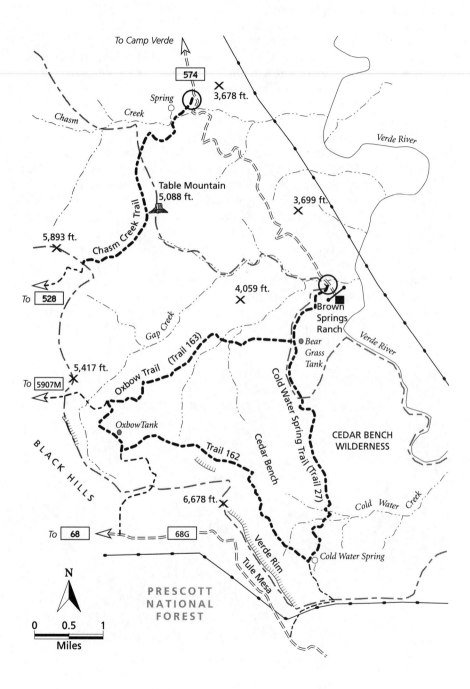

To Camp Verde

574

Spring ○

3,678 ft. ✕

Chasm   Creek

Verde River

Table Mountain
5,088 ft.

3,699 ft. ✕

5,893 ft. ✕

Chasm Creek Trail

To 528

4,059 ft. ✕

Brown
Springs
Ranch

● Bear
Grass
Tank

Verde River

Gap Creek

5,417 ft. ✕

To 5907M

Oxbow Trail (Trail 163)

Cold Water Spring Trail (Trail 27)

CEDAR BENCH
WILDERNESS

OxbowTank

Trail 162

Cedar Bench

B L A C K   H I L L S

6,678 ft. ✕

Cold Water Creek

To 68

68G

Verde Rim

Tule Mesa

○ Cold Water Spring

N

PRESCOTT
NATIONAL
FOREST

0   0.5   1
Miles

The hike: Although most of the trail is easy to follow, there are faint sections since it receives little use. It's a good idea to have the topographic map, which shows the trail correctly. The trail is marked by rock cairns and tree blazes.

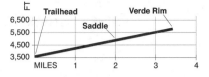

From the trailhead, go through the wire gate and follow the trail as it descends into Chasm Creek. The section of trail along the creek bed was destroyed in a huge flood in February 1993. Stay generally on the left side of the creek for about 200 yards. The trail climbs out on the left just before a series of rockbound pools and small cascades. There is no more water on the trail after this point. Climbing steeply, the trail heads south, away from Chasm Creek itself, but stays in the Chasm Creek drainage all the way to the Verde Rim. After the steep climb the grade moderates somewhat as the trail turns more to the west, traversing pleasant pinyon-juniper forest. More steep sections lead to the west slopes of Table Mountain, the prominent flat mesa visible from the approach road. The Verde Rim is visible to the west, across the Chasm Creek basin. About 2 miles from the trailhead, the trail reaches a saddle on the ridge west of Table Mountain, and the view to the south opens up. The Verde River canyon is visible, as are the rugged Mazatzal Mountains and the Mogollon Rim. Finally, the trail follows the ridge southwest and skirts a hill to reach a broad, grassy saddle on the Verde Rim, with views of the distant Bradshaw Mountains to the west. Although the trail continues to FR 528 in another 3 miles, this point on the Verde Rim makes a good turnaround point.

Hiking the Chasm Creek Trail, Cedar Bench Wilderness.

107 Cold Water Spring

See Map on Page 239

Description: This is a challenging hike on rarely used trails in the Cedar Bench Wilderness. It is a remote area with fine views of the Verde River canyon.

Location: 16.5 miles south of Camp Verde.

Type of trail: Loop.

Type of trip: Day hike or overnight backpack.

Difficulty: Difficult.

Total distance: 14.4 miles.

Elevation change: 2,720 feet.

Time required: 10 hours.

Water: Cold Water Spring.

Best season: Spring and fall.

Maps: Tule Mesa, Horner Mountain USGS quads; Prescott National Forest.

Permits and restrictions: None.

For more information: Verde Ranger District, Prescott National Forest.

Finding the trailhead: From Camp Verde, drive south on the General Crook Trail (Forest Highway 9) and turn right on paved County Road 163. This turnoff is just before the Verde River Bridge. Continue generally south and east 16.5 miles to a locked gate near the Brown Springs Ranch. The road becomes Forest Road 574 and will change from paved to maintained gravel and then to unmaintained dirt, but it is passable to most cars with care. Trailhead parking is to the left of the ranch buildings in a clearing next to Gap Creek.

Key points:

0.0	Brown Springs Ranch Trailhead.
1.0	Junction with the Oxbow Trail; continue straight ahead.
4.6	Cold Water Spring; turn right on Trail 162.
9.2	Turn right onto unsigned Oxbow Trail.
10.2	Turn right again at an unsigned junction to stay on the Oxbow Trail.
13.4	Turn left at an unsigned junction to stay on the Oxbow Trail.
14.4	Brown Springs Ranch Trailhead.

The hike: All of the trails in this loop hike are little used and are faint in places. It will be necessary to watch for tree blazes, rock cairns, and even the cut limbs on trees to stay on the trail. In difficult sections, don't leave the last cairn or blaze until you have located the next one. The trail is rocky, and some sections are brushy—allow extra time. You should have good route finding and map reading skills before attempting this hike. The reward for your efforts is a continuously changing view of the rugged Verde River canyon, the Mogollon Rim, and in the distance, San Francisco Mountain and the Mazatzal Mountains.

Walk up the road past the locked gate about 200 yards and turn right on a much rougher road that climbs steeply west up the ridge. After another 200 yards, the road swings sharply left, and a small sign marks the beginning of Trail 163 (Oxbow Trail). Follow the trail another 200 yards to a gate in a saddle. Two fences cross at right angles here. Turn left (south) and go through the gate in the east–west fence. Do not go through the gate in the north–south fence. The trail becomes more distinct as it climbs south along the ridge. At Bear Grass Tank, about 1 mile from the trailhead, the unsigned Oxbow Trail goes right (west)—this will be the return trail. Continue straight ahead (south) on the Cold Water Spring Trail (Trail 27). The trail climbs through an open forest of pinyon pine and juniper as it skirts the east slopes of Cedar Bench and climbs sharply up the headwaters of Cold Water Creek to reach Cold Water Spring. The spring appears to be reliable, and there are numerous campsites for those who wish to do this loop as an overnight hike.

Turn right on Trail 162. (The Cold Water Spring Trail continues south another 2 miles, and ends at FR 68G on the Verde Rim.) This junction is unsigned and difficult to find. Just above the spring, which is marked by an old water trough, turn right (northwest) and contour along the slope. Watch for a length of black plastic pipe and a series of cairns and blazes. After a short distance the trail becomes clearer but is still more difficult to follow than the Cold Water Spring trail. The trail contours the steep slopes below the Verde Rim and then climbs onto the upper slopes of Cedar Bench, clearly visible ahead. After crossing Cedar Bench the trail swings more to the west and crosses steep, brushy slopes that offer panoramic views of the Verde Valley to the north. About 4 miles from Cold Water Spring the trail crosses through a broad, grassy saddle. Carefully follow the cairns about 0.5 mile to an unsigned trail junction at a fence. Turn right (north) and follow the cairned trail (Oxbow Trail) downhill to Oxbow Tank. Pass the tank on the left then continue on the trail as it descends the deepening canyon. Just above a cliff, the trail veers right and crosses the drainage. It then contours around the slope above the cliff, generally in a northeast direction. About 1 mile from the last trail junction, an unsigned trail forks left and descends into Gap Creek. (This trail goes to FR 5907M.) Continue straight ahead on the Oxbow Trail as it contours the north-facing slope for about a mile then comes out on a ridge and starts descending. The trail is distinct and well marked with rock cairns. In another mile the trail turns south, leaves the ridge, and crosses a series of drainages. It then climbs slightly to reach the junction at Bear Grass Tank. Turn left and return to the trailhead, now a mile away.

108 Towel Creek

Description:	This unique hike leads to the Verde River, one of the only remaining free-flowing rivers in Arizona. It's also the lowest-elevation hike in this book.
Location:	15.6 miles south of Camp Verde.
Type of trail:	Out and back.
Type of trip:	Long day hike, or overnight backpack.
Difficulty:	Moderate.
Total distance:	14.2 miles.
Elevation change:	1,600 feet.
Time required:	8 hours.
Water:	Verde River.
Best season:	All year.
Maps:	Hackberry Mountain, Horner Mountain USGS quads; Coconino National Forest.
Permits and restrictions:	None.
For more information:	Beaver Creek Ranger District, Coconino National Forest.

Finding the trailhead: From Camp Verde, drive about 7.6 miles east on Arizona Highway 260 and turn right on Forest Road 708. Continue 8.0 miles to the trailhead, which is on the right.

Key points:
- 0.0 Trailhead.
- 0.8 Saddle.
- 2.3 Towel Tank.
- 2.8 Towel Spring junction.
- 7.1 Verde River.

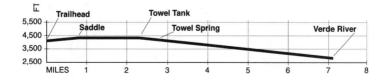

Towel Creek

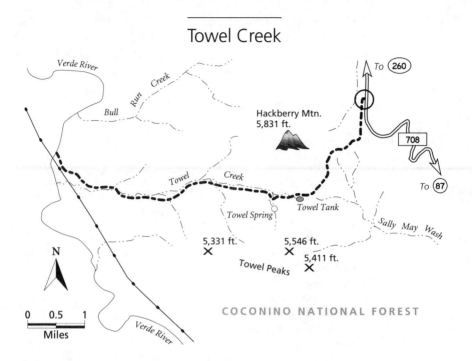

The hike: At first, the trail heads south, nearly parallel to the road. It climbs through a saddle and contours southwest across the slopes of Hackberry Mountain. It then swings west and crosses into the head of Towel Creek at Towel Tank. As you continue west, you'll pass a side canyon coming in from the south. A short spur trail leads to Towel Spring, which is in this side canyon. The main trail continues west, loosely following Towel Creek all the way to the Verde River.

This is a remote section of the river. There is a ranch across the river to the west and road access a few miles downstream at Childs, but otherwise the Verde flows through a wilderness canyon. The river is prime habitat for desert bald eagles, and if you're lucky you may see one of these striking birds.

Mogollon Rim

East of Oak Creek Canyon, the Mogollon Rim turns southeast to form the eastern boundary of the Verde Valley. At Fossil Creek, the Rim resumes its general east–southeast orientation. A series of long, spectacular canyons cuts into the Rim; most are remote and are protected as wilderness areas. Several of the following hikes are in these canyons; others are on the southeast portion of the Coconino Plateau.

109 Bell Trail

Description:	This is a popular summer hike along Wet Beaver Creek in the Wet Beaver Wilderness. The trail climbs to the Mogollon Rim for some good views.
Location:	16 miles southeast of Sedona.
Type of trail:	Out and back.
Type of trip:	Day hike.
Difficulty:	Moderate.
Total distance:	8.4 miles.
Elevation change:	1,320 feet.
Time required:	5 hours.
Water:	Wet Beaver Creek.
Best season:	All year.
Maps:	Casner Butte USGS quad; Coconino National Forest.
Permits and restrictions:	None.
For more information:	Beaver Creek Ranger District, Coconino National Forest.

Finding the trailhead: From Sedona, drive about 14 miles southeast on Arizona Highway 179 and go under the Interstate 17 interchange. Continue 2.1 miles on the Beaver Creek Road (Forest Road 618) and then turn left into the Wet Beaver Creek trailhead.

Key points:
- 0.0 Wet Beaver Creek Trailhead.
- 2.1 Apache Maid Trail.
- 3.1 Cross Wet Beaver Creek.
- 4.2 Mogollon Rim.

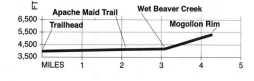

The hike: The trail stays along the north side of Wet Beaver Creek. Stands of Fremont cottonwood and other riparian vegetation crowd the creek, but there are several short side trails down to the water. One of several permanent streams flowing through the canyons below the Mogollon Rim, Wet Beaver Creek is very popular during the summer. As you continue up the

245

Bell Trail • Walker Basin Trail • Buckhorn Trail

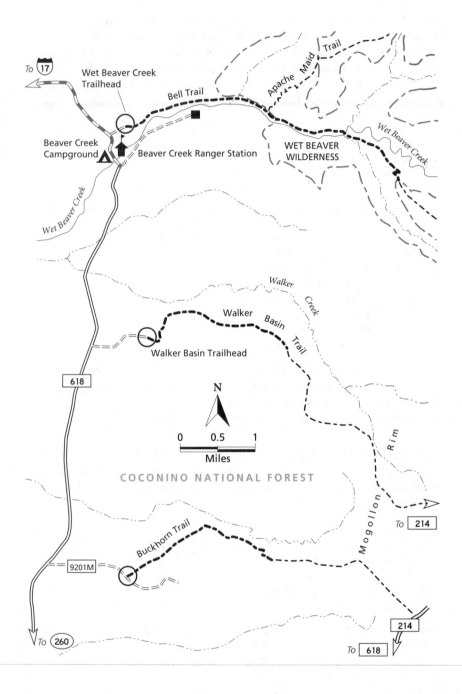

The Bell Trail in Wet Beaver Creek.

canyon, notice how the slope to the left, which is sunnier and drier, features a nearly pure stand of juniper trees. On the other hand, the slope to the right, which faces north and is cooler and moister, supports a mixed stand of juniper and pinyon. Evidently pinyon pine require just a bit more moisture, and possibly cooler temperatures, than juniper trees. Very slight changes in climate can have a dramatic effect on plant and animal communities.

At 2.1 miles you'll pass the Apache Maid Trail. Continue east along the canyon on the Bell Trail. There are a number of good swimming holes along the creek, just below the trail. After another mile, the trail crosses the creek and climbs up a steep ridge to the Mogollon Rim. Although the trail continues to FR 214, this scenic spot makes a good turnaround point for the hike.

As an option, you can also reach the rim via the Apache Maid Trail, which climbs the north slope of the canyon. The juniper forest is open, and the first section of the trail provides good views down Wet Beaver Creek. A series of switchbacks leads up to the base of Casner Butte. The trail then crosses the drainage to the north and angles up to the Mogollon Rim. Here the view ranges from San Francisco Mountain on the north to the Verde Valley on the west and southwest. Originally built for access to the Apache Maid fire tower, the remainder of the trail is faint and difficult to follow, so this is a good place to turn around for this optional side hike. This hike adds 2.8 miles and 1,050 feet of elevation gain to the main hike.

110 Walker Basin Trail

See Map on Page 246

Description:	A hike on a little-used, historic trail to the Mogollon Rim.
Location:	15.5 miles northeast of Camp Verde.
Type of trail:	Out and back.
Type of trip:	Day hike.
Difficulty:	Moderate.
Total distance:	4.8 miles.
Elevation change:	1,350 feet.
Time required:	3 hours.
Water:	None.
Best season:	Fall through spring.
Maps:	Casner Butte USGS quad; Coconino National Forest.
Permits and restrictions:	None.
For more information:	Beaver Creek Ranger District, Coconino National Forest.

Finding the trailhead: From Camp Verde, drive east about 5.7 miles on the General Crook Trail (Forest Highway 9) and turn left on maintained dirt Forest Road 618. Continue about 9.0 miles, turn right, and then drive 0.8 mile to the Walker Basin Trailhead. Low clearance vehicles may have to be left on FR 618.

The Walker Basin Trail turnoff can also be reached from the north. Take the Arizona Highway 179 exit from Interstate 17 and go southeast on FR 618, which is paved to the Beaver Creek Campground. The signed Walker Basin Trail turnoff is 5.0 miles from the interstate.

Key points:

0.0   Trailhead.
0.7   Start of steeper climb.
1.9   Climb moderates a bit.
2.4   Mogollon Rim.

The hike: The historic Walker Basin Trail, built to move stock between summer and winter pastures, starts out as an old, closed road, wandering northeast through juniper forest toward a low ridge visible ahead. It climbs this gentle ridge along its crest, and the views start to open up. The trail starts to climb more steeply just over a mile from the trailhead. The reward for this exertion is ever more sweeping views of the Verde Valley. The ridge merges with the steep slopes of a point that looms above, and the trail attacks the slope with steep, rocky switchbacks. The views are some of the best of the hike—plenty of excuses for rest stops. Most of the Verde Rim is visible from Pine Mountain on the south to Mingus Mountain and Woodchute Mountain to the west. A large section of the western Mogollon Rim is visible as well, including the Sedona area and San Francisco Mountain. At the top of the steep climb, the trail crosses the flat top of the point before making a short, final climb to the rim at 5,350 feet. Our hike ends here, having covered the most scenic part of the trail.

As an option, you could hike another 3.5 miles across the plateau to FR 214.

111 Buckhorn Trail

See Map on Page 246

Description: This hike takes you up a rarely used trail to the Mogollon Rim, with expansive views of the Verde Valley.
Location: About 13 miles northeast of Camp Verde.
Type of trail: Out and back.
Type of trip: Day hike.
Difficulty: Moderate.
Total distance: 4.6 miles.
Elevation change: 1,130 feet.
Time required: 3 hours.
Water: None.
Best season: Fall, winter, spring.
Maps: Walker Mountain USGS quad; Coconino National Forest.
Permits and restrictions: None.
For more information: Beaver Creek Ranger District, Coconino National Forest.

Finding the trailhead: From Camp Verde, drive east about 5.7 miles on the General Crook Trail (Forest Highway 9) and turn left (north) on maintained dirt Forest Road 618. Continue 6.1 miles and turn right (east) on FR 9201M. This unmaintained road is just past the sign for Wickiup Draw. Go 1.1 miles to the third closed road on the left (north). The trailhead is not signed, and there is minimal parking.

FR 9201M can also be reached from the north. Take the Arizona Highway 179 exit from Interstate 17 and go southeast on FR 618, which is paved to the Beaver Creek Campground. FR 9201M is 8.1 miles from the interstate, and just before the Wickiup Draw sign.

Key points:
0.0   Trailhead.
1.3   Fenceline.
2.3   Mogollon Rim.

The hike: Initially, the Buckhorn Trail is an old jeep road that the Forest Service has closed by bulldozing a pile of dirt at its beginning. The trail leads northeast across a flat and then climbs onto a juniper-covered mesa. It is a pleasant walk about 1.3 miles to a fenceline, where the trail turns southeast and starts to climb along a ridge crest. The view becomes wider as the ridge gains elevation and becomes narrower. Pinyon pine begin to compete with the junipers. Finally, the ridge runs into the slopes below the Mogollon Rim, and the trail becomes very steep and rocky. Mercifully, this section is short, and the trail soon reaches a saddle on the ridge leading to Hollingshead Point. Above this saddle the trail becomes difficult to follow, so the hike ends here.

The Verde Valley (verde means "green" in Spanish) to the west was named by the members of Coronado's Spanish expedition, which explored Arizona in the early 1540s. After their long, hot journey from Mexico City through the Sonoran desert, the Verde Valley, with its river and several permanent streams, must have been a relief. The valley and the surrounding canyons contain numerous cliff dwellings, pueblos, and other ruins left by the Sinagua people about 900 years ago. Examples are preserved in Montezuma Castle and Tuzigoot National Monuments.

As an option, you can continue 2.4 miles across the plateau to the east end of the trail at FR 214.

112 Tramway Trail

Description:	This short trail in the West Clear Creek Wilderness is an enjoyable hike, and it provides access to spectacular West Clear Creek.
Location:	About 60 miles southeast of Flagstaff.
Type of trail:	Out and back.
Type of trip:	Day hike.
Difficulty:	Moderate.
Total distance:	0.8 mile.
Elevation change:	840 feet.
Time required:	1.5 hours.
Water:	West Clear Creek.
Best season:	Spring through fall.
Maps:	Calloway Butte USGS quad; Coconino National Forest.
Permits and restrictions:	None.
For more information:	Blue Ridge Ranger District, Coconino National Forest.

Finding the trailhead: From Flagstaff, drive about 50 miles southeast on the Lake Mary Road (Forest Highway 3) and turn right (west) on Forest Road 81. Stay on this maintained dirt road 3.0 miles and turn left on FR 81E. After 3.6 miles, turn right on FR 693. Go 1.2 miles on this unmaintained road, turn left at a fork, and continue 0.3 mile to the end of the road. The last 1.5 miles of road may be impassable during wet weather, and a high clearance vehicle is recommended.

Tramway Trail • Maxwell Trail • Willow Crossing Trail

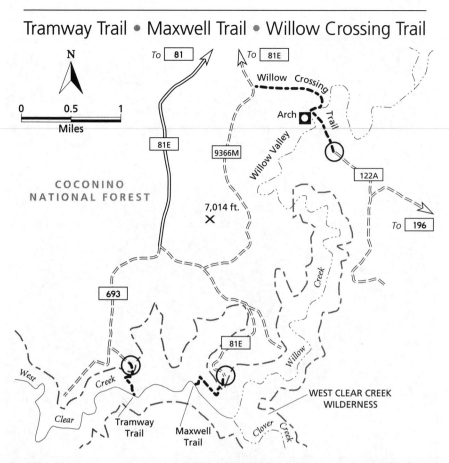

You may also reach FR 81 from Camp Verde by driving about 30 miles east on the General Crook Trail (FH 9). Turn left (north) on Arizona Highway 87 and continue 11 miles. Turn left (northwest) on the Lake Mary Road (FH 3). Go 7.0 miles and turn left on FR 81.

Key points:

0.0   Trailhead.
0.4   West Clear Creek.

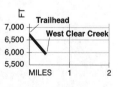

The hike: The short but spectacular trail descends into the gorge of West Clear Creek, affording fine views both up and down the canyon. It follows the route of an old aerial tramway. The Kaibab limestone forms the rim. This fossil-rich layer was deposited in a shallow ocean and forms the edge of the Mogollon Rim in this area. Below the Kaibab limestone, the cross-bedded Coconino sandstone appears, with its layers of overlapping petrified sand dunes.

The trail ends at the bottom of the canyon. One option is to hike crosscountry upstream and climb out via the Maxwell Trail (see Hike 113 for details). Another is to hike and swim the entire 25-mile length of West Clear

251

Clear Creek from the Tramway Trail.

Creek downstream to the Bull Pen Ranch trailhead. This is a difficult, multi-day backpack trip that requires swimming and floating your pack across numerous pools. It should be attempted only in warm, stable weather by experienced canyon hikers.

113 Maxwell Trail

See Map on Page 251

Description: Another short trail in the West Clear Creek Wilderness providing access to West Clear Creek.
Location: 58 miles southeast of Flagstaff.
Type of trail: Out and back.
Type of trip: Day hike.
Difficulty: Moderate.
Total distance: 1.0 mile.
Elevation change: 840 feet.
Time required: 1.5 hours.
Water: West Clear Creek.
Best season: Spring through fall.
Maps: Calloway Butte USGS quad; Coconino National Forest.
Permits and restrictions: None.
For more information: Blue Ridge Ranger District, Coconino National Forest.

Finding the trailhead: From Flagstaff, drive about 50 miles southeast on the Lake Mary Road (Forest Highway 3) and turn right (west) on Forest Road 81. Stay on this maintained dirt road 3.0 miles and then turn left on FR 81E. After 3.6 miles, turn left to stay on FR 81E, which is not maintained after this point. Turn right at all later forks to stay on FR 81E to its end. The last few miles of road may be impassable during wet weather, and a high clearance vehicle is recommended.

You may also reach FR 81 from Camp Verde by driving about 30 miles east on the General Crook Trail (FH 9). Turn left (north) on Arizona Highway 87 and continue 11 miles. Turn left (northwest) on the Lake Mary Road (FH 3). Go 7.0 miles and turn left on FR 81.

Key points:
0.0   Trailhead.
0.5   West Clear Creek.

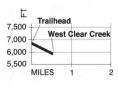

The hike: The Maxwell Trail descends in a series of switchbacks and then traverses to the west for a short distance before resuming the steep descent to the canyon bottom. At the creek, which flows all year, a lush, riparian habitat is encountered, a strong contrast to the dry plateau at the trailhead. It is very rewarding to explore cross-country both upstream and downstream from the end of the trail.

114 Willow Crossing Trail

See Map on Page 251

Description: This trail follows the route of a historic crossing of Willow Valley, a tributary of West Clear Creek, and also takes you to a natural arch.

Location: About 58 miles southeast of Flagstaff.

Type of trail: Out and back.

Type of trip: Day hike.

Difficulty: Easy.

Total distance: 2.4 miles.

Elevation change: 300 feet.

Time required: 2 hours.

Water: None.

Best season: Spring through fall.

Maps: Calloway Butte USGS quad; Coconino National Forest.

Permits and restrictions: None.

For more information: Blue Ridge Ranger District, Coconino National Forest.

Finding the trailhead: From Flagstaff, drive about 53 miles southeast on the Lake Mary Road (Forest Highway 3) and turn right (west) on Forest Road 196. (FR 196 is not well marked; it is 13.2 miles south of the Happy Jack Ranger Station.) Stay on this maintained dirt road 1.9 miles and then turn right onto FR 122A, an unmaintained dirt road. After only 0.1 mile, turn left (west) and continue on FR 122A. Continue another 0.7 mile on FR 122A across a shallow valley and turn right (northwest) on FR 122A. (The main road continues straight ahead; do not take this road.) Drive 1.1 miles to a point where the road reaches the bottom of a drainage, turn sharply right (north) on FR 122A, and go 0.7 mile to the end of the road in a grassy valley just beyond a gate. The last few miles of the road may be impassable during wet weather.

You may also reach FR 196 from Camp Verde by driving about 30 miles east on the General Crook Trail (FH 9). Turn left (north) on Arizona Highway 87 and continue 11 miles. Turn left (northwest) on Lake Mary Road (FH 3). Go 3.0 miles and turn left (west) on FR 196.

Key points:

0.0   Trailhead.

0.4   Willow Valley and natural arch.

0.6   West rim.

1.2   End of trail at FR 9366M.

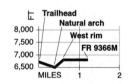

The hike: The Willow Crossing Trail is not shown on the topographic map, but a sign marks the beginning of the trail. It follows the drainage in a gentle descent through tall ponderosa pine for about 0.4 mile. As the side canyon becomes steeper, the trail abandons it for the ridge to the west and then stays on the ridge to the canyon bottom. Watch for poison ivy along

254

the canyon floor. Here the trail turns north to cross the normally dry creek bed and climbs the west side of the canyon to reach the rim. It's an easy walk across the pine-covered flat to the end of the trail at FR 9366M. After retracing your steps to the bottom of Willow Valley, go downstream a few yards and you will spot the natural arch on the west wall. It is not easily seen from the trail.

Options include cross-country exploration both up- and downstream. The experienced canyon hiker can boulder-hop 9 miles downstream to West Clear Creek and the Maxwell Trail.

115 Fossil Springs Trail

Description:	This trail takes you to Fossil Springs and a historic diversion dam on Fossil Creek in the Fossil Springs Wilderness.
Location:	About 5 miles east of Strawberry.
Type of trail:	Out and back.
Type of trip:	Day hike.
Difficulty:	Moderate.
Total distance:	6.8 miles.
Elevation change:	1,400 feet.
Time required:	4 hours.
Water:	Fossil Springs.
Best season:	Spring through fall.
Maps:	Strawberry USGS quad; Tonto National Forest.
Permits and restrictions:	None.
For more information:	Payson Ranger District, Tonto National Forest; Beaver Creek Ranger District, Coconino National Forest.

Finding the trailhead: From Strawberry on Arizona Highway 87, go west 4.7 miles on the main road through town. This becomes Forest Road 708, a maintained dirt road. Turn right after 4.7 miles and go another 0.4 mile to the Fossil Springs Trailhead.

Key points:
  0.0   Fossil Springs Trailhead.
  2.8   Fossil Creek.
  3.4   Dam.

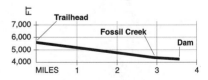

The hike: The trail descends northeast below the rim of the canyon. It soon turns northwest and continues its descent through pinyon-juniper woodland to reach Fossil Creek. Turn left and hike downstream. Though upper Fossil Creek often flows, there's no mistaking the added volume when you reach Fossil Springs. These warm springs gush from the left bank of the creek. A short distance below the springs, you'll leave the wilderness area and reach an old concrete dam,

Fossil Springs Trail

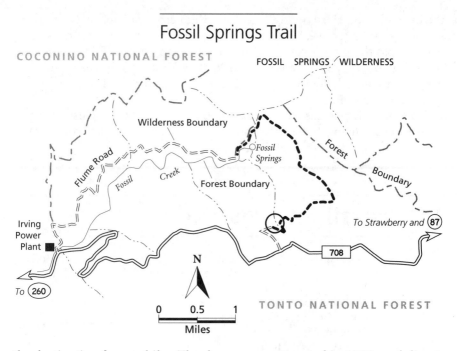

COCONINO NATIONAL FOREST

FOSSIL SPRINGS WILDERNESS

Wilderness Boundary

Flume Road

Fossil Creek

Fossil Springs

Forest Boundary

Forest Boundary

Irving Power Plant

To Strawberry and (87)

708

N

To (260)

0   0.5   1

Miles

TONTO NATIONAL FOREST

the destination for our hike. The dam was constructed in 1916, and diverts water into a flume. Several miles downstream, the water spins the turbines at the Irving Power Plant. Another power plant at the mouth of Fossil Creek, on the Verde River, harnesses the power of Fossil Creek a second time. These facilities were among Arizona's first hydroelectric generators and are still producing power. Arizona Public Service, the owner of the power system, has announced a plan to decommission the power plants and return the full flow of Fossil Springs to the lower canyon.

An option is to hike the access road to the dam, FR 154. It's closed to private vehicles; however, it is open to hikers to its end at the Irving Power Plant and FR 708. Other options are to hike cross-country upstream in Fossil Creek from the point where the trail first reached the canyon bottom. The bulk of the wilderness lies up stream and encompasses two major side canyons, Calf Pen and Sandrock Canyons.

116 Horse Crossing Trail

Description:	A historic trail providing access to East Clear Creek.
Location:	70 miles southeast of Flagstaff.
Type of trail:	Out and back.
Type of trip:	Day hike.
Difficulty:	Easy.
Total distance:	1.4 miles.
Elevation change:	500 feet.
Time required:	1 hour.
Water:	East Clear Creek.
Best season:	Spring through fall.
Maps:	Blue Ridge Reservoir USGS quad; Coconino National Forest.
Permits and restrictions:	None.
For more information:	Blue Ridge Ranger District, Coconino National Forest.

Horse Crossing Trail • Kinder Crossing Trail

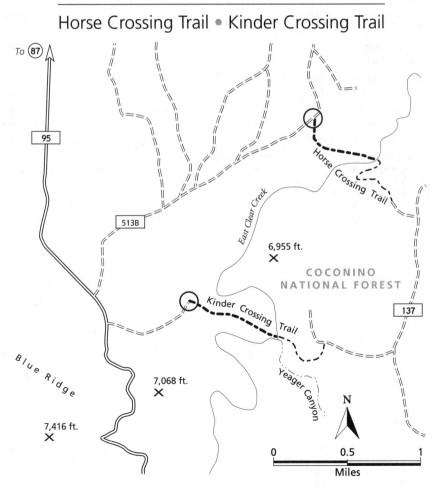

Finding the trailhead: From Flagstaff, drive about 55 miles southeast on Lake Mary Road (Forest Highway 3) to Clints Well. Turn left on Arizona Highway 87 and drive 9 miles. Now, turn right on Forest Road 95. Continue 4.0 miles on this maintained road and turn left on FR 513B, which is signed Horse Crossing Trail. Drive 2.0 miles on this unmaintained road and park at the signed Horse Crossing Trailhead on the right.

Clints Well can also be reached from Camp Verde by driving 30 miles east on the General Crook Trail (Forest Highway 9), turning left (north) on AZ 87, and continuing 11 miles.

Key points:
    0.0   Horse Crossing Trailhead.
    0.7   East Clear Creek.

The hike: The Horse Crossing Trail is shown incorrectly on the topographic map. From the trailhead it descends to the south through a fine forest of pine and oak and follows a gentle ridge for the final descent. East Clear Creek drains north from the Mogollon Rim and forms a major barrier to travel on the Coconino Plateau. A number of crossings were established by the early settlers, and some, like Horse Crossing, survive today. Others have been replaced by high speed logging roads, but East Clear Creek's long canyon is crossed by roads in only three places.

The delightful creek runs all year, making the canyon bottom easy to explore. Optionally, you can hike upstream about 3 miles to Kinder Crossing (see Hike 117 for details). East Clear Creek is much easier to hike than West Clear Creek, although it is still cross-country and requires wading. It is best hiked in warm weather, when the occasional deep pools are irresistible swimming holes instead of chilly obstacles.

Another option is to hike up the remainder of the Horse Crossing Trail to FR 137 on the east rim of the canyon.

117 Kinder Crossing Trail

See Map on Page 257

Description: Another historic trail providing access to East Clear Creek.
Location: 68.8 miles southeast of Flagstaff.
Difficulty: Easy.
Type of trail: Out and back.
Type of trip: Day hike.
Total distance: 1.2 miles.
Elevation change: 500 feet.
Time required: 1 hour.
Water: East Clear Creek.
Best season: Spring through fall.
Permits and restrictions: None.
For more information: Blue Ridge Ranger District, Coconino National Forest.

Finding the trailhead: From Flagstaff, drive about 55 miles southeast on Lake Mary Road (Forest Highway 3) to Clints Well. Turn left on Arizona Highway 87 and drive 9 miles. Now, turn right on Forest Road 95. Continue 4.2 miles on this maintained road and turn left on the unmaintained road to the Kinder Crossing Trail. Continue 0.6 mile to the end of the road.

Clints Well can also be reached from Camp Verde by driving 30 miles east on the General Crook Trail (FH 9), turning left (north) on AZ 87, and continuing 11 miles.

Key points:
0.0   Kinder Crossing Trailhead.
0.6   East Clear Creek.

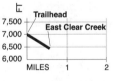

The hike: The Kinder Crossing Trail descends into East Clear Creek by following the ridge to the east, reaching the creek at the confluence of East Clear Creek and Yeager Canyon. There is a large and very inviting swimming hole at the confluence. After cooling off it is fun to explore the canyon, both up and down stream. Another option is to follow the remainder of the Kinder Crossing Trail, which climbs out the west side of the canyon to a spur road from FR 137. Yet another option, with a car shuttle, is to hike cross-country downstream about three miles to Horse Crossing. See the Horse Crossing Trail for details.

118 U-Bar Trail

Description:	A hike on a historic trail featuring historic cabins near the Mogollon Rim.
Location:	About 76 miles southeast of Flagstaff.
Type of trail:	Out and back.
Type of trip:	Day hike or overnight backpack.
Difficulty:	Moderate.
Total distance:	15.8 miles.
Elevation change:	620 feet.
Time required:	9 hours.
Water:	Barbershop Canyon, Dane Canyon, and Dane Spring.
Best season:	Spring through fall.
Maps:	Blue Ridge Reservoir, Dane Canyon USGS quads; Coconino National Forest.
Permits and restrictions:	None.
For more information:	Blue Ridge Ranger District, Coconino National Forest.

Finding the trailhead: From Flagstaff, drive about 55 miles southeast on Lake Mary Road (Forest Highway 3) to Clints Well. Turn left on Arizona Highway 87, go north 9 miles, and then turn right on Forest Road 95. Continue 11.1 miles on this maintained road and turn left on FR 139A. After just over 0.1 mile, turn left on an unsigned, rough road (park low clearance vehicles here). The road drops into Houston Draw and ends at Pinchot Cabin, the trailhead, in 0.5 mile.

Clints Well can also be reached from Camp Verde by driving 30 miles east on the General Crook Trail (FH 9), turning left on AZ 87, and continuing 11 miles.

Key points:

0.0	Pinchot Cabin Trailhead.
0.8	Turn right on a road.
1.0	T intersection; cross the road and follow the blazed trees east.
1.6	Turn left (north) along a closed road.
1.8	Pass a steel water tank, turn right, and follow the blazed trail east.
2.3	Cross FR 139.
2.8	Barbershop Canyon.
3.5	McClintock Spring.
4.0	Dane Canyon.
5.6	Dane Spring.
7.2	Coyote Spring.
7.9	Buck Springs Cabin.

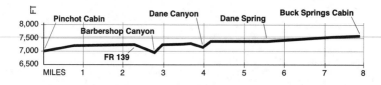

260

U-Bar Trail • Houston Brothers Trail • Barbershop Trail

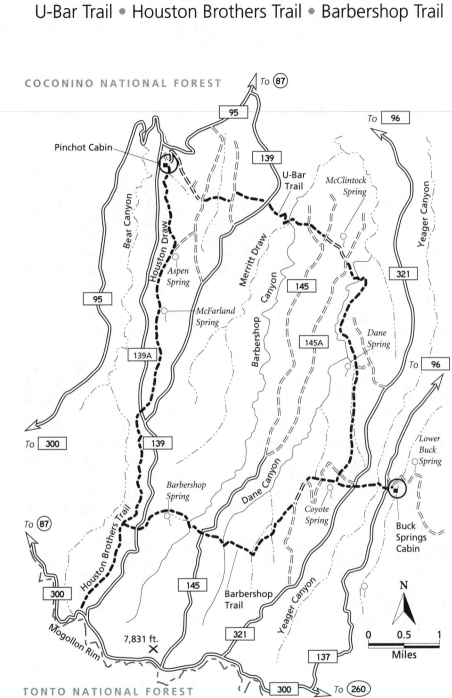

COCONINO NATIONAL FOREST

To (87)

95

139

Pinchot Cabin

U-Bar
Trail

McClintock
Spring

To 96

Bear Canyon

Houston Draw

Aspen
Spring

Merritt Draw

145

321

McFarland
Spring

Barbershop Canyon

Yeager Canyon

145A

Dane
Spring

To 96

95

139A

139

To 300

Lower
Buck
Spring

Barbershop
Spring

Dane Canyon

Houston Brothers Trail

Coyote
Spring

Buck
Springs
Cabin

To (87)

300

145

Barbershop
Trail

Yeager Canyon

N

Mogollon Rim

7,831 ft.
✕

321

137

0   0.5   1

Miles

TONTO NATIONAL FOREST

300

To (260)

The hike: This hike is part of the Cabin Loop, a system of trails that connects three historic cabins in the Mogollon Rim country. (None of the trails in this system are shown on the topographic maps.) Pinchot Cabin is named for Gifford Pinchot, the first Chief of the USDA Forest Service. It was used for many years as a fire guard station. The trail system provided the main transportation routes through this remote country during the early days of ranching and forestry. Most of the trails have been lost during the development of the forest road system, but several, including the U-Bar, have recently been relocated and restored. Sections of the trail are cross-country but are well marked by recent tree blazes.

Initially, the U-Bar Trail route follows the road past the cabin and up the hill to the east. Note the fresh tree blazes. The entire trail is blazed with the same style blazes. After 0.8 mile, turn right (south) onto another road (note the blaze and right arrow), and continue 0.2 mile to a third road intersection. The trail crosses the road and continues east into the forest, ignoring both roads. In this section there is no trail, but walking through the forest is easy and pleasant if you follow the blazes carefully. The trick to following the blazes is to walk from blaze to blaze, always keeping the last blaze in sight. If the route is lost, return to the last known blaze and locate the next one before continuing.

The route crosses Dick Hart Draw and meets another road in 0.6 mile. The route now turns left (north) and follows the road past a large, steel water tank. After about 0.3 mile the route turns sharply right (east) and leaves the road. After another 0.5 mile the blazed trail crosses a maintained dirt road (FR 139), and a sign calls out the U-Bar Trail. The route veers somewhat left as it crosses the road; follow the blazes carefully. The U-Bar route goes to the southeast out onto a point and then descends through a gate.

After the fence, the trail becomes obvious as it descends into Barbershop Canyon, which is 0.5 mile from FR 139. Serious trail construction was done on this section. Barbershop Canyon has a fine, little permanent stream, and this would make a good goal for hikers wanting an easy day.

The trail, still distinct, climbs the east wall of the canyon and crosses a faint road. After this, the trail becomes a blazed route again. About 0.7 mile from Barbershop Canyon, the route crosses a road at right angles, and a sign marks the U-Bar Trail. On the east side of the main road, the U-Bar Trail follows an unmaintained road past a fine little meadow bordered by pines, aspens, and McClintock Spring. About 0.4 mile from the sign, the road joins another road, and the route continues across the road and descends into Dane Canyon. The historic trail is distinct again in this section. Dane Canyon has a permanent stream and offers plentiful campsites on grassy meadows. A lush forest of Douglas-fir and ponderosa pine covers the canyon walls, spiced by an occasional aspen, limber pine, or white fir.

After crossing the creek, the trail climbs east out of the canyon then turns south along the east rim. This is one of the prettiest sections of the trail since it stays below the heavily logged ridgetop. About 1.6 miles from Dane Canyon, the U-Bar Trail reaches Dane Spring and the ruins of an old cabin. This is an excellent goal for a more ambitious day hike.

The ruins of an old cabin at Dane Spring along the U-Bar Trail.

The trail continues south along the east side of a shallow drainage, crosses the drainage, and climbs to cross a road on a ridgetop. It descends into the next drainage to end at the junction with the Barbershop Trail, 1.5 miles from Dane Spring. Turn left (east) on the Barbershop Trail to reach a trailhead at Buck Springs Cabin in an additional 0.5 mile.

One option is to shuttle a car to Buck Springs Cabin (see Hike 120 for access instructions) and do the trail as a one-way hike. Another is to do a loop overnight backpack using the Barbershop and Houston Brothers Trails.

119 Houston Brothers Trail

See Map on Page 261

Description: This is a historic trail that starts at an old cabin and ends at the Mogollon Rim. It's also a delightful hike through ponderosa pine and across aspen-lined meadows.

Location: 76 miles southeast of Flagstaff.

Type of trail: Out and back.

Type of trip: Day hike or overnight backpack.

Difficulty: Moderate.

Total distance: 13.2 miles.

Elevation change: 800 feet.

Time required: 7 hours.

Water: Aspen Spring, Houston Draw.

Best season: Spring through fall.

Maps: Blue Ridge Reservoir, Dane Canyon USGS quads; Coconino National Forest.

Permits and restrictions: None.

For more information: Blue Ridge Ranger District, Coconino National Forest.

Finding the trailhead: From Flagstaff, drive about 55 miles southeast on Lake Mary Road (Forest Highway 3) to Clints Well. Turn left on Arizona Highway 87, go north 9 miles, and then turn right on Forest Road 95. Continue 11.1 miles on this maintained road and turn left on FR 139A. After just over 0.1 mile, turn left on an unsigned, rough road (park low clearance vehicles here). The road drops into Houston Draw and ends at Pinchot Cabin, the trailhead, in 0.5 mile.

Clints Well can also be reached from Camp Verde by driving 30 miles east on the General Crook Trail (FH 9), turning left on AZ 87, and continuing 11 miles.

Key points:

0.0	Pinchot Cabin Trailhead.
1.4	Aspen Spring.
2.2	McFarland Spring.
3.8	FR 139A.
5.2	Barbershop Trail.
6.6	FR 300 and the Mogollon Rim.

The hike: This hike is part of the Cabin Loop, a system of trails that connects three historic cabins in the rim country. (None of the trails in this system are shown on the topographic maps.) The trailhead is signed and starts along the east side of Houston Draw.

264

The historic Houston Brothers Trail in the Mogollon Rim country follows beautiful Houston Draw through stands of ponderosa pine and quaking aspen.

Water is usually present in the creek, and the valley bottom makes for a pleasant hike. There is little sign of the heavy logging that has taken place on the ridges, and large ponderosa pine and graceful quaking aspen line the grassy meadows. About 1.4 miles from the trailhead, you'll pass Aspen Spring, where a road comes down to the trail. Less than a mile of easy hiking through open meadows leads to McFarland Spring. When you near the head of Houston Draw, the forest becomes more alpine: a mix of Douglas-fir, white fir, and ponderosa pine. After climbing out of Houston Draw the trail crosses FR 139A, a maintained road. Beyond this point, very little of the actual trail remains. Carefully follow the blazed trees, which are often too far apart. If you lose the trail, turn directly east and walk to FR 139, which is never more than 0.2 mile away. After 1.6 miles, you'll pass the signed junction with the Barbershop Trail. Continue south another 1.4 miles on the Houston Brothers Trail to reach FR 300. Cross the road to the edge of the Mogollon Rim. The view of the rim country and the central mountains to the south is a treat, marred only slightly by the damage from the Dude Fire, which roared onto the rim in 1990.

120 Barbershop Trail

See Map on Page 261

Description: This is a fine walk on an historic trail through beautiful forest near the Mogollon Rim.

Location: About 81 miles southeast of Flagstaff.

Type of trail: Out and back.

Type of trip: Day hike or overnight backpack.

Difficulty: Moderate.

Total distance: 9.0 miles.

Elevation change: 320 feet.

Time required: 5 hours.

Water: Usually at Coyote Spring, Barbershop Canyon and Barbershop Spring.

Best season: Summer through fall.

Maps: Dane Canyon USGS quad; Coconino National Forest.

Permits and restrictions: None.

For more information: Coconino National Forest.

Finding the trailhead: From Flagstaff, drive about 55 miles southeast on Lake Mary Road (Forest Highway 3) to Clints Well. Turn left on Arizona Highway 87, go north 9 miles, and then turn right on Forest Road 95. Continue 6.5 miles on this maintained road and turn left on FR 96, a maintained dirt road signed for Buck Springs Ridge. Go 4.6 miles and turn right on FR 137. After 5.4 miles, turn left on an unmaintained road signed for Buck Springs. After 0.1 mile, park at the signed trailhead near Buck Springs Cabin.

Key points:

0.0	Buck Springs Trailhead.
0.3	Cross Buck Springs Canyon.
0.7	Coyote Spring.
2.7	Dane Canyon.
3.3	Barbershop Canyon.
3.7	Barbershop Spring.
4.3	FR 139.
4.5	End of the trail at the junction with the Houston Brothers Trail.

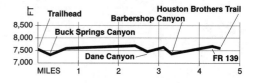

The hike: Like the U-Bar and Houston Brothers Trails, the Barbershop Trail is in a multiple use area and is not a wilderness trail, but the trail is interesting because of its historical significance and the beauty of the forest of pine, fir, and aspen. About 0.7 mile of the trail follows dirt roads, and it crosses several other roads, generally on the broad ridgetops, where it is important to follow the blazed route carefully. The trail is indistinct and can easily be missed where it leaves the roads. The trail crosses several shallow canyons and is obvious in these sections; old trail construction is plainly visible. It is not shown on the topographic map.

Buck Springs Cabin at the eastern end of Barbershop Trail.

From the trailhead, it climbs past a water tank and crosses FR 137 at a small trail sign. It then angles left (southwest) and descends into Yeager Canyon. The trail climbs onto Dane Ridge and crosses maintained dirt FR 321 at a trail sign. It immediately descends into a drainage and meets the U-Bar Trail at a signed junction, 0.8 mile from the trailhead. Coyote Spring is about 0.2 mile farther down the drainage. The trail, now a two-track road, follows the drainage west to Bill McClintock Draw and then climbs southwest to cross a low ridge. For the next 1.5 miles or so, the trail crosses several drainages and follows several roads for short distances. Follow the blazes carefully so that you don't miss the places where the trail leaves the roads.

About 2 miles from the junction with the U-Bar Trail, the Barbershop Trail crosses Dane Canyon at a sign. It climbs up a drainage to the west, crosses a maintained road, and then drops into Barbershop Canyon, which usually has flowing water. The trail climbs steeply for a couple of hundred yards then contours into a meadow at Barbershop Spring. After the spring, the trail goes up the bed of a shallow drainage to the west and climbs out on the right to cross FR 139, a maintained dirt road. The Barbershop Trail ends about 0.2 mile west of the road at the signed junction with the Houston Brothers Trail.

An option is to turn left onto the Houston Brothers Trail and hike 1.4 miles to the Mogollon Rim.

Wilderness

It doesn't take long for a hiker to begin to appreciate wild country. Although hiking in semi-urban settings can be pleasant, natural settings are more enjoyable. The idea behind the wilderness conservation movement is to preserve the opportunity for primitive, non-motorized recreation and to protect wild plants and animals in their natural habitats.

Aldo Leopold of the USDA Forest Service began to promote the idea of preserving wild country within the national forests in the 1920s. Under his influence, the agency soon began designating wilderness and primitive areas. Roads and other permanent manmade structures were excluded from such areas, although trails and activities considered compatible such as hunting, fishing, grazing, and limited mining were allowed. Most of the land within the national parks was also managed as wilderness. This protection was under the control of the land management agencies, which could rescind the wilderness designation at any time. After a long campaign, conservationists succeeded in convincing Congress to take the wilderness concept further in 1964, when it passed the Wilderness Act. This landmark law established the National Wilderness Preservation System. Most of the existing designated Wilderness and Primitive Areas on the national forests were included in the system. Since then, Congress has added many deserving areas to the national wilderness system.

When I started hiking in Arizona in the 1960s, there were only a few protected wilderness areas. Interests such as ranching, mining, and even tourism fought to prevent any wilderness protection. As time passed, more people began to appreciate wild country as a priceless asset to the state. Now, Arizona is a leader in wilderness protection. In recent years many wild areas in Arizona have been protected by Congress as national wilderness areas administered by the USDA Forest Service or the US Bureau of Land Management. Other wilderness areas have been protected in National Monuments administered by the National Park Service. Private organizations such as the Nature Conservancy have also become managers of wild areas on private trust lands.

We owe this change to the dedication of the hard working people in the conservation groups, government agencies, and US Congress who believe in protecting what remains of the American wilderness.

While protecting existing roadless areas is vital, more attention is now being paid to the protection of intact ecosystems. As we learn more about plant and animal habitats, we find that survival of individual species is linked to the health of other plants and animals as well as the quality of the air and water. Instead of protecting a few isolated wild areas and ignoring the consequences of unrestricted human activities on the rest of the land, we have to consider entire watersheds and entire forests and consider how proposed activities will affect them. In addition, cities such as Flagstaff and Sedona have recognized that the federal lands surrounding them are a valuable open-space resource, and these cities are connecting their urban trail systems with the national forest trails.

Appendix A

FURTHER READING

Aitchison, Stewart, and Grubbs, Bruce. *Hiking Arizona,* Falcon Press, Helena, Montana, 1992.

Aitchison, Stewart. *A Guide to Exploring Oak Creek and the Sedona Area,* RNM Press, Salt Lake City, Utah, 1989.

———. *Red Rock Sacred Mountain: the Canyon and Peaks from Sedona to Flagstaff,* Voyager Press, Stillwater, Minnesota, 1992.

Ashworth, Donna. *Biography of a Small Mountain,* Small Mountain Books, Flagstaff, Arizona, 1991.

Fletcher, Colin. *The Complete Walker III,* Alfred A. Knopf, New York, 1989.

Grubbs, Bruce. *Desert Hiking Tips,* Falcon Publishing, Helena, Montana, 1999.

Harmon, Will. *Leave No Trace,* Falcon Publishing, Helena, Montana, 1997.

———. *Wild Country Companion,* Falcon Publishing, Helena, Montana, 1994.

Kricher, John C., and Morrison, Gordon. *Ecology of Western Forests,* Houghton Mifflin, New York, 1993.

Larson, Peggy. *Sierra Club Naturalist's Guide to the Deserts of the Southwest.* Sierra Club Books, San Francisco, California, 1977.

Perry, John and Jane Greverus. *Guide to the Natural Areas of New Mexico, Arizona, and Nevada.* Sierra Club Books, San Francisco, California, 1985.

Wilkerson, James A. *Medicine for Mountaineering,* The Mountaineers, Seattle, Washington, 1985.

Appendix B

OUTDOOR SUPPLIERS

LOCAL SHOPS

Flagstaff

Aspen Sports, 15 North San Francisco Street, Flagstaff, AZ 86001, (520) 779-1935.

Babbitts Backcountry Outfitters, 12 East Aspen Avenue, Flagstaff, AZ 86001, (520) 774-4775.

Mountain Sports, 1800 South Milton Road, Flagstaff, AZ 86001, (520) 779-5156.

Peace Surplus, 14 West Route 66, Flagstaff, AZ 86001, (520) 779-4521.

Popular Outdoor Outfitters, 901 South Milton Road, Flagstaff, AZ 86001, (520) 774-0598.

Jerome

Ghost Town Gear, 415 Hull, Jerome, AZ 86331, (520) 634-3113.

Sedona

Canyon Outfitters, 2701 West Highway 89A, Sedona, AZ 86336, (520) 282-5293.

MAIL ORDER

Beartooth Maps, P.O. Box 160728, Big Sky, MT 59716, (406) 995-3280.

Campmor, P.O. Box 700-C, Saddle River, NJ 07458-0700, (800) 226-7667, customer-service@campmor.com, www.campmor.com.

Mountain Gear, North 730 Hamilton, Spokane, WA 99202 (800) 829-2009, info@mGear.com, www.mountain-gear.com.

National Geographic (formerly Wildflower Productions), 375 Alabama Street, Suite 230, San Francisco, CA 94110, (415) 558-8700, info@topo.com, www.info.com.

Recreational Equipment, Inc., Sumner, WA 98352, (800) 426-4840, www.rei.com.

Trails Illustrated, P.O. Box 3610, Evergreen, CO 80439-3425, (800) 962-1643, www.trailsillustrated.com.

Appendix C

LOCAL HIKING CLUBS AND CONSERVATION GROUPS

Arizona Mountaineering Club, P.O. Box 1695, Phoenix, AZ 85001-1695, (623) 878-2485, azmtnclub@abilnet.com.

Arizona Trail Association, P.O. Box 36736, Phoenix, AZ 85067, (602) 252-4794, aztrail@primenet.com, www.primenet.com/~aztrail.

Maricopa Audubon Society, 4619 East Arcadia Lane, Phoenix, AZ 85018.

Nature Conservancy, 333 East Virginia Avenue, Suite 216, Phoenix, AZ 85004, (602) 712-0048.

Sierra Club, Grand Canyon Chapter, 516 East Portland Street, Phoenix, AZ 85004, (602) 267-1649.

Appendix D

PUBLIC AGENCIES

CITY

Flagstaff Parks and Recreation, 211 West Aspen, Flagstaff, AZ 86001, (928) 779-7690.

Sedona Parks and Recreation, 525 Posse Grounds Road, Sedona, AZ 86336, (928) 282-7098.

Williams Parks and Recreation, 2200 North Country Club Road, Williams, AZ 86046, (928) 635-1496.

STATE

Arizona Game and Fish, 3500 South Lake Mary Road, Flagstaff, AZ 86001, (928) 774-5045.

Arizona State Land Department, 3650 Lake Mary Road, Flagstaff, AZ 86001, (928) 774-1425.

Arizona State Parks, 1300 West Washington, Phoenix, AZ 85007, (602) 542-4174.

Arizona Trail Steward, Arizona State Parks, 1300 West Washington, Phoenix, AZ 85007, (602) 542-7120, clovely@pr.state.az.us, www.pr.state.az.us.

Red Rock State Park, HC - Box 886, Sedona, AZ 86336, (928) 282-6907.

COCONINO NATIONAL FOREST

Beaver Creek Ranger District, HC 64, Box 240, Rimrock, AZ 86335, (928) 567-4121.

Blue Ridge Ranger District, H.C. 31, Box 300, Happy Jack, AZ 86024, (928) 477-2255.

Mormon Lake Ranger District, 4373 South Lake Mary Road, Flagstaff, AZ 86001, (928) 774-1147.

Peaks Ranger District, 5075 North Highway 89, Flagstaff, AZ 86004, (928) 526-0866.

Sedona Ranger District, P.O. Box 300, Sedona, AZ 86336-0300, (928) 282-4119.

Supervisors Office, 2323 East Greenlaw Lane, Flagstaff, AZ 86001, (928) 527-3600.

NATIONAL PARK SERVICE

Grand Canyon National Park, P.O. Box 129, Grand Canyon, AZ 86023, (928) 638-7888.

Sunset Crater National Monument, 6400 North Highway 89, Flagstaff, AZ 86004, (928) 526-0502.

Walnut Canyon National Monument, 6400 North Highway 89, Flagstaff, AZ 86004, (928) 526-3367.

Wupatki National Monument, 6400 North Highway 89, Flagstaff, AZ 86004, (928) 679-2365.

KAIBAB NATIONAL FOREST

Chalender Ranger District, 501 West Bill Williams Avenue, Williams, AZ 86046, (928) 635-2676.

North Kaibab Ranger District, P.O. Box 248, Fredonia, AZ 86022, (928) 643-7395.

Supervisor's Office, 800 South Sixth Street, Williams, AZ 86046, (928) 635-8200.

Tusayan Ranger District, P.O. Box 3088, Tusayan, AZ 86023, (928) 638-2443.

Williams Ranger District, Route 1 Box 142, Williams, AZ 86046, (928) 635-2633.

PRESCOTT NATIONAL FOREST

Bradshaw Ranger District, 2230 East Highway 69, Prescott, AZ 86301, (928) 445-7253.

Chino Valley Ranger District, P.O. Box 485, 735 North Highway 89, Chino Valley, AZ 86323, (928) 636-2302.

Supervisor's Office, 344 South Cortez Street, Prescott, AZ 86303, (928) 771-4700.

Verde Ranger District, P.O. Box 670, Camp Verde, AZ 86322-0670, (928) 567-4121.

TONTO NATIONAL FOREST

Payson Ranger District, 1009 East Highway 260, Payson, AZ 85541, (928) 474-7900.

OTHER

U.S. Geological Survey, Information Services, Box 25286, Denver, CO 80225, (800) HELP-MAP, http://mapping.usgs.gov

Appendix E

HIKER'S CHECKLIST

This checklist may be useful for ensuring that nothing essential is forgotten. Of course, it contains far more items than are needed on any individual hiking trip.

Clothing
- ☐ Shirt
- ☐ Pants
- ☐ Extra underwear
- ☐ Swim suit
- ☐ Walking shorts
- ☐ Belt or suspenders
- ☐ Windbreaker
- ☐ Jacket or parka
- ☐ Rain gear
- ☐ Gloves or mittens
- ☐ Sun hat
- ☐ Watch cap or balaclava
- ☐ Sweater
- ☐ Bandanna

Footwear
- ☐ Boots
- ☐ Extra socks
- ☐ Boot wax
- ☐ Camp shoes

Sleeping
- ☐ Tarp or tent with fly
- ☐ Groundsheet
- ☐ Sleeping pad
- ☐ Sleeping bag

Packing
- ☐ Backpack
- ☐ Day pack
- ☐ Fanny pack

Cooking
- ☐ Matches or lighter
- ☐ Waterproof match case
- ☐ Fire starter
- ☐ Stove
- ☐ Fuel
- ☐ Stove maintenance kit
- ☐ Cooking pot(s)
- ☐ Cup
- ☐ Bowl or plate
- ☐ Utensils
- ☐ Pot scrubber
- ☐ Plastic water bottles with water
- ☐ Collapsible water containers

Food
- ☐ Cereal
- ☐ Bread
- ☐ Crackers
- ☐ Cheese
- ☐ Margarine
- ☐ Dry soup
- ☐ Packaged dinners
- ☐ Snacks
- ☐ Hot chocolate
- ☐ Tea
- ☐ Powdered milk
- ☐ Powdered drink mixes

Navigation
- ☐ Maps
- ☐ Compass
- ☐ GPS receiver

Emergency/Repair
- ☐ Pocket knife
- ☐ First aid kit
- ☐ Snakebite kit
- ☐ Nylon cord
- ☐ Plastic bags
- ☐ Wallet or ID card
- ☐ Coins for phone calls
- ☐ Space blanket
- ☐ Emergency fishing gear (hooks and a few feet of line)
- ☐ Signal mirror

- ☐ Pack parts
- ☐ Stove parts
- ☐ Tent parts
- ☐ Flashlight bulbs, batteries
- ☐ Scissors
- ☐ Safety pins

Miscellaneous
- ☐ Fishing gear
- ☐ Photographic gear
- ☐ Sunglasses
- ☐ Flashlight
- ☐ Candle lantern
- ☐ Sunscreen
- ☐ Insect repellent
- ☐ Toilet paper
- ☐ Trowel
- ☐ Binoculars
- ☐ Trash bags
- ☐ Notebook and pencils
- ☐ Field guides
- ☐ Book or game
- ☐ Dental and personal items
- ☐ Towel
- ☐ Water purification tablets or water filter
- ☐ Car key
- ☐ Watch
- ☐ Calendar

In the Car
- ☐ Extra water
- ☐ Extra food
- ☐ Extra clothes

About the Author

Bruce Grubbs is an avid hiker, climber, mountain biker, and cross-country skier who has been exploring the American West for over 30 years. An outdoor writer and photographer, he's written twelve other FalconGuides. He lives in Flagstaff, Arizona.

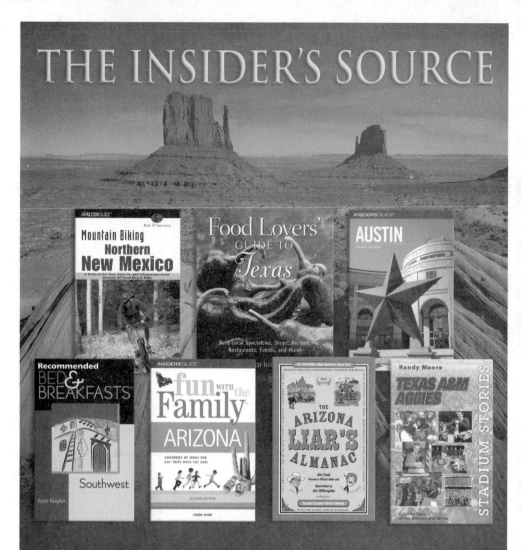